KNOWING

THE

SCRIPTURES

KNOWING THE SCRIPTURES

By
Arthur T. Pierson

AMG Publishers
Chattanooga, TN 37422

KNOWING THE
SCRIPTURES

Originally published by
Gospel Publishing House in 1910.

ISBN 0-89957-203-0

Printed in the United States of America

Contents

Foreword

Originally published by Gospel Publishing House of New York in 1910, Arthur T. Pierson's *Knowing the Scriptures* is a detailed survey of numerous features of the Bible. Pierson, a graduate of Union Seminary, thoroughly explicates the literal elements of Scripture and expounds on their spiritual significance. His analysis includes comprehensive tables and charts that give Bible students and general readers alike a straightforward description of the specifics of Scripture.

In creating this new edition of *Knowing the Scriptures*, we at AMG Publishers have made some minor changes to the original work to help make its content more clear to modern readers: We have updated the spelling in accordance with how our language has changed over the years; some portions have been modified in format to ease readability; however, the information Pierson provides has not been altered in any way.

Readers should note that the information presented regarding dates and authorship of the books of Scripture is from the early 1900s and does not take into consideration more recent biblical scholarship.

Introduction

"Thou hast magnified Thy Word above all Thy name"—
Psalm 138:2.

This saying of the Psalmist may primarily refer to some specific word of God, some promise, like that recorded about the future of David's own house (2 Sam. 7:11, 19); but the larger truth it contains and conveys is capable of so much wider scope and broader application that it may well be said to include the whole body of Holy Scripture.

Calvin translates: "Thou hast magnified Thy name, above all things, by Thy Word"; and Luther, "Thou has made Thy Name glorious, above all, through Thy Word." But, with Hengstenberg, the majority of the best Bible students favor substantially the common rendering: "Above all Thy Name, Thou has made glorious Thy Word"—meaning that, beyond all works of Creation and Providence, or other means whereby God has made Himself known, He has exalted His written Word.

To those to whom it is addressed, it has power to convict and convert, sanctify and edify; but it has even a higher power and province: *it is the mirror of its Author;* meant, first of all, to reveal, unveil, magnify and glorify Him from whom it originally went forth.

This high tribute found expression when as yet there was only the Written Word. Without doubt the Living Word is a fuller unveiling of God's inmost self. In the incarnation, "the Word was made flesh and dwelt among men," as a living Presence. In the Person of His Son, the Logos, the Word Incarnate, the Father made Himself known as never before, with new clearness and fullness of revelation.

Yet it still remains true that, in the Inspired Scriptures, He has glorified His own Name, or nature: revealing His mind, heart, will—His whole character—and, especially, His gracious attitude toward sinners; and, in such manner and measure, as to make all other revelations of Himself in the creation of the material universe and the control of human history comparatively dim and indistinct, only as the first faint flushes of the dawn in comparison with the fuller light of day.

One of the main uses of the Word of God is to supply us with a divine standard of both doctrine and duty. In his travels in the Dark Continent, Dr. Livingstone found his native guides either so ignorant or so determined to deceive and mislead, that he could do better without them than with them; and so he constantly referred to his own compass and sextant to determine direction and location. What would he have done if, by any accident, or defect in his instruments, he had found even these scientific guides utterly untrustworthy?

For God's written Word no substitute has ever been found. Where other ancient civilized nations, such as Egypt, Assyria, Persia, Rome, and Greece, have left monuments in law and letters, mechanic arts and fine arts, Judea, as Dr. Jamieson remarks, while leaving us no legacy of secular achievements, rose immeasurably above all other lands in the possession and transmission of the Living Oracles of God. In fact, the Hebrews were rather warned against some things in which other nations prided themselves. The fine arts, for instance, were so often the handmaids of polytheism and the promoters of idolatry, finding their highest sphere in glorifying image-worship, that Jehovah required His people to be, in this as in many other respects, separate from the nations (Ex. 20:25; Is. 2:16).

In every department of life the need for some exact and unvarying *standard*, as in weights and measures, time, etc., compels resort to the works of God for guidance, for here alone are found perfect forms and changeless models. Man's best watches and chronometers have to be corrected by nature's horologium—God's sidereal clock, which has not varied the one-thousandth part of a second, since He appointed sun, moon and stars for times and seasons. And, so, from all human oracles, however self-confident, we turn at last to the Inspired Word where instead of ambiguous and untrustworthy utterances we find teachings distinct and definite, authoritative and infallible.

One very conspicuous feature of the Word of God is its *Self-Interpreting power*. In the mastery of human books help is needful from large libraries and patient research in the realms of science and philosophy. Grammars, and glossaries, histories and biographies, copious lexicons and learned encyclopedias, often become necessary to furnish the mere sidelights to interpret the terms and illumine the sense of human literature. But, in studying this Divine Book, confessedly the crown of all literature, other writings, though often helpful, are never indispensable. To a remarkable degree, God's Word explains and interprets its own contents, is its own grammar and lexicon, library and encyclopedia. Within itself may be found a philosophy which interprets its history, and a history which illustrates its philosophy. Even what in it is most obscure and mysterious is not dependent upon outside helps for its complete unlocking or unveiling. The humblest reader, if shut up by circumstances to this one Book, as was Bunyan, almost literally, in Bedford jail, might, without any other guide than the Bible itself, by careful, prayerful searching, come to know the Word; exploring its contents till he became another Apollos, mighty in the Scriptures. This statement has been often verified by fact, as in the experience of believers, actually imprisoned for Christ's sake but carrying their Bibles with them as companions in solitude, and coming forth enriched in the knowledge of God.

The highest secret of Bible study, however, is that teachable spirit which is inseparable from obedience. Spiritual vision, like the physical, is binocular: it depends on both reason and conscience. If the intellectual faculties are beclouded, the moral sense is apt to err in its decisions; and, if the conscience be seared, the reason is blinded. Our Lord says, "If any man will *do* His will he shall *know* of the doctrine" (John 7:17); in other words, *obedience is the organ of spiritual revelation*. Insight into the Scriptures is never independent of the obedient frame, but is conditioned upon actual conformity to their precepts and sympathy with their spirit. *True biblical learning is not so much mental as experimental*. There are professed teachers and preachers who no more grasp the truth they nominally hold than does the sparrow grasp the message that passes through the telegraph wire on which it perches—as Normal McLeod quaintly put it.

It is sometimes worse than vain to read, or even to search the Scriptures, with mere intellect, as though they were merely literary productions to be examined and understood with no higher faculties than those which are associated with an unsanctified scholarship. Many a man who has approached the Word of God without prayer for God's help, without reverent attitude, or any ultimate end beyond a critical, intellectual analysis, has been left to grope his way blindly while persuading himself that he had even exceptional insight. On the other hand, many a humble and uneducated believer has had his eyes unveiled to behold wondrous things out of God's law (Ps. 119:18), and become and expert in its "mysteries."

Critical study is not to be discouraged; it is not only proper but helpful in its proper sphere, when conducted with a proper spirit. But there is a sort of analysis that is destructive; like the vivisection that invades the domain of life, in cutting in pieces the organic body of truth, it sacrifices vitality, and leaves only dead, disconnected fragments of what was one living organism. The Bible is such a living organism. Its various parts are members of a common body; they have a vital connection and relation, and must be examined, not in isolation and separation, but in union as integral parts of a great whole. Then criticism, instead of being arrogant and destructive, will be reverent and constructive.

The late Dr. A. J. Gordon of Boston—in that memorable visit to Scotland with the writer, in 1888—used to relate an anecdote which the great Scotchman, Principal Cairns, declared to be the best illustration he had ever met of the mistakes of modern "critics." In a conversation with a deacon of a colored church in his neighborhood, Dr. Gordon drew out from him the fact that the people did not like the new pastor "berry much"; and, when pressed for an explanation, the deacon added that the pastor told too many "antidotes in the pulpit"; and, when Dr. Gordon expressed surprise, saying that he had supposed his pastor to be a great Bible man, the deacon replied, "Well, 'I'll tell yer how it is. *He's de best man I ebber seed to tak' de Bible apart, but he dunno how to put it togedder agin!*" Modern critics have proved adept in pulling to pieces the blessed Word, but they are too much like those to whom Asaph referred, who in his day had broken down the carved work of the sanctuary with axes and hammers, and burned up the synagogues (Ps. 74:3–8).

No student of Holy Scripture should forget that, to see the highest truth man needs the *verifying faculty*. "The light of the body is the eye," because the condition on which depend the perception and reception of all light is a healthy organ of vision, without which there is in effect no light. This is a thought of profound outreach. Objective testimony, or external evidence of truth is never enough; there must be also subjected capacity, integral receptivity to its witness. We must not be so absorbed in simply gathering proofs or evidences of Christianity, as to overlook the need and value of an inward readiness to receive and feel the force of proof, when furnished. The candid mind, the clean conscience, the obedient will, are all necessary to the open eye. Their opposites, an uncandid mind, corrupt conscience, perverse will, are in Scripture compared to an eye *veiled*, voluntarily *closed*, or judicially *blinded*.*

To understand the importance of this verifying faculty in ourselves is very rare. A mind, candidly open to conviction, asking only to know "what is Truth?" and a will that turns to truth, when found, and yields to its sway, as the needle to the pole—how seldom those conditions are found—probably never where persistent unbelief reigns. The two veils of prejudice and self-interest are still as common and as effective hindrances as in our Lord's day. The Pharisees and Scribes were so built into the errors of that time, that to accept His teaching meant turning their little world upside down—upsetting the whole fabric of their individual, social and religious life; and hence their invention of every possible pretext for opposing and rejecting Him (John 11:47, 48). Prejudice implies that a wrong or partial view has been formed which leads to antagonism; there is no longer a clear eye to see truth. Self-interest warps the whole mind, so that conviction cannot fit the demands of truth even if recognized; and, often unconsciously, men devise excuses or invent difficulties, which would at once disappear were there a fair, impartial judgment.

* Compare 1 Cor. 14:37; 1 John 2:27; 4:1; 2 Cor. 3:14–18; John 3:19–21; Acts 26:18, 19; 28:26, 27; 1 Tim. 1:19; Rom. 8:6, 7; 2 Cor. 4:3, 4; John 7:17; 2 Cor. 11:3.

Gregory the Great, left us a sublime maxim: *"Discere cor Dei in verbis Dei"*—"We are to learn the mind of God from the words of God." True, but we must be both prepared and willing to be taught. Our Lord rebuked even professed leaders among the Jews, because, while claiming to be exponents of the Law, they "knew not the Scriptures nor the power of God." This reminds us of the necessity, if we are to have a true acquaintance with Scripture teaching, that we should feel the force of truth, not only as directly declared, but as *inferentially taught*. This rebuke was especially to the Sadducees, who denied both separate spiritual existence apart from the body, and the reality of the future state. And yet Jehovah had declared: "I am the God of Abraham, and the God of Isaac and the God of Jacob"; referring to them, not as dead but as living; and these Sadducees might have deduced from this declaration the doctrine of the survival of the spirit at death, and of the future state which they denied. While we are to be on our guard against those *false* inferences which are due to careless reasoning, we are not to forget that prejudice will blind us to true and safe deductions.

This unique peculiarity which has been adverted to, the self disclosure of the Word of God, it will be the main purpose of what follows to exhibit and illustrate. This is a convincing proof of a supernatural origin, and shows the universal fitness of the Scripture for man, as man, while it both incites and inspires a reverent and searching study.

As a possible help to the appreciation and interpretation of the Scriptures, attention will be called to some of the leading ways in which the close study of this divine book had been found to disclose its meaning, even in cases where at first there seemed to be not only obscurity but contradiction. The year of the issue of this book marks the completion of a half century since the writer entered upon the full work of the gospel ministry; and it is intended as a sort of gathering up of some results of fifty years of Bible study, putting in form some of the laws, principles and methods found by actual trial to yield the best fruit, and so promising to be of like service to others.

A rightly conducted examination of God's Word will be found to yield not only rich results in homiletics and hermeneutics, but in apologetics. In the structure and contents of Holy Scripture may be found a triumphant answer to all assaults upon its inspiration and authority as a divine Book and the standard of doctrine and duty. The Bible is its own witness; and whoever, turning from all external defenses to the book itself, will seek to make himself master of its contents and to enter sympathetically into its spirit, will find himself lodged in an impregnable fortress where he laughs in derision at all who, like Voltaire, threaten to overthrow it, while he holds in scarcely less contempt the timidity which fears such threats. The Ark of the Covenant needs no help from puny human hands to steady it, nor is the Shekinah fire in danger of being quenched by those who blow upon it to put it out. Light needs only to be let shine and it become its own witness. A lion has only to be let loose and he needs no defender. Give the Word of God free course and it will be victor over all assault.

Let us intimate the Bereans who "*searched* the Scriptures daily." That word "search" is emphatic, implying a thorough examination, a judicial investigation, reminding of the work of the civil engineer, mapping out a newly-explored coast line, with triangulation of every bay and inlet. Search into the Scriptures should be thorough, systematic, habitual, tarrying over peculiarities of conception and expression, emphatic words and phrases, and seeking to know the exact meaning and order of words used by the Spirit of God. It is safe to assume that nothing is purposeless; and that to the great end of the whole every part, however minute, contributes, somewhat as, in creation, every whit subserves God's great design. Whether or not all these mutual bearings are seen, they exist; and our dimness and narrowness of vision cannot obliterate what they only obscure.

Nothing like an exhaustive treatment is attempted in the pages which follow. No doubt many a devout reader might, out of his own treasure bring forth things new and old, outranking in importance what is here found. Perhaps, however, others who have not digged so deep into this mine of celestial wealth may find somewhat here to incite to a more painstaking study. But all who, for themselves, will prayerfully search, will find the Scriptures testifying to their own divine original, and will reap the reward of the explorer who, from new paths of investigation and discovery, brings new trophies; or of the miner who digs up new nuggets of gold, or gems. Here are to be found ever new truths, precious stones of beauty and radiance surpassing the gold of Ophir, the precious onyx and the sapphire.

ARTHUR T. PIERSON

May, 1910.

Bible Study
Some of its Laws, Methods and Principles

As History teaches philosophy by examples, both exhibiting and testing ethical principles, so practical results both manifest and prove the utility of methods. For many years certain laws and modes of Scripture research have been adopted and approved in actual daily practice, and with such growing confidence in their value and helpfulness as to suggest their formal statement and illustration, in hope of aiding, in some measure, other Bible students, and especially those who are either comparatively beginning such study or who, by reason of other necessary secular labors, have less leisure for systematic search into the Word of God. We are all dependent in part upon the experience of others. It is a necessity that there should be a division of labor, for we cannot all, in one short life, do everything; and so each of us is appointed of God, to some specific form of activity, both to accomplish and accumulate somewhat for ourselves and to contribute somewhat to the common store and stock of knowledge and experience from which others may draw. It is a law both of privilege and of obligation, that we should pass on what we learn, give what we get, communicate what we receive. It is only selfishness that is content to hoard; all noble living spends; and so one naturally desires to suggest what had been tried and proven to be valuable and useful in that first of all the sciences and fine arts, the accurate understanding of the inspired Word of God. The method here followed will be to indicate, first, a law, principle, or mode of Scripture study, and then give some amplifications, applications, corroborations and illustrations of it.

Manifestly the Word of God consists of *form* and *substance*, expression and conception, what is external and what is internal; and the natural and normal method in study will be from what is without to what is within. That famous saying of Wordsworth, however, "Language is the incarnation of thought," suggests that the ideas and the words which embody them are inseparable, and cannot really be studied wholly apart from each other. The shell of a nut is so related to the kernel, and the shell of a mollusk, to the animal that inhabits it, that each variety has its own peculiar enclosure or tenement, adapted to its nature and uses, and could not exchange with another; and we shall find, as we examine closely the *literal* element in the Word of God, that we are passing, by unconscious and gradual steps, into the *spiritual* content.

We shall, however, approach our great subject as from the outside, proceeding from what is general to what is special, and from the letter to the spirit; seeking to begin at the beginning, with what is fundamental and rudimental, and as far as practicable advancing, step by step, from vestibule and outer court to inner chambers and inmost shrine. There should be in all this advance no careless prayerless step; the place where we stand is holy ground, and should be trodden with reverent feet; and, if such an attitude is imperative for one who ventures to act as guide, it is scarcely less needful for those who would follow. We trust, therefore, that the reader will peruse these pages in sympathy with the spirit and motive with which they have been written, seeking only to "know the Scriptures" and "the power of God."

First, then, we take a glimpse of this divine book as a *whole;* then look at its language and literary features, its words as indexes of its thought; then at its ideas, ideals and conceptions, advancing toward what is mystic and mysterious.

1

Supreme Authority of the Word of God

IN REVELATION 5, IS FOUND a pictorial exhibit of the authority and majesty of Holy Scripture.

A scroll, written within and on the backside, and sealed with seven seals, is seen in the right hand of Him who is seated on the Throne, and it partakes of His own unapproachable glory.

A seal stands in Scripture for silence, mystery, completeness, but especially for the sacredness connected with authority, authenticity, inviolability. Whatever this particular scroll is, it represents some written word of God. We cannot escape the suggestion of divine sanction or authority as stamped upon Holy Scripture, and there is a hint of a sevenfold attestation which makes His Word the mirror of His attributes. It also bears seven seals:

1. The seal of omnipresence, eternity, immutability, in its production, independent and irrespective of time and place, variety of matter and diversity of human writers.

2. The seal of sovereignty and majesty, in the providential control of historic events, and of individual and collective history.

3. The seal of omniscience, wisdom, in its forecasts of the future and its revelations of the events of a remote and unhistoried past.

4. The seal of truth, veracity, verity, infallibility, in its general accuracy, not only in the ethical and spiritual realm, but in the whole sphere and domain of truth.

5. The Seal of Righteousness and Justice in its immaculate, moral and spiritual standards of character, conduct and administration.

6. The Seal of Omnipotence, Benevolence, Love, in its moral and spiritual transformations and miracles of grace, its purpose and promise of regeneration.

7. The Seal of Infiniteness and Holiness in the superhuman revelation of the absolute perfection and glory of the divine character.

Such multiplied testimony puts upon the Word of God a sevenfold sanction of supreme authority. It asserts its divine origin with an emphasis to which nothing can be added.

This most notable chapter is unique, as showing *God's opinion of His own Book:* for, even if the scroll, here referred to, be only the Apocalypse itself, what is true of a *part* is true of the *whole*. Scanning the whole chapter we further see:

1. The unparalleled *majesty of the Scriptures*. No created intelligence, even though angelic, worthy to open the seals, take the scroll in hand or even to look upon it.

2. The inviolable *mystery* of the Scriptures—sealed up with sevenfold secrecy apart from the one and only interpreting Power.

3. The inseparable *unity* of the Book and the Lamb—the written Word and the living Word. He only is worthy to take the scroll or capable of unloosing the seals.

4. The complex character of the *Person of Christ*—Lion and Lamb are one, King and a Priest. Hence able to make us kings and priests.

5. The solvent power of the *blood* of Christ, which alone unlooses the seals and interprets the contents. Two thoughts pervade the Word—Priesthood and Kingship—and the Lamb and the Lion explain both.

It is necessary also to settle the question of the Inspiration of Scripture. It is divinely declared to be *"theopneustic"*—that is, "God-in-breathed" (2 Tim. 3:16). This language suggests a body of language, in-breathed with a spirit of divine life, somewhat as the body of the first man was when God breathed into his nostrils the breath of life and he became a living soul: this is a living Book.

We need to distinguish between *revelation, interpretation, illumination* and *inspiration*.

Revelation is the divine impartation and communication of truth to the mind of man, whatever be its mode or channel (Rom. 1:17; 16:25; Eph. 3:3–5; Amos 3:7).

Interpretation is the science of discovering and disclosing the true meaning of the holy oracles. It is sometimes a function of inspiration to enable a prophet or teacher to give an authoritative meaning to a divine utterance (Dan. 4:24–28; 5:17–28).

Illumination refers more to the province of the Spirit in so enlightening the mind of the believer as to enable him to discern, and in a measure beyond his natural, unaided powers to apprehend and comprehend the beauty and glory of a divine revelation (Eph. 1:17, 18; 3:16–19).

Inspiration is rather the method of revelation rendering its subject capable of receiving and transmitting revealed truth, communicating to others without error, either by tongue or pen. Obviously the value of a written revelation must depend upon its inspiration.

As to the *method* of inspiration—the *modus operandi* of the Holy Spirit in revealing truth—it is inscrutable, wrapped in the mystery of silence, like His other operations in regeneration and miracle working (John 3:8). All we know or need to know about it is its *effects;* and these may be learned from the didactic statements of the Word itself, and the phenomena of its operation, as we may know the wind by its working. Inspiration rendered whomsoever it controlled an adequate medium or vehicle of God's utterance, His mouthpiece or spokesman, so that "He spake by the mouth of His holy prophets who have been since the World began" (Luke 1:70; Heb. 1:1).

We need also carefully to define the *measure of authority* which Inspiration carries. The Bible is, in part, a *record*, embracing narratives of fact which form part of the history it records, and the sayings and doings of fallible and fallen human beings. In such cases, Inspiration assures only the essential accuracy of the narrative, not the sanction of God's approval of the utterances or conduct of the parties. But, in all cases where God speaks directly in His own Person or by His appointed agents, Inspiration covers not only the truthfulness of the record but the sanction of the statements expressed.

"*Verbal Inspiration*" is a term much misunderstood. It does not, of course, mean that every word found in Scripture is God's word or represents His mind, for some words record the acts of the erring and the ungodly, or are their sayings, and in some instances Satan is the speaker. Any theory would be absurd that clothes all words found in Scripture with equal authority or importance. But whatever is meant to convey God's thought is used with a purpose and adapted to its end, so that, as the Angel said to John, on Patmos: "These are the true sayings of God" (Rev. 19:9).

Every student must observe what in Holy Scripture carries authority, and what only accuracy. Satan's words to Eve (Gen. 3:1–5), though accurately recorded, are false and misleading in intention and sentiment, exactly contrary to God's mind. The greater part of the Book of Job, though an inspired record of events and sayings, is expressly disowned of God as *not* rightly *spoken* (Job 42:7). More than this, many other well meant words and deeds of men, embodied in the history, here recorded, may lack authority because due to imperfect knowledge of the mind of God or partial obedience to His will. Even prophets and apostles, *apart from their character and capacity as such*, being only fallible men, were liable to mistakes (1 Kgs. 19:4; Gal. 2:11–14).

A very instructive instance of the principle may be found in 2 Samuel 7:2 through 7. David declares his purpose to build God a house, and his reasons are both devout and unselfish: he is unwilling to have his own palace outshine the dwelling place of Jehovah. Not only so but, on communicating to the prophet Nathan his purpose, he meets with entire approval; the prophet bids him do all that is in his heart, assuring him that the Lord is with him. Did the narrative give no further light, we should infer this to be a God-inspired thought of David; but the prophet is bidden to go to the King and tell him that he is not to build the house—that privilege being reserved for Solomon. Here the narrative is inspired, but the proposed action is not. It was well meant but not in God's plan—a very conspicuous example of the principle that many a good man says and does what is not authorized by God; and that the fact that such words or deeds are recorded in Scripture carries no necessary sanction of them as prompted of God.

We must, therefore, discriminate and distinguish *three degrees of authority* in the inspired record:

1. An authoritative narrative where sentiments and acts are not sanctioned and may be disowned as disapproved of God.

2. An authoritative narrative where sentiments and acts are not expressly approved or disapproved and must be judged by the general standards of Scripture teaching.

3. An authoritative narrative where the sentiments and acts are inspired and controlled by the Spirit of God, and therefore represent His mind and will (2 Sam. 7:4–17).

Lack of proper discrimination in matters such as these has often led to much confusion and needless controversy.

But, with these careful limitations, Verbal Inspiration is an absolute necessity if, in any proper sense, there be divine inspiration at all. As Dean Burgon has expressed it, what music would be without notes, a mathematical sum without figures, so would an inspired book be without words controlled by the inspiring Spirit.

We have taken pains to determine this principle at the outset, for without such foundation we have no solid bottom for the studies which follow. The more carefully this Book of God is examined, the more exact do its choice and use of words appear, and the more precise its phrases and terms and even grammatical forms. It is a matter of great importance to scrutinize the very language God employs to convey His mind, and in all the details which follow part of the purpose is both to demonstrate and illustrate the significance of every atom of Scripture—what our Lord called every "jot and tittle."

The following important considerations should always be borne in mind:

1. It is not necessary that the man inspired shall always understand his own message, for even the "prophets inquired and searched diligently" after the meaning of their own predictions which were an enigma even to themselves (1 Pet. 1:11, 12).

2. It is not necessary to comprehend the mode of inspiration. All we are concerned with is the result, the investment of the message with unique authority as from God, who was pleased thus to supply to men a final standard of doctrine and duty.

3. Inspiration is affirmed, of course, only of the original documents, now no longer extant. Many mistakes may have been made by copyists,

and some interpolations by officious scribes and translators are fallible. It is the part of reverent criticism to seek, by careful examination
and comparison of all existing documents, to detect errors and restore
as far as possible the Scriptures in their original purity.

4. Inspiration is not affected by minor differences in various narratives. While God used men as media of communication, they were
not mere machines, but were left to use their faculties in individual
freedom. Hence arose peculiarities, not only of style, but of treatment,
according as the same utterances or occurrences might impress each
observer or narrator. But this, instead of impairing, rather increases
the trustworthiness of the record, as it proves that there could have
been no prior agreement or conspiracy among the various writers.

5. Most so-called discrepancies or disagreements disappear, when
the various records are regarded as partial, rather than complete, as
each of the four Gospel narratives may present some features not
found in the rest, but capable of being combined with the others in
one full statement. For example, the complete inscription over the cross
was: "This is Jesus of Nazareth, the King of the Jews." Of this inscription of ten words, Matthew records eight, Mark five, Luke
seven, and John eight, and not the same in any two cases; but the full
inscription includes all the words found in any record. There is,
therefore, no antagonism or contradiction.

6. That which is essential in inspiration is the *action of the mind of
God upon the mind of man,* in such way and measure as to quicken and
qualify the human medium for the true conveyance of the Divine message. Revelation expresses the *informing* process, and inspiration the
imparting.

2

The High Level of the Word of God

THE WORKMAN IS known by his work, and the more perfect the product the fuller the exhibition of the producer. The Bible, being God's workmanship, will, like the heavens, declare His Glory and show forth His handiwork (Ps. 19).

He expressly declares: "My thoughts are not your thoughts; neither are your ways, My ways; for as the heavens are higher than the earth so are My ways higher than your ways and My thoughts than your thoughts" (Is. 55:8, 9).

This states a pervasive principle of the entire Scripture: "thoughts" —literally, "weavings"—include the whole fabric of Scripture conceptions, contrivances, devices, imaginations (cf. Ps. 33:10; 40:5; 92:5; 94:11). In the last reference, "The Lord knoweth the thoughts of man that they are vanity"—there is a designed contrast between man's devices and God's, man's being compared in the same prophecy of Isaiah (59:5, 6), to *cobwebs* which never become *garments*.

God's "thoughts" and "ways" are by no means equivalent. His ideas or ways of *thinking* are as far above the level of man's as the heavens are above the earth—a distance illimitable and immeasurable. And so of His *ways* of *doing*, as of His ways of *thinking*—the distance and difference is infinite. Human notions all fall immeasurably short of God's, as when the Jews conceived of Messiah as a temporal monarch and His kingdom an earthly one, and had no thought of that new man to be made of twain, in the union of Jew and Gentile (Eph. 2:15). His way was to make the gospel a highway for all nations, and the whole earth, even the dark places and habitations of cruelty, a fruitful field and garden of the Lord. But, even after the gospel era had begun, how slow was Peter himself to apprehend it (Acts 9:11).

We must be ready to meet, at every point in Bible study, the evidence that we are communing with an infinite Being and, as Coleridge discriminatingly said, *consent to apprehend much that we cannot comprehend.*

God has, to begin with, His own unique constitution of Being. He is the *eternal* God, and therefore independent of all time limits, as the Persians defined Him—*Zeruane Akerene*—Time without bounds. He is the "I AM"—to whom past, present and future are equally *today,* who is alike without beginning and without end, without succession of days or change of conditions. He is the *Omniscient* One, to whom all things are so absolutely known that there can neither be anything hidden from Him nor any increase of knowledge or intelligence. He is the *Omnipresent* One, so pervading all space and time with His presence that it is only in an accommodated sense that He can be said to be at any point of time or place any more than any other. He is the *Immutable* One, who changes not. His absolute perfection at once forbids change for the worse which would be declension and degeneration, or for the better which would be improvement and imply previous imperfection, since perfection cannot be improved. Such a unique and solitary Being must have His own ways, both of thinking and doing. We shall find evidence that He has His own *lexicon*, using language in a unique sense and defining His own terms; that He has His own *arithmetic* and *mathematics,* not limited to man's addition and multiplication tables; His own *calendar,* reckoning time in His own fashion, and dividing all duration into ages and dispensations, to suit His eternal plan; that He has His own *annals* and *chronicles,* writing up history according to methods of His own, leaving great gaps of silence, chasms of oblivion, where He deems nothing worthy of record; that He has His own *grammar,* using all the nice distinctions of conjugation and declension, voice and mood, tense and person, gender and number, with discrimination and design. In a word, everything about God and His methods shows that He lives on a different plane from man and cannot be either restricted to man's notions or judged by man's standards.

We shall meet in the study of Scripture many original and peculiar divine devices. Certain features appear prominent, as connected with unique patterns, models and standards. These, designed to arrest attention and embodying permanent lessons, should be grouped by themselves, as both related to one another and contributing to one common, ultimate end. They are divine ideals, expressing divine ideas; concrete forms for abstract truths, making them easier of apprehension and more lasting in impression.

Examples will readily recur to the bible student. First, there are three pictorial parables of higher truths, all needing higher explanation: the Tabernacle, the one house which God planned and built, the Temple, being essential on the same model; the *Ceremonial*, the one order of worship and service in connection with His house, which He decreed and directed; and again the *Calendar*, the one series of fasts, feasts and festivals which He arranged and ordained.

These three parables He meant to be the constant study of His devout people, and to be illustrated and illuminated by the subsequent events and teachings of all history. About each of these there seems to be a sevenfold completeness. In the Tabernacle the conspicuous features were the brazen and golden altars, the lampstand and shewbread table, the laver, ark and mercy seat. In the Ceremonial the five offerings—sin and trespass, meal, peace, and burnt—then the red heifer, first fruits and tithes. In the Calendar, a sacred seventh day, week, month, year, a seven times seventh year, and a seventy times seventh, or four hundred and ninetieth, with a dimly forecast final millennium or sabbatical thousand years.

Three *standards of measurement* are also suggested, as indexes of His divine Power, Wisdom and Love.

1. The wonders connected with the Exodus from Egypt, referred to hundreds of times (Mic. 7:15).

2. The miracle promised in the Regathering of the scattered tribes of Israel, a second time out of all lands (Jer. 16:14, 15).

3. The supreme marvel, of the Raising of Christ from the Dead and exalting Him to His own Right Hand (Eph. 1:19–23). Phil. 2:9–11).

The phrase "according to," so often used suggests that His design is to give His people a standard by which to estimate both His ability and willingness to do great things for them.

To the wonders of the Exodus He perpetually appeals in the Old Testament. "I am Jehovah who brought you forth out of the Land of Egypt, out of the House of Bondage." By this He perpetually rebuked their unbelief and stimulated faith and fearlessness in the presence of foes.

There are indications that the second return or restoration of scattered Israel will be attended by events so stupendous and supernatural as to more than equal those of the Exodus, and having absolutely no parallel in ordinary human history.

And as to the Resurrection and exaltation of our Lord, that went far beyond all dreams of even divine power, defying death and the devil, invading the uniformity of natural law and annulling the power of gravitation—the miracle of all ages, all wonders in one.

These three Standards of Power all have to do with an Exodus: the first from Egypt as the land of Bondage; the second from all lands of exile and disperson; the third our Lord's Exodus from the realms of Death and the grave—and as such referred to in the converse on the Mount of Transfiguration by Moses and Elijah.

Many minor points of resemblance are suggested, particularly between the deliverance from Egypt and the Resurrection and ascension of the Son of God. In the former, four wonders were very conspicuous: the passing by the blood-stained portals; the crossing of the Red Sea; the overwhelming of the pursuing foes; and the covenant guidance by the Pillar of Cloud.

In our Lord's Exodus, how correspondent the fourfold marvel: the divine passing over of the blood-sprinkled sinner; the emergence of Christ and with Him His believing people from the place of death and judgment; the overthrow of Satanic foes by that same Resurrection and ascension; and the bestowment of the new Pillar of Cloud in the Pentecostal gift of the Spirit.

As God has thus His own scales for weight, and standards for measure, some things which to man are small, to Him are great; what man accounts long is to Him short and conversely. To attempt to crowd divine things into human compass is both to misapprehend God and to belittle Him. We must accustom ourselves to His standards, so far as possible to adopt them, or adapt ourselves to them; or, if no more, recognize them as far above our own. We need a sense of Proportion.

The Time element must be kept in its proper relations to Scripture and the plans of God. "One day is with the Lord as a thousand years and a thousand years as one day"; that is, with the Eternal One, human time measurements count nothing—a prolonged interval is but as a moment.

The High Priest, on the great day of Atonement, went from the altar of sacrifice into the Holiest and shortly returned to bless the people. These few moments which elapsed between his disappearance within the veil, and his reappearance in the court, typify the whole interval between our Lord's ascension and second advent, already protracted over nearly nineteen centuries. God's "little while" often proves man's long while, and especially when events are seen in *perspective* as in prophetic vision. We must not stumble over the difficulty of delay. "Long" and "short" are relative terms: everything depends upon the scale.

At a time of political panic, due to local issues, the Earl of Salisbury counseled alarmists to quiet their fears and get a wider view of events by procuring *larger maps*. Students of prophecy and of Scripture, generally, need to understand God's larger maps and eternal plans—His worldwide campaign and age-long battle—to get some glimpse of the magnitude and magnificence of the whole scheme of Redemption which takes in two eternities. All time is but an instant in eternal movements. *Delay* is so far recognized in the Scripture as possible that the duty of persistent faith, persevering hope and patient waiting is based upon such deferment (Hab. 2:3).

Much of the mystery of Scripture is inseparable from its exalted level. What is eternal cannot be expressed or explained in terms of the temporal, and what is celestial must essentially differ from what is terrestrial. If all that is divine could be comprehended by what is human it would cease to be divine. Perfect understanding implies equality of intellect and intelligence: the tiny cup of a flower might as well attempt to contain the ocean as a man's mind to grasp the infinite.

A man, passing a church with Daniel Webster, asked him how he could reconcile the doctrine of the Trinity with reason; and the great statesman of giant intellect replied by another question: "Do you expect to understand the arithmetic of Heaven?"

Such expressions as "God said," "the Lord spake, saying," "the Lord commanded," "the Word of the Lord came unto me saying," etc., occur in the Pentateuch alone 680 times. How strange it would be if in all these nearly 700 communications from Jehovah, there was nothing too high for man to comprehend? Sin was born of presumptuous intelligence: Milton's Satan is the portrait of intellect without God, and the first temptation was an act of human revolt against the mystery of a divine command and an attempt to break through into the realm of the unknown. All rationalism is the worship of human reason and denial of any higher level in divine truth than man can reach or any deeper abyss in divine mystery than man can sound: it is in effect a claim to man's equality with God and a virtual denial of any God at all. Francis Bacon, who was called the "wisest and brightest of mankind," said, "I do much condemn that interpretation of Scripture which is only after the manner of men, as they use to interpret a profane book."

It is because the Word of God belongs to a superhuman level that man's investigation of it never reaches its limit of new discovery. Every new study of it brings new unveiling. As a distinguished author says: "In the Divine Word, the letter is stationary; the meaning progressive."

3

The Identity of the Written and Living Word

OUR LORD IS found in the Word, in the letter; the Word is found in Him in the life. It is of the highest importance to guard the written Word from losing its firm hold upon us as God's Revelation of Christ. There are two forms or modes of such revelation: first, *to* the soul in the Scriptures; second, *in* the soul by the Spirit, in the experience of His indwelling; but the scriptural precedes the experimental as its basis, so that, without the former the latter is impossible in all ordinary cases.

It is therefore a delusion to suppose that, even if the Scriptures were destroyed or impaired we should still have Christ. This may in a sense be true in the case of one who has already known Christ experimentally, but two important questions arise; first, how did the believer get experimental knowledge of Him except through the Scriptures? and, secondly, how are others who do not yet believe in Christ and have no inner revelation of Him, to find the way to faith if confidence in the Scriptures is destroyed or undermined? Even if our faith in the Lord Jesus survives loss of faith in the written Word, what becomes of the authoritative note in preaching?

The teaching of our Lord Himself on this matter is very explicit: "Search the Scriptures; for they are they that testify of Me." "They have Moses and the prophets; let them hear them; for if they believe not Moses and the prophets neither will they be persuaded though one rose from the dead." "Had ye believed Moses ye would have believed Me, for he wrote of Me; but if ye believe not his writings how shall ye believe my words?"*

Here is a progressive testimony. First those who honestly search the Scriptures find in them sufficient testimony to Christ; second, where there is faith in their witness there will be faith in His words; and, third, if men reject their testimony, even the miracle of His resurrection will fail to convince.

Here, curiously enough, is an outline of the whole history of modern rationalistic "criticism." It began by not believing "Moses' writings"; then it assailed the testimony of "the prophets," then it proceeded to undermine the authority of Christ's words; and at last, the confidence in His Resurrection from the dead. Our Lord thus in a few words hinted the course of rationalistic thought nineteen centuries later.

Explicitly, our Lord, in His post-resurrection interview, declares that in the whole Old Testament He is revealed (Luke 24:28–44). His words are unmistakable and His witness is repeated: "Beginning at Moses and all the prophets, He expounded unto them in all the Scriptures, the things concerning Himself," declaring that "all things must be fulfilled which are written in the Law of Moses and in the prophets and in the Psalms concerning Me." Thus, on the way to Emmaus, He traced one progressive Messianic revelation throughout the three popular divisions in which the Old Testament workings were arranged. To understand New Testament records of Christ, then, we must know the whole Old Testament, from Genesis to Malachi, for the two are as closely related as a medallion and its mold.

The whole Scripture is the *Mirror* of the Messiah. This is verified from several points of view, as will appear later:

1. The Prophetical. Directly and indirectly His Image is forecast and foreshadowed (Gen. 3:15; Ps. 22, 110; Is. 53).

2. The Sacramental. Under the Covenant of the Law circumcision and sacrifices, both sweet savor and ill savor. Under the Covenant of Grace, Baptism and the Lord's Supper.

*Luke 16:31; John 5:39, 45, 47.

3. Ceremonial. The whole Levitical System, Tabernacle and Priesthood; with the specific provisions and ordinances. Passover, Day of Atonement, Red Heifer, Leper's cleansing, etc.

4. Historical. Events like the Deluge, Exodus, Desert Journey, Conquest of Canaan; persons like Adam, Abel, Abram, Melchizedek, Isaac, Joseph, Moses, Aaron, Joshua, David, Solomon, etc.

5. Evangelical. The four gospel narratives separately mirroring Him from as many different points of view; and jointly projecting His figure before us in a combined and complete witness.

6. Autobiographical. His testimony concerning Himself when its scattered fragments are gathered together witness to Him as the Son of Man and Son of God, prophet, priest and King; His parables and miracles forming part of His witness, and above all the crowning miracle, His Resurrection.

7. Apostolical. The writings of the New Testament generally, the Epistles to the Churches, to the Hebrews, the epistles, individual and general, all center in Him and exhibit His teaching and character—officium propheticum, officium sacerdotale, officium regium.

The Scriptures portray our Lord in His three great offices, as Prophet, Priest, King; each incomplete without the others—prophet, to instruct and inform; priest, to atone and intercede; king, to subdue and control. As has been well said, as Shepherd, He bears the crook; as Suffering Savior, the Cross; as Victorious King, the Crown.*

There is a strange, almost mystic, similarity between the Written and Incarnate Word, traceable even in many minor matters.

For instance, the one Bible is a compound of a Hebrew and a Greek portion; the composition of the Old Testament covered about a thousand years, and that of the New, about one-tenth that time. The life of our Lord on earth spans about 33 years, in two marked divisions, the latter, the period of public ministry, about one-tenth of the former. The Old Testament dealt in types and parables, and the New in clear and direct doctrine and fact. Our Lord taught largely in parable, promising in the Paraclete a fuller, clearer revelation. Again, as the whole inspired Word consists of body and spirit, the letter and the deeper insight that interprets it and gives it force and value,

---

* Rev. Hubert Brooke.

so our Lord had a body of flesh, indwelt by the living Eternal Spirit. The parallel may be further followed in many lesser particulars, both suggestive and instructive.

The Supreme Importance of Prophecy arises, most of all, from its being the link between the written and the living word. Prophecy, in its larger sense, covers two-thirds at least of all Scripture. It is not necessarily *predictive*, but may be *preceptive*, the result of insight into truth as well as foresight of the future. A prophet was one who *spoke in behalf of God*. Whatever therefore represents God's message to man is prophecy: even history is indirectly prophetic so far as it has an ethical or typical bearing. Special study needs therefore to be centered upon the prophetic element in Scripture, and most of all with reference to Him who was the Supreme Head of all the Prophetic succession.

The Scriptures represent the Lord Jesus Christ as the *Final and Supreme Prophet of God* (Deut. 18:15–19; Heb. 1:1).

Though other prophets were both called and qualified of God, they were finite and fallible, human and necessarily imperfect. Their inferiority to Him will appear if they are contrasted with Him, in the following particulars:

1. In numbers, many.	He one, alone, solitary.
2. In limitations of knowledge.	He without limitations.
3. In scope of power.	He having all power.
4. They sinful and imperfect.	He sinless and perfect.
5. They inspired at times only.	He always the divine mouthpiece.
6. They not always understanding.	He omniscient and original.
7. They but partially foreseeing.	He framer and controller of the ages.
8. They witnessing to the Light.	He Himself the Light of the world.
9. They revealing truth in part.	He Himself the Truth.
10. They giving place to others.	He without rival or successor.

The only way to read the two testaments, intelligently and adequately, is to compare them, to set them side by side; to remember Augustine's great motto, and be prepared to find the Lord Jesus Christ *"latent"* in the Old as He is *"patent"* in the New. The entire old Economy, including its history and prophecy, ritual and ceremony, is a *parable* of Christ, which finds its amplification, explanation and illustration in the history and economy of the new. If the Bible, in its two great divisions, be thus regarded and studied, correspondences will continually reveal themselves, sometimes so exact and varied as to remind us of the counterparts, so often found in nature, between forms and colors, vegetable and animal life, causes and effects; or of the rhythmic harmony of lines in a poem, where the words differ, but the metrical flow is the same.

Not only is the Old Testament the *parable*, it is also the *prophecy* of the New; it forecasts the future which the New reveals and records. A devout writer has compared the Old Testament to a dissected map which he once gave to his children for their amusement, and which, when all its parts were accurately fitted, and the map turned over, revealed on the back the figure of a man, so that his form might be the key to the true place which each fragment was to fill. Were we sufficiently familiar with the entire structure of the Old Testament, we might find in it at every point his analogy with the New. The superficial reader overlooks the correspondence; but the close and careful searcher finds it in multiplied details, until he wonders that he could ever have failed to detect it. This, we take to be a most valuable department of apologetics. It imparts to the whole Old Testament a prophetic character, making it like the mystic memorials of Egypt, whose inscriptions waited for centuries for a Champollion to decipher and interpret them. Niebuhr reckoned these results the crowning achievement of the century; and the Word of God is still waiting for its Champollion fully to read its deep meaning, and discover everywhere the Christ of God.

The true way to know the Scriptures is to regard them as what Bunyan called "The House of the Interpreter," to all whose apartments and chambers of mystery, the Lord Jesus Christ is the Magic Key.

Obviously only thus can the Messianic chamber be opened and entered; the 300 predictions, there stored up, are enigmas whose only adequate solution is Himself. The Symbolical Chamber, with its Tabernacle symbolism, its priestly robes and rites, its fasts and feasts, sacrifices and offerings are meaningless until He is seen as the Tabernacle of God with man, at once High Priest and victim, offering and offerer. The Historical chamber is a picture gallery, with scenic paintings and personal portraits, and He, the living guide to explain the events and characters of all ages. There is the Sacramental chamber, with its ceremonies and ordinances of separation and purification; its anointings and washings, its symbols of fleshly mortification, of burial and resurrection, and perpetual feeding on heavenly food: all these are without meaning until they serve to typify identification with Him in suffering and service, victory and glory.

The Inspired Written Word and the Eternal Living Word are forever inseparable. The Bible is Christ portrayed; Christ is the Bible fulfilled. One is the picture, the other is the Person, but the features are the same and proclaim their identity.

4

The Prophetic Element in Scripture

THE WORDS "PROPHET" AND "PROPHECY," ETC., occur so frequently, over 400 times, that they suggest special study.

"Prophet" is always used in one of two senses, and prophecy
is regarded from two corresponding points of view. When a prophet
predicts or foretells, he sees and represents the future in the light of
the present; when he rebukes, reproves, counsels, or admonishes, as
Jehovah's representative messenger—*forth*-telling rather than *fore*-
telling, he portrays the present in the light of the future.*

Hence there are two sorts of prophetic teaching: the *preceptive* and the
predictive. Elijah, Elisha, John the Baptist belong to the former; David,
Daniel, Isaiah, John, to the latter; Moses, Hosea, Malachi, to both.

Predictive prophecy is the foremost proof to which the Word of
God appeals in its own behalf. It was the standing miracle by which
God challenged faith in His inspired Word, defying all the worshipers of other gods and their sages and seers to produce any such
proofs that their gods were worthy of worship or their prophets true
representatives of a divine religion (cf. Is. 41:21–23).

Prophecy characterizes one of the three main divisions of Old
Testament Scripture, the others being the historic and the poetic or
devotional. The common Hebrew word, *Nabi*, from a root, meaning
to boil up, or bubble as a spring, suggests the impulse of inspiration

---

* Compare Edersheim.

(2 Pet. 1:21) as a mouthpiece of God giving utterance to an outflow of divine thought. The divine message was communicated by dreams, visions, trance or ecstasy, or in ways not revealed. Prophets were known as *seers*—men who had supernatural insight or foresight or both. The *ecstatic state* predominates in the Old Testament, and is not the highest, for neither Moses nor our Lord ever was in it.

The prophetic office was mainly one of *teaching*, and intensely practical, meant to rebuke and reform, rouse and incite to action; hence the "schools of prophets" in the later days of Elijah and Elisha, associations of men, more or less endowed with the Spirit, out of whom a succession of prophets might come. Eichorn discriminatingly calls Moses' Song (Deut. 32) the "Magna Charta of Prophecy."

For a *transient* inspiration, or a special occasion men might have the prophetic gift, irrespective of *character*, as in Saul's and Balaam's cases: but those who had a *continuous mission* as prophets were men of deep piety like Isaiah and Daniel. The main criteria of a true prophet were:

1. The accordance of his messages with the Revealed Law.

2. His not promising prosperity to the rebellious and unrepentant.

3. His own conscious call and assurance of his mission (Jer. 20:8, 9; 26:12).

4. His consequent power to produce in others conviction of truth.

5. His foresight of the Messiah and His career.

Fulfilled predictions and miracles were only confirmatory proofs when his teaching was in harmony with previous revelations of God's mind in Scripture (Deut. 13:2).

The promulgation of the prophetic message might be *oral* or *written*; sometimes what was first by word of mouth was afterwards committed to writing for preservation and wider dissemination. Probably all prophecies thus put in scroll form are yet extant, though some oral utterances may have been lost to us.

Prebendary Horne has attempted to arrange the Old Testament "seers" in chronological order, but even scholars disagree as to the exact place of several of the prophets in the prophetic succession. It may help students to embody here the results of Horne's investigations, specifying only the times of the Kings of Judah to promote simplicity and avoid burdening the memory.

Prophets	Approximate Times	"Burden," or Subject	Date, B.C.
	Kings of Judah:		
JONAH	Joash; Amaziah, or Azariah.	Nineveh.	860–784
AMOS	Uzziah.	Syria; Philistia; Tyre; Edom; Moab; Israel's Captivity.	810–785
HOSEA	Uzziah; Jotham; Ahaz; Hezekiah.	The Jews; Messiah; Latter days.	810–725
ISAIAH	Uzziah; Jotham; Ahaz; Hezekiah; Manasseh.	Deliverance from Captivity; Rejection of Israel; Calling of Gentiles; Glories of Christ's Kingdom.	800–700
JOEL	Uzziah, or Manasseh.	Judah.	810–660
MICAH	Jotham; Ahaz;	Judah and Israel; Messiah's birthplace.	758–699
NAHUM	Hezekiah.	Downfall of Assyria.	720–698
ZEPHANIAH	Josiah.	Captivity.	640–609
JEREMIAH	Josiah; Jehoahaz; Jehoakim; Jehoiachin; Zedekiah.	Desolation of Jerusalem, Judah, etc. Captivity. Messiah.	628–586
HABAKKUK	Jehoiakim.	Destruction of Chaldean and Babylonian Empire.	620–598
DANIEL	During the Captivity.	Messiah's kingdom.	606–534
OBADIAH	After the siege of Jerusalem by Nebuchadnezzar.	Edom.	588–583
EZEKIEL	In the Captivity.	To comfort and warn the captives.	595–536
HAGGAI	After return from Captivity.	Encouraging Jews in rebuilding the temple; Christ's coming.	520–518
ZECHARIAH	Ditto.	Same as Haggai; Glory of Messiah.	520–518
MALACHI	Days of Nehemiah.	Reproving the priesthood: announcing near approach of Messiah.	436–420

The word "prophet" has come from the medieval use of the Greek word (*propheteia*) to carry the sense of *prediction*, but the larger idea of *interpretation* should not be lost, and in the latter sense the church still has the prophetic gift, so far as godly preachers and teachers unfold and declare to men the Word of God. We know now how far the Holy Spirit may, even now, empower believers with spiritual insight, though foresight is very rare.

God seems to have meant that something corresponding to the regal, sacerdotal, and prophetical orders should always exist in the church—in those fitted to guide and govern; in others, called to administer ordinances and act as media of communion with God and worship; and again in others who by clear apprehension of divine truth are prepared to teach. But, in no proper sense are there any *priests*, for all believers constitute a priesthood with privileges of immediate access to God.

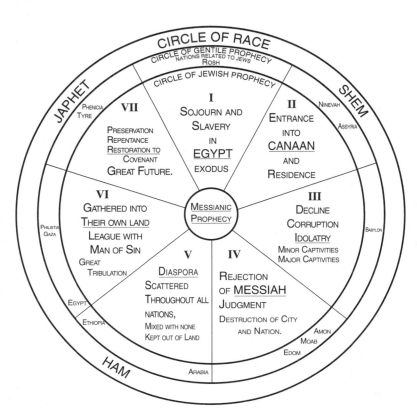

A peculiar and very significant fact about the whole prophetic element is that, when its fragmentary utterances are brought together they are found to constitute *one organic body*. All predictions of the Word of God may be arranged in concentric circles—the innermost pertaining to our Lord Jesus Christ, as heart and center of all prophecy, then, next outside, the circle of predictions pertaining to the Hebrews as God's chosen people, then, next, the circle of national predictions having reference to the various peoples located about, and having special connection with Jewish history; and then outside of all, the earliest forecast of the history of the race. We can best convey this idea by the two diagrams which accompany this section.*

In predictive prophecy we have an impregnable rock fortress for rational faith, defying all successful assault. It is a double defense—it

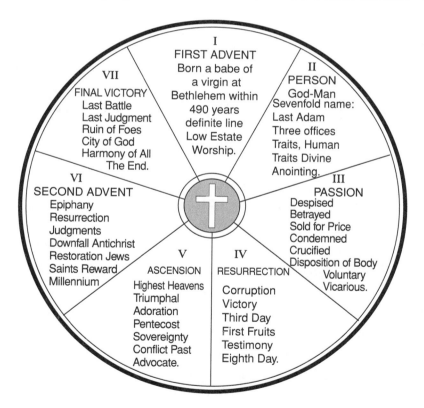

* From the *Bible and Spiritual Life,* by the author.

proves the divine origin, inspiration and authority of Scripture; and because at least one-half of all its forecasts converge upon the Lord Jesus
Christ, it vindicates His Deity and Messiahship. The central Messianic
prediction (Is. 52:13 —53:12) is alone sufficient. Jewish and Christian writers agree that it is a portrait of the coming Messiah, differing
only as to the historic person to whom it refers and who answers to the
portrait.*

The highest crown of the prophetic office was found in the fullness and clearness of Messianic revelation; hence Isaiah has been
known as the "Evangelical Prophet," because in his writings are
found more predictions about the coming Christ than in any one or
all of the others. Hence also the master device of Satan in seeking to
impugn and impair the prophetic value of Isaiah's writings.

---

* Compare Edersheim.

5
Structural Form in Scripture

The unity of the scriptures reminds us literally of a structure with its architectural symmetry and mathematical proportion. As a Doric or Ionic column had a fixed relation of circumference to height, so, in the Word of God singular correspondences are traceable, as between the five books of Moses, the five poetical and five major prophetical books, the five historical narratives that begin the New Testament; and again the twelve minor histories, and twelve minor prophecies of the Old Testament. These correspondences can scarcely be accidental.

If we look into more minute matters, we shall find these signs of a mathematical mind pervading the individual books, as in a perfect building, even the smallest peculiarity, like a pinnacle, or a capital, conforms to the general design and belongs to the same order and style of architecture. The great Architect and Builder had before Him the finished Temple of Truth, before the first stone was laid; and so perfect were all the details of His plan that no sound of "hammer, nor axe, nor any tool of iron was heard in the house while it was in building"—all being made ready beforehand, and needing no human agency to accommodate each part to its place (1 Kgs. 6:7).

To conceive of the Word of God *as a structure*, and so to picture it before the mind's eye, the imagination is very helpful. It suggests many other thoughts which aid a fuller understanding of the character of the Scriptures as a whole.

For example, every structure implies a *constructor;* one mind planning and designing behind the workmen who simply wrought upon successive parts and stages of the building but had no part in the plan.

It suggests also the originality and sublimity and universality of the divine design, the incorporation of divine ideas in sensible ideals and patterns; and the line of proportion and harmony traceable throughout.

It suggests unity, symmetry and completeness; the variety and multiplicity of the various parts, all contributing to the perfection of the whole, the individual beauty of all subordinate features, and the structural law pervading, controlling, unifying all, and determining their mutual relations.

It suggests the progressive development of the building toward completion, the impossibility of either defect or addition when finished, and the inhabitation of the divine Spirit, as a temple, irradiating and glorifying it by the Presence of God.

This thought of the Word of God in its totality and entirety we would fix in mind before examining its parts in detail.

Though a composite product of sixty-six different books, or, counting double, and those which belong together, as one, of fifty-six and by some forty human writers and prepared through fifteen centuries or more, the Bible is still *one* Book, as truly as though it had but one human writer as well as divine Author. This unity, of itself, is one of the strongest proofs of its superhuman origin. Take those great structures the pyramids of Egypt, or the cathedrals of Europe, that took centuries and hundreds of thousands of workmen to erect, one original designer must have been behind all the work of the mere laborers: the building was not due to their brawn but to the architect's brain.

Evidences of this pervasive structural law everywhere appear, as further study will show.

For example, structural unity is seen first of all in the great *ideas* embodied in Scripture, somewhat as all architectural orders are the expression of certain conceptions—the Egyptian, of strength and massiveness, the Greek of symmetry and beauty, the Gothic, of aspiration and adoration. God's Word is a Temple of Truth, in which supreme facts and forms of thought find the highest artistic expression.

About a few grand ideas or concepts all Scripture as a *whole*, centralizes and crystallizes; for example,

1. God;
2. Man, regarded as a whole—a race of humanity;
3. Man, regarded as an individual, alienated by sin, both from God and his fellowman;
4. The God-Man, uniting in one person the two natures, divine and human;.
5. Man, as reconciled to God, through the God-Man and to his fellowman;
6. God in man, in the Holy Spirit, dwelling and working and transforming;
7. God over man, re-established in His proper sovereignty and supremacy.

Here in seven simple and progressive conceptions is a complete outline both of biblical theology and of redemptive history from creation to the new creation. Under these few heads all else may be easily embraced. The idea of God suggests His nature, attributes and activities; the idea of man, his creation, original character and condition; and his fall, the origin of sin, its consequences and condemnation. The God-Man hints the mystery of the Incarnation, Salvation by Atonement, God's manifestation to man and the righteousness which is by faith; the Holy Spirit, the mystery of regeneration and sanctification, fitness for service, access to God in prayer, fellowship with Him and with saints, and the unseen spirit realm. God's ultimate rule over a regenerate race gives a glimpse of the final consummation of His redemptive plan and of man's redeemed estate.

Thus, whatever variety and diversity appears in Holy Scripture, the unity is more conspicuous, and to that all else contributes as many different musical notes and chords blend in one harmony or symphony. Or, better still, we may liken it to the solar system, with its one central orb, around which all else revolves—a Holy, Infinite Eternal God—then subordinate facts and truths, like planets with their satellites, smaller systems with their correlated interests, but all belonging to one larger system. Or, again, to find the center of unity brings order out of confusion, and shows all roads, from whatever quarter or direction converging toward one "golden milestone."

Unity does not forbid multiplicity and diversity, provided all parts combine in one and contribute to one end. "God in many parts and many ways spake in time past to the others by the prophets," and "in these last days, by His Son" (Heb. 1:1). But it was *He* who spake through all.

Structure, so far from forbidding multiplicity and variety of parts, rather implies them. The word, from *struō*—to build—suggests materials of different nature, size, shape and pattern, brought to one site, and arranged and combined into one harmonious whole, which we call a "building." An ideal structure therefore will have certain prominent characteristics: first of all, it must be the embodiment and expression of some idea or conception; then it must have definite form; must also have a purpose or specific end, and variety of parts; otherwise there is no *structure* for there is nothing with which to build; and all this implies a thinker, designer, builder. An idea, embodied, insures beauty; form, consistency and symmetry; a purpose, serviceableness and utility; variety of parts, adaptation to the end; and a builder as the source of all.

On some of these peculiarities of biblical structure we have already commented, but as we advance to the consideration of the materials of which the Bible is made up, we need to understand intelligently their contribution to its unity and completeness.

Let us not forget the two ideas that are implied in *form*, namely *inclusiveness* and *exclusiveness;* it includes all that is essential to its perfection, and as rigidly excludes all that is superfluous and needless. If anything necessary to completeness be absent, there is a lack—the defect of insufficiency; if anything unnecessary be present, there is an excess—the defect of excrescence.

To illustrate this, take the human hand, which in its perfection is one of the most remarkable of the Creator's works. Sir Charles Bell, one of the famous eight distinguished men selected to write the celebrated "Bridgewater Treatises," chose "The Hand, its mechanism and vital endowments, as evincing design." He finds over 8,000 words insufficient to describe the construction and adaptations of this one member of the human body. Consider one peculiarity of the hand: it has four fingers of unequal lengths, and one thumb; and the thumb is so placed as to be in opposition to the fingers; and these five subordinate members so arranged that, when the ends of fingers and thumb touch, they form, within, a hollow sphere, and would just meet about a small ball. Were there one finger less or more, no thumb or two thumbs; or were the fineries of the same lengths, or differently arranged on the hand, all this perfection of adaptation and cooperation would be forfeited, and what is now a perfect structure would be imperfect and *de-formed*, that is, without form, in its true and technical sense. And this is but one feature out of many which evince creative design. Again, if the fingers and thumbs be outspread, it will be found that from the center of the palm, the same radius would describe a perfect arc of a circle about the ends of thumb and fingers, another evidence of a symmetry and proportion which few ever observe.

Now transfer such correspondences as these to the structure of the Word of God. Here all that is, is necessary, and there is nothing superfluous. We do not find here much that men might have desired, because it is not essential to the end for which the Holy Scriptures were designed. For example, there were great nations of antiquity of whose history we should be glad to have fuller records, such as Egypt, Persia, Phoenicia, Assyria, Greece and Rome; yet in God's Book they are scarcely mentioned, while one obscure people, for whose annals the human historian cares but little, occupies twelve whole books, and is the nucleus of all biblical history. But the reason is that the Bible is the book of Salvation, and because the Jew figures so largely in the redemption of the race, Jewish history is made conspicuous, and other nations are referred to only as in some way connected with the Hebrews.

Again, mankind craves knowledge upon matters connected with science. Yet the Holy Scriptures touch scientific mysteries only incidentally, never disclosing the hidden laws and facts that it has taken centuries to bring to light. And all this is to be accounted for by the fact that form excludes what is superfluous. The Bible was not meant as a scientific textbook, but a spiritual guide—to teach man what he cannot find out for himself otherwise—the way of salvation. To have made the Word of God an encyclopedia of general information would have not only obscured its greater design, but diverted human attention to minor issues. The perfection of Holy Scripture is found in part in its absolute singleness of aim.

But on the other hand, whatever contributes to this supreme purpose is found in the Scriptures, as in the hand there is a marvelous combination of bones and joints, muscles and tendon, blood vessels and nerves, all that is needful or helpful to the end in view.

Nothing but minute examination and careful consideration can make this apparent. We need to separate the various parts of the Bible, for individual examination, then set them side by side for comparison, and then combine them again, to understand their mutual relations, as we can best appreciate a skeleton by taking it apart, studying all its hingejoints and ball-and-socket joints, its cervical axis and vertebrae, and then once more restoring each to its place. This is the method we propose in these Bible studies; both the analytic and the synthetic; the examination of the individual parts, and then of the collective whole.

One result may be confidently reckoned on in advance: We shall find nothing lacking and nothing excessive. As in any true structure, timbers meet and join with mortise and tenon, and stones fit each other in shape, size and angle; pillars are set on bases and crowned with appropriate capitals; so, in the Holy Scripture, all parts contribute to each other and to the whole. Every book serves some end not answered by any other; every historic event or personage; every rite or ceremony; every action or utterance, have something to do to fill out the grand central design.

Another result may be predicted: We shall discover new and unsuspected consistencies and harmonies; even where there is apparent contradiction at first, there will be found real coordination and cooperation, afterward. It is one of the marked characteristics of the Inspired Word, that its agreements, like other deep things of God, lie beneath the surface, like the hidden watercourses that connect far separated springs, or the great strata of bedrock that pop out at widely parted points. We must be content to dig deep and not trust surface appearances. Truth's harmonies are not such as are heard by the common ear, but to those whose bearing is divinely quickened, the whole Word of God is a glorious anthem, in which many voices and instruments combine in one symphony.

6

Mutual Relations of the Two Testaments

A S WE HAVE ALREADY SEEN, the Word of God is a unit—a symmetrical, complete structure, one organic whole. Yet it is composed of two main parts, and many subordinate and diverse members. It should, first of all, be viewed as a *whole*, in its essential totality and entirety; then, its consistency and harmony being seen, any apparent discord or discrepancy will lead us to distrust the accuracy of our own vision and perception rather than its own consistency and perfection.

Unity does not exclude *duality*. This book is in two principal parts, the Old and New Testaments, not independent of each other but, like the two sides of the human body, organically one; the two hands and feet both by their likeness and unlikeness contribute to mutual efficiency. The two Testaments must be studied together, to secure the best results, as right and left hands and feet, eyes and ears, must be united in working and walking, seeing and hearing. The whole Bible has one central idea and controlling purpose: so has each Testament, and every subordinate part. To grasp intelligently these guiding, leading conceptions is to hold the key to the contents of the inspired Word.

Broadly speaking, the Old Testament is prophetic; the New, historic; the former teaches truth, typically; the later directly, doctrinally.

31

In the one, the prominent, dominant feature is *Law,* as operative in God's dealing with man; in the other, *Grace,* in fuller exhibition and illustration. The Old Testament forecasts and foreshadows, often in enigma, what the New reveals, more clearly, in substance, and with that variety and vividness of color that so differs from the dull, dead monotony of a shadow.

There is a persistent attempt in some quarters, to depreciate the Old Testament, with a lamentable result that it is comparatively neglected. Yet the New Testament itself unmistakably teaches the organic unity of the two Testaments, and in various ways exhibits their mutual relations.

There are often definite statements of a practical moral and spiritual purpose and purport of Old Testament writings, as when Paul says, "Whatsoever things were written aforetime were written for our learning that we through patience and comfort of the Scriptures, might have hope" (Rom. 15:4). Here two main purposes are hinted— warnings and encouragement—records of evil doing with its penalty that we may be strengthened patiently to withstand temptation; records of well doing with its rewards that we may be comforted and encouraged in doing and bearing the will of God. And again, in reciting the history of Israel, "Now all these things happened unto them for examples, and are written for our learning and admonition" (1 Cor. 10:14).

The two Testaments are like the two cherubim of the mercy seat, facing in opposite directions, yet facing each other and overshadowing with glory one mercy seat; or again, they are like the human body bound together by joints and bands and ligaments; by one brain and heart, one pair of lungs, one system of respiration, circulation, digestion, sensor and motor nerves, where division is destruction.

Observe how our Lord constantly quoted from, or referred to, the Old Testament, its various books, and authors; persons and places mentioned in it; how He recognized its types—like the brazen serpent; how He lent the sanction of His authority to its commandments in the Sermon on the Mount, etc. Its teachings and terms thread His own discourses and sometimes are their woof and warp as well as pattern. He does not contradict but confirms it, explaining and interpreting its true meaning, and clearing away the rubbish of tradition or superstition which has covered and obscured it, as an artist washes off the dust which hides a masterpiece of painting, or the explorer unearths ancient buried treasures. There can be no doubt what our Lord thought of the practical value, immutable truth and bearing upon the New.

Westcott and Hort, in their edition of the Greek New Testament, have done a great service by indicating in capitals, the quotations of sentences and phrases from the Old Testament in the New. They have traced more than 1,500 such in the twenty-seven New Testament books. It is both a curious and significant fact that frequently these citations are in the very center of some paragraph and are a sort of turning point of the whole argument or mark the heart of the treatment, as in Paul's great portrait of charity, in 1 Corinthians 13, where the phrase, *"thinketh no evil"*—from Zechariah 8:17, marks the central feature in the portrait. The verbiage of the Septuagint translation of the Old Testament is so interwoven with the New, that the threads are mingled and cannot be separated. The New Testament is largely framed in the dialect of the Old, and again reminds us of the points and bands and ligaments which make the body one. The Book of God, taken as a whole, is a seamless robe yet a coat of may colors; a grand oratorio with one musical theme, yet many orchestral performers with a variety of instruments and voices.

There are not only general correspondences between the two Testaments, but between individual books, and often to a very remarkable degree, so that they serve to throw light upon each other. When placed side by side and studied as companion books this complementary character and relation become very apparent. For example, we place in opposite columns some of the books having this close mutual relation:

The Pentateuch, Genesis to Deuteronomy	The New Testament Pentateuch; The first five books—historical.
Genesis—Book of Beginnings.	John—Beginning of the Word.
Exodus—Book of Pilgrimage.	Epistles of Peter.
Leviticus—Book of Priesthood.	Epistle to Hebrews.
Joshua—Wars of the Lord.	Acts and Peaceful Conquests.

Judges—Period of Anarchy. Second Timothy, Jude.
Books of Wisdom—Job to Epistle of James.
    Solomon's Song.
Daniel, O.T. Apocalypse. Revelation.

These are a few examples of correspondence which might be carried much father; but these suffice to show some of the ligaments which bind the two Testaments together. And the effect upon Biblical study is somewhat as in a stereoscope, companion pictures blend into one so that objects stand out in relief, exhibiting not only outlines but proportions and dimensions.

Two great texts on Faith, both quoted from the Old Testament, thrice in the new, are introduced each time in a separate epistle, and at the turning point of the argument.

Compare Genesis 15:6; Romans 1:17; 4:3; Galatians 3:6, 11; Hebrews 10:38; James 2:23; Habakkuk 2:4 and the relation of each to the Epistle it appears in may be indicated by the *emphasis* on a particular word. Thus, "Abram believed and it was counted for righteousness."

In Romans the emphasis is on "*counted.*"
Galatians, on "*believed.*"
James, on "*righteousness.*"
"The Just shall live by his faith."
In Romans the emphasis in on "*just.*"
Galatians, on "*faith.*"
Hebrews on "*live*"—i.e., made alive and kept alive.

The correspondence between the two Testaments extends to so many very minute particulars that one is a commentary upon the other. How often, for example, the Old is both interpreted and illuminated by the New. Casual references to Old Testament characters and events bathe them in a flood of light.

When Melchizedek is first mentioned (Gen. 14:18 *et seq.*) there is scarce a hint of historic character, dignity, and relation to our blessed Lord—a simple narrative with no suggestion of its mystic meaning. But in the Epistle to the Hebrews the very names, "Melchizedek," or "King of Righteousness," and "King of Salem," or "King of Peace," are shown to be typical of Christ, and even in their *order*, "first righteousness; after that peace" (Heb. 5:6—6:20).

Similarly as to Balaam. His real character and vile conspiracy are only hinted in the narrative in Numbers (22:31). But the comments of Peter, Jude and John lend new meaning to the whole story (2 Pet 2:15; Jude 1:11; Rev. 2:14). Thus not until we turn to the last of the sixty-six books, the very close of the whole volume of Scripture, do we know how much this soothsayer of Mesopotamia had to do with that awful plunge of Jehovah's people into the abyss of sensuality. In Numbers, the facts are registered of their sin and crime, followed by an obscure hint of Balaam's complicity with it; but the Apocalypse finally withdraws the veil and discloses his full agency as the chief conspirator. The word "stumblingblock" in Revelation 2:14, means, literally that part of a trap wherein bait is laid, and which, when touched by the animal as it seizes the bait, caused the trap to spring and shut so as to catch the prey. What a darkly suggestive word to describe that human bait of female charms that made this trip so seductively effectual! Here also for the first time, we learn that Balaam set a double snare, entangling Israel in idolatry as well as immorality.

And so, after many centuries, evil reappears in its older forms and complications. As Balak and the Moabites had literally been Balaam's followers and accomplices in encouraging idol sacrifices and sensual sins, so the Pergamites had in both forms followed Balaam's doctrine, and accompanied these literal sins of the flesh by spiritual idolatry and adultery, corrupting the worship of God, and encouraging infidelity to the sacred bridal vows of the church to the heavenly Bridegroom!

In many like cases, the language of the New Testament finds its explanation and interpretation in the Old.

In the midst of our Lord's hour of betrayal and the agonies of the passion week, He reminded the impetuous Peter that He had infinite resources of power had He chosen to draw upon them. "Thinkest thou not that I could pray to My Father, and He should presently give Me more than twelve legions of angels?" (Matt. 26:53). We have but to turn back to 1 Chronicles 27:1–15, to find a hint of why He referred thus to "twelve legions," and get an illuminative illustration of His meaning; for there we read how David, His kingly type, surrounded himself with twelve legions of servant-soldiers, each legion numbering 24,000 and all together, therefore, 288,000, or, including the 12,000 officers that naturally waited on the chief princes, an immense bodyguard of 300,000! How beautifully our Lord thus taught His disciple who was eager to draw a sword to smite His foes, that David's greater Son had at command resources far greater than Judea's King; and if in one night one angel of the Lord had smitten with death 185,000 Assyrians, what might not twelve legions have done in that hour of distress! Such a host could depopulate thirty-seven worlds like ours!

Psalm 68:18 is an example of the illumination shed upon an Old Testament obscurity and perplexity by New Testament quotation and application.

> Thou hast ascended on high!
> Thou hast led in procession a body of captives;
> Thou has received gifts among men;
> Yea, among the rebellious also;
> That Jehovah Elohim might dwell with them.

"Thou hast ascended on *high*": It is referred to, in Ephesians 1:20–23—and indirectly expounded in 4:8, where it is referred to the ascension of our Lord, raised far above all rule and authority and power and dominion, seated at God's own right hand in the heavenlies. In fact, the whole epistle sheds light upon it.

"Thou hast received gifts"—compare Acts 2:33. "Being by the right hand of God exalted, and having received of the Father the promise of the Holy Spirit, He hath poured forth this." The Spirit seems to have been the great gift received to be distributed among men, giving apostles, prophets, evangelists, pastors and teachers, etc.—not only that the Body of Christ might be built up and perfected, but that even the rebellious might be turned into disciples and habitations of the Spirit. The Old Testament enigma is thus solved— the mystery becomes a revelation, an apocalypse.

7

The Bible as a Book Among Books

A TRUE CRITICISM descends to what is minute, counting nothing trivial, especially where God's Word is concerned. There are not only two Testaments, but each of these, a compound of many lesser, individual books, each having a purposed character of its own. Of all these scores of books no two cover the same ground; they are like the members of an organism, the least of all having its own definite place, sphere, function and work, and to find the exact end for which each is meant and fitted is to get the key to its contents and to its relations to all the rest.

Then, in each book, there are subdivisions of historic event, prophetic utterance or doctrinal teaching. These must be seen, if the plan is to be perceived, and the unfolding of it traced. What is true on a larger scale of the whole Bible, and each book in it, is on a smaller scale equally true of every section of each book. The historic scene may shift and so change the current of discourse; new events, a new locality, a new personage, or a new and trifling circumstance, may determine important personage, or a new and trifling circumstance, may determine important changes in the contents. Transitions in thought are often due to transitions in scene or circumstances and take their form accordingly.

First of all, there are historical questions to settle. There is a law of period or time. The preparation of these more than sixty books occupied from fifteen to forty centuries: the exact time it is not necessary or possible to determine, as even earlier tradition, as well as later written documents, may have contributed to the result. But the exact or approximate time when each book was prepared affects two great questions: first, the form and fullness of revelation; and second the progressive development of revealed truth. If an accurate chronology of the books could be framed, it might throw great light on their logical and theological relations; and especially might it show how some books came to be written, and how some events, of more or less importance became the occasion or suggestion of utterances; as when national crises led prophets to exhort or rebuke, or individual occurrences, as in David's experience, prompted a psalm. Compare 2 Samuel 21:15 to 22:51, where the repulse of the Philistines, and the slaughter of four giant foes, formidable like Goliath, led to an outburst of praise to Jehovah, as a Deliverer. How new is the flood of light cast upon that psalm when it is read in the remembrance of the signal triumphs just won!

There is a law of *personality*.

We must, therefore, study the *human media* of revelation. God, at sundry times, in diverse manners and portions, and by various human instruments, made known His will. These forty writers were, however, not mere machines; no violence was done to their native temperaments or natural characteristics. When God used them as His organs of utterance, He fitted their peculiarities to His purpose; their individual traits, and training, their previous associations and surroundings, employments and habits of life, all were a part of His plan in choosing them for this service. Moses' schooling in the Court of Pharaoh and at the "backside of the desert"; Ezra's education as a scribe, Luke's experience as a physician, Paul's scholarship, gathered at Gamaliel's feet and in the Greek schools of Cilicia, Peter's life as a Galilean fisherman, Matthew's as a publican; the philosophic mind of John, the ethical conscience of James—all these tinge their writings, help to determine why certain things specially impressed them and are made by them prominent. To study these individual characteristics and clearly carry in mind the portrait of each writer with his own marked features, makes what they wrote the more intelligible, and gives to their records verisimilitude and consistence as well as variety.

There is also a Law of *Locality* or place. Every book was written somewhere: the writer had, therefore, his local surroundings. To know where he lived and wrote, and amid what scenes, through what experiences he was passing and whom he met; whether he was in palace or prison, at home or in a strange land; all this throws a flood of light upon what he spoke and wrote, explains local references, forms of appeal, modes of illustration and figures of speech, and interprets his teachings. His writings become intelligible, take on new meaning and attraction: his pen often becomes a pencil, and his product a picture, with the lineaments of life and local coloring. Such knowledge helps even to exposition.

What is true of all literature cannot but be true of sacred literature. If we read with new interest and intelligence the oration of Demosthenes' "De Corona" when we know his relations to Aeschines; or the address of Lincoln at Gettysburg when we know the story of the war which turned its crisis there, we can understand better the prophets of the Captivity when we know that Daniel was in Babylon, Ezekiel by the river Chebar, Joel in Judea during a twofold plague of drought and locusts; and it helps us to understand Paul's letter to Corinth when we locate the writer at Ephesus; or, to Philippi, when we imagine him in Rome, a prisoner; or to appreciate the Apocalypse when we know that John was on the isle called Patmos for the sake of his testimony of Christ!

It is believed that our Lord's discourses are often, perhaps always, suggested by something appropriate at the time. So understood, what new meaning they acquire! A shepherd with his flock suggests His words on Himself as the good shepherd. The artificial vine, about the beautiful Temple gate, led Him to say, "I am the True Vine"; the appeal to divide property between brethren, to the discourse on Covetousness; the miracle of the feeding of the 5,000, to the discourse following on the Bread of Life, etc. To know why He spoke on a theme may show what He meant when He spoke. It may do even more: it may guard us against misconstruction and perversion of His words. This is most conspicuously illustrated in the case of His warning as to the one unforgivable sin—blasphemy against the Holy Ghost, which is seen to be attributing His work of love and mercy to the agency of demons

(Mark 2:22–30), a sin arguing so hard a heart and perverse a will as to reveal a hopeless state of voluntary alienation from God.

We need also to study *historic connection.* Facts are often exegetes and expositors—history and biography indirectly explain and interpret doctrine, serving to throw light on truth taught, and becoming the key to occult references. Thus a narrative may serve a threefold end; interpretation, illustration, illumination. Facts and philosophy are wedded and must not be divorced: facts are *factors;* they are of great value in solving problems, in helping to correct an instructive exposition, in not a few cases opening the way to the heart and meaning of Scripture lessons.

A very fine illustration of this may be found in 1 Corinthians 3. This was written after Paul had been to Ephesus, and in fact while there (16:8), and should be read with Acts 18 and 19 in view. Hence his plain references to the famous temple of Diana—to the difficulty of finding a safe "foundation" in the swampy ground, making necessary immense substructions (v. 2); to the immensity, magnitude and magnificence of this wonder of the world with its "gold, silver and precious stones"; to the dwellings of the poor round about, made of "wood, hay, stubble"; to the successful attempt of Erostratus 400 years before to set it afire, suggesting "the fire that shall try every man's work," etc. A building may be destroyed notwithstanding its indestructible foundation.

Psalm 90, inscribed as "a Prayer of Moses," becomes most luminous if construed as his dying son, when, reviewing his 120 years of life, and especially the last forty when a whole generation was swept away in the desert like the sand in a storm. The unique circumstances of his career give form to this prayer, determine its language, its laments and its petitions, and control its whole structure.

For example, compare its poetic stanzas with such prominent features of that forty years of sorrow and of divine dealing as the following:

1. The perpetual changes of that wandering, in contrast with the unchanging Eternity of Jehovah.

2. The destruction of whole generations, as contrasted with the ever living One, whose years do not fail.

3. The open iniquities and secret sins of man, and the justice and righteous wrath of a holy God.

4. The transient, temporal, carnal experience of man, and the permanent, eternal, spiritual elements in the Godhead.

5. The beauty of the Lord our God as the crowning adornment of human character.

6. The identity of man's work and God's work as the only assurance of its permanent establishment.

There is a subordinate law of historic *interval*. Narratives are often condensed, only bold outlines being drawn, somewhat as the peaks of far distant and separated mountains may be seen in close proximity on a landscape or the horizon, while vast valleys stretch between. It is unsafe to infer the immediate succession of events from proximate mention of them in Scripture: while their logical connection may be most intimate, their historical separation may be quite as remote.

We shall learn if we search closely that "the Day of the Lord" covers not twenty-four hours, but it may be twenty-four centuries; that His "judgments are a great deep" which, like the ocean, laves many shores and exhibits successive storms; that, because He is Eternal, a thousand years are in His sight like "yesterday when it is past, or as a watch n the night." What is to us, with our three score years and ten, as an interminable suspense, is to Him as an instant's delay. These things the Bible student must learn, and not attempt to map out immensity and measure eternity by the foot measure of time. Everything about the Infinite One is on a grand scale.

There is also a law of *perspective*. As in nature objects are seen in line and appear nearby or far off, according to the station point or point of sight, which determines the plane of delineation and the perspective lines; so in the Scripture, much depends upon the supposed position of the observer. He may see events as from the head of a column of soldiery, one behind another; or, from the side of a column, where they will be discerned with the relative distances between rows and ranks. The point of view must be found before the relations of things can be known.

There is also a law of historic *objective*—that is, the end in view may bring near together events far apart in occurrence, or put far apart what are in close succession. If a principle is to be illustrated or a lesson enforced the sacred narrator may leap over a wide interval to bring some incident into his record at that point where it best serves the purpose: the logical relation may be more important than the actual succession. The Bible student who nearest gets God's point of vision will most nearly see as He sees, and discern the hidden relations of events and truths.

Beside these historic matters of person, place, time, event, all the purely *literary* features demand careful examination. Each writer has his own style. Personal traits affect the mode of his utterance, and largely determine what he will make most prominent. There are laws of grammar and logic and rhetoric which control all composition. Words have specific meanings, and are used for a reason. Even a tense of a verb or the number of a noun we shall see hereafter may be of much consequence. We may call this the law of *literary construction* which will be seen to have many important applications. But our object just at this point is to emphasize the fact that the Scriptures are in a book form, are written by human pens, that God's messages have flowed through human minds as channels; that all these writings have to do with persons, places, times, events, geographical and historical surroundings, and are framed in human speech and according to the laws of grammar and the usages of language; and all these things must be considered and examined if we are to know the Scriptures and the power of God in them. The brilliance of a diamond depends in part upon the delicate angles into which the many minute faces have been ground and polished by the lapidary.

8

Numerical and Mathematical Features

THERE IS UNQUESTIONABLE EVIDENCE of a *numerical* proportion and symmetry in this marvelous book.

Numbers and mathematical proportion mark it as a whole, and appear in its individual parts, with such frequency and in such definite relations and conditions as to evince a mathematical mind. Often this numerical structure is hidden, but like the fixed proportions of an Ionic column, are disclosed after patient examination. There is a crystalline symmetry and beauty, at first unsuspected, which reminds, when unveiled, of the walls of the celestial city.

It need not surprise us to find such numerical law pervading Scripture. In the works of God it is manifest; why not in His Word? A mathematical mind is manifest in the universe, in the planetary and stellar worlds, their distances and dimensions, densities, proportions, orbits and periods of revolution. In the most minute as in the most majestic objects in nature the same laws govern. In the mineral realm, crystallization shows its squares, triangles, circles and polygons— cubes, cylinders and pyramids or cones, all with exact angles and perfection of proportion. The million snowflakes have a million exquisite forms each, under the microscope, revealing indescribable complexity and beauty.

In the vegetable realm, we find fixed numbers of stamens and pistils, regular proportions in leaf structure and blossom, and a strange recurrence of numbers, 1, 2, 3, 5, etc., in the arrangement of leaf buds in spirals round the stems.

Mathematics, like morals, belong to the eternal, unchangeable order, not to the temporal and transient, and therefore to the Eternal, Immutable God. We might expect to trace the same mathematical mind in the Author of the Word, as in the Creator of worlds. And such is the fact. The numerical system of nature is repeated in Scripture, and to a surprising degree; so that, if the two are placed side by side, and compared, it will be seen that not only do mathematical laws govern both, but there is a strange correspondence in the numbers and forms which prevail in both realms, and in their significance in both.

Even a superficial glance shows, in the structure of the Bible as a whole, a singular mathematical symmetry. Five books of history—the Pentateuch—succeeded by twelve of minor history—Joshua to Esther; then five poetic books, five of major prophecy, and then twelve minor prophecies. Again, in the New Testament, five historic books—another Pentateuch—then three times seven Epistles, and one crowning, dome-like, apocalypse to complete the hole. This recurrence of five and twelve, three sevens, etc., can neither be accidental, nor on the part of human writers, intentional. Not one contributor to the contents of this complex book ever saw it in its completeness, even John who wrote 25 years after the rest had all completed their work. The so-called "canon" of Scripture was not compiled and completed till all the writers were dead. Hence no one who thus wrought in the work had any conception how the finished revelation of God would appear when the capstone was laid. While the workmen were doing, each his part, the building was like some great temple, hidden by its own scaffolding. Yet, when the scaffolding was removed, a certain definite symmetry and proportion were revealed which could not have been suspected in the course of construction.

If this fact and feature are repeatedly and emphatically referred to in these studies, it is partly because of their conspicuousness in the construction of the Bible and partly because of their convincing tribute to its divine origin. In a day when there is a combined assault upon the supernatural element in the Word of God, it is of first importance to recognize its unique claims to supreme authority. There are two ways of destroying this authority: first, by letting it down to a common level, and second, by lifting other books to its level: in both cases it ceases to be superior or supreme. Every mark of the uniqueness and solitariness of the Holy Scriptures should be noted and emphasized, and this is one: that they contain a system of mathematical number and order which cannot be due to any intention on the part of any human writer, or to an agreement between them all; and hence must be attributable to a divine design.

If we examine more closely we discover certain prominent numbers, such as three, five, seven, twelve, constantly reappearing in the structure of individual books, as in the five sacrifices or offerings in Leviticus, in the "Pentateuch," of Psalms, etc., the Epistles to the seven churches, both by Paul and John, etc.

The correspondence reaches to matters even more minute. In nature, seven is divided into four and three, as in the octave of sounds, where the half notes as on the piano keyboard separate the keys into two groups, or, in the octave of colors, with its three primary and four secondary. Twelve, both in nature and Scripture, represents the multiple of three and four, as in the pyramid with its four sides and three dimensions, length, breadth, height, etc.

All this shows that the God of the Worlds is the God of the Word, and that He works by fixed laws and methods, and nothing is accidental or imperfect, or insignificant.* We do well to search for concealed proportion, not expressed by any enumeration, but embedded in the structure, as when we find seven pregnant sentences spoken by our Lord on the cross, seven statements about Christ's relation to the church in Ephesians 5:25, 32, etc., seven features of church unity in Ephesians 5:4–6, seven marks of final perfection, Revelation 22:3–5.

The Book of Daniel is happily so divided as to indicate its contents: twelve chapters, the first six recording as many tests in which the worldly wisdom and policy of Babylon and its magi are seen in competition with the superior wisdom and principles of the captives of Judea: and the loyalty of the holy children enters into successive con-

---

* These matters are followed more closely in detail in the author's *Exeter Hall Lectures—God's Living Oracles* and *The Bible and Spiritual Criticism.*

flicts with idolatry, and God's servants are in each case more than conquerors; then six more chapters, recording as many visions of God and the future which constitute this book the Old Testament apocalypse.

The structure of the Book of *Esther* shows peculiar symmetry. It towers far above the other historical narratives of the Old Testament, its composition being nearly perfect, as Professor Schultz has remarked. The history develops scene after scene in swift succession and advancing toward the climax in a series of acts which have a fascinating interest, and reminds us of a well-planned drama and masterly novel, both in one. The first chapter is an introduction, the last a supplement. Between lie eight chapters, four of which show how the knot was tied, another plot formed; the other four, how the knot was untied and the plot defeated and reversed, or to adopt a phrase from the book, "turned to the contrary." Two of these eight chapters regularly belong together in the first part because of the relation of plot to counterplot; in the second part, because they refer to the removal of an identical difficulty.

The Pentateuch of Psalms, already referred to, is seen not only in the five books in which the whole 150 are arranged, but in the close correspondence with the Mosaic Pentateuch:

1. Psalms 1–41. Correspondent to Genesis;
2. Psalms 42–72. Correspondent to Exodus;
3. Psalms 73–89. Correspondent to Leviticus;
4. Psalms 90–106. Correspondent to Numbers;
5. Psalms 107–150. Correspondent to Deuteronomy.

The resemblances are not fanciful; the studious and devout Hebrews long ago found in Psalm 1, the reference to the Tree of Life in Eden; in Psalm 42, to the oppression of their fathers in Egypt; in Psalm 73, the despair of the alien and the privilege of drawing near to Jehovah; in Psalm 90, the disastrous story of the wilderness wandering and a generation's graves; and in Psalm 107, the approach to the Promised Land.

The fivefold structure in the great forecast of Messiah in the very heart of Isaiah's prophecy is very striking, though not at first apparent (Is. 52:13; 53:12).

1. 52:13–15. Jehovah's estimate of His Servant, however marred.
2. 53:1–3. The despisers' and rejecters' estimate of Him.
3. 53:4–6. The believers' estimate of Him as Savior.
4. 53:7–9. His vicarious character and sufferings.
5. 53:10–12. His ultimate achievement, victory and glory.

Of numerical structure, many students, like F. W. Grant, in his "Numerical Bible," find numbers so embedded in the very structure of the Word of God that they believe it to be one method of stamping divine design upon the Scriptures; and close investigation shows amazing numerical symmetry where a careless reader would never suspect it, as in Exodus 14:19–21, in each of the three verses in the Hebrew there are seventy-two letters. This seems a trifling thing, but these verses form the heart of the narrative.

An English writer reckons in case of Elijah, eight miracles, and in Elisha's ministry, a "double portion," sixteen; and he thinks Paul, as a "chosen vessel" corresponds to Elisha, and was permitted to work exactly double the number of recorded miracles of our Lord, or of those mentioned as directly blessed by his ministry. The writer curiously reckons the latter to be 153—the number of fishes particularized as enclosed in the miraculous draught recorded in John 21:11; and he finds Paul's recorded instances 306—just double.*

Whatever may be thought of the exactness of these calculations, this whole matter of numbers as bearing on the structure of Scripture may yet become one of the most conspicuous proofs of a divine mind. To attribute all this to a deliberate intention of the human writers taxes credulity. This numerical law lies so embedded in the very construction of the Word of God that it is only now beginning, after all these centuries, to be discovered by the most minute search.

A striking instance of numerical structure is found in Philippians 2:5–11, where the contrast is so vivid between the humiliation and exaltation of our Lord Jesus Christ. If the words be counted from the sixth verse to the end of the eleventh, there are about 120 in the English, divided into two almost exactly equal parts, the first half describing His descension, and the second, His ascension, as though to hint that the one must be measured by the other somewhat as the

---

* *A Double Portion,* by Lieutenant Colonel F. Roberts.

height of one of the Alpine mountains we are told, is exactly correspondent to the depth of the lake at its foot. When we know how far
our Lord went up, we may know how far He came down.

In the Greek the numerical proportion is even more striking. If the
introductory phrase, "Let this mind be in you which was also in
Christ Jesus"—be placed by itself, with the companion phrase,
"wherefore God also," which introduces the second half—there remains seventy-two words—half of which refer to the descent and the
other half to the ascent.

Some correspondences are very unique and striking. Not only are
there five historical books which begin both the Old and New Testaments, but there were twelve tribes beside Levi in Canaan, and twelve
apostles beside Paul in Judea; there were three disciples to whom our
Lord was manifested on the Mount of Transfiguration, James, John
and Peter; and three to whom He appeared after His ascension—
Stephen the martyr, Saul the persecutor, and John the revelator.

But mathematics is also the science of *proportion*, and deals with
forms like the triangle and pyramid, the square and cube, the circle
and sphere. In the Tabernacle, the square and cube are prominent. It
was a threefold cube thirty cubits long, ten broad and ten high, the
Holiest of all being a perfect cube. The Laver seems to have been cir-
cular, and the golden lampstand suggested the inverted triangle.
These proportions reappear in the Temple of Solomon and City of
God in Revelation 21:22.

There are many who think that the ideal structures, referred to in
Scripture metaphors, are *pyramidal*. For example, the spiritual Temple so sublimely outlined by Paul and Peter (Eph. 2; 1 Pet. 2) of
which Christ is both cornerstone and capstone—"Headstone of the
corner"—(Ps. 118:22; Zech. 4:7). Zechariah particularly seems to have
in mind a stone which when laid, completes the structure; and it is
a beautiful conception that this Holy Temple is one which both
commences in our Lord as cornerstone and culminates in Him as capstone: for in a pyramid there can be but one crowning stone, itself a
perfect pyramid and an image of the whole; and by the lines and
angles of the two—the corner and capstones, all the other lines and
angles must be controlled.

9

The Law of Grammatical Construction

THE SCRIPTURES, being a form of sacred literature, need to be interpreted, in part, by literary methods though not exclusively as if they were a merely human product. The need to be examined in the following ways:

1. Structurally—to find out how the body of divine truth is framed and fitted together; of what parts composed, how those parts are combined, and what is their mutual relation and bearing upon the whole results.

2. Philologically—with reference to the three or four original languages in which the Bible was written or which mold its forms of speech, the Hebrew and Chaldaic, Greek and Aramaic with the peculiarities of each.

3. Historically, with relation to the times and places, persons and events connected with its preparation, and the effect of temporal circumstances and conditions upon its character as a book and its mission to mankind.

4. Spiritually, as a book of salvation, pre-eminently, and a revelation of God in His essential character, and dealings with the human race, all else being incidental and subordinate.

With such fundamental principles kept in view, Scripture studies cannot be too minute and critical, and will only discover more and more the consistency of the Word of God with itself and its Divine Author.

A general orderly arrangement is everywhere manifest in this inspired book. "Order is Heaven's first law," wrote the poet Pope, and this law pervades all God's handiwork. In hundreds of instances, the order is part of the inspiration, and therefore inviolable, to be reverently regarded as conveying an integral part of the lesson to be learned. The succession of thoughts, words and deeds is often also a progression of procession, in which there is constant advance toward a complete unfolding of some truth, even the order being tributary to the purpose in view. The whole grammatical and rhetorical arrangement of inspired utterances is therefore to be held as sacred, keeping asunder what God has not joined, and what He has joined not putting asunder.

Some of these laws and principles, in the grammatical sphere, we are now about to illustrate.

Inspiration covers grammar, for it controls the exact forms of language in which God expresses Himself. In the Word of God we are taught that we must not disregard or change anything or count it as of no consequence. This will appear if the following passages are carefully compared:

Hebrews 12:27, Galatians 4:9, John 8:58, John 10:34–36, Matthew 23:37, Galatians 3:16, Matthew 5:18.

If these passages are examined it will be seen how important is a single *phrase*, for in the first quotation the argument turns on one phrase, "Yet once more"; in the second, on the *passive*, rather than the *active voice* of a verb; in the third, on the *present*, rather than the past *tense*; and in the fourth, on the *mood* of a verb; in the fifth, on the inviolability of a single *word*; in the sixth, on the *singular number* rather than the plural of a noun; and in the last, on the retention of a single *letter*, and that the smallest in the Hebrew alphabet, and even a little stroke or mark used to distinguish one letter from another. Taken together, these Scripture utterances so guard the Word of God that they forbid the alteration or omission of a phrase or word, the change of voice, mood or tense in a verb, or the number of a noun, or even a letter or stroke of a letter.

The Jews showed a jealousy for even the letter of Scripture that we, Christian believers, might well emulate and imitate. They found in every detail a significance, and copyists sought to make the Old Testament manuscripts exhibit the sense which devout scribes thought they had detected, as in the use of *majascula*, or larger letters at times, as in Deuteronomy 6:4, which we shall refer to later.

The Massorites, so-called, so critically examined the text of the Old Testament, that they marked not only its divisions, but is grammatical forms, letters, vowels, accents, etc. They counted words and even letters and recorded the numbers at the end of each book, enumerating in the Pentateuch, for example, 18 greater, and 43 smaller portions; 1,534 verses, 63,467 words, 70,100 letters, etc. While much of their work was elaborate and minute, and led to fanciful notions and interpretations, it served two great ends: first, to detect most minute peculiarities in the Holy Writings, which otherwise would escape careless readers: and to preserve the original Scriptures in their purity by making alterations impossible without detection.

Grammar teaches us to examine closely the exact meaning of words.

Take the word, "*watch*," found in the New Testament twenty-seven times as applied to spiritual vigilance, and being the equivalent of three Greek words (*agrypneō, grēgoreō* and *nēphō*). The first means to abstain from sleep, to keep awake; the second, to arouse oneself, and shake off lethargy, a stronger word, implying activity as on the part of one who is fully awake; the third means to abstain from drink which produces stupor as well as sleep, and therefore conveys the additional idea of sobriety—keeping sober as well as awake. Only as all these meanings are combined do we get the full force of the Scripture exhortations to watchfulness. We are not only to keep awake, but to keep active, and in order to both, to keep sober minded, avoiding the intoxication of this world's destructive pleasures. Here grammatical study not only reveals the exact force of Scripture language but the moral and spiritual lesson to be conveyed.

Another very important grammatical feature is *emphasis*. Both in the Hebrew and Greek tongues the stress upon a word is indicated by its place in the sentence and some other signs of comparative prominence. Context and circumstances so often guide to correct emphasis that they should be regarded as necessary to exposition, as when our Lord contrasting earlier and imperfect teachers with Himself, says:

"Ye have heard that it hath been said by them of old time: But *I* say unto you."

Here the obvious emphasis is one of the first personal pronoun, "I." And so, when contrasting the worldly spirit of Pharisees, seeking human applause, with the true worshiper doing his alms and offering prayers to the unseen God, He says:

"They *have* their reward; but He *shall* reward thee," it is equally plain that the emphasis lies upon the present and future tenses.

Sometimes emphasis is determined by *idiom*, but this again demands special study of idiomatic forms of speech.

Few readers have any proper conception of the importance and significance of emphasis upon which the entire meaning often hinges. The order of words will often either obscure or reveal the sense. In the original of Matthew 27:47, the words stand thus: "Elias called this man," but, when the cases of the nouns are examined, it becomes plain that the grammar changes the order and emphasis: "This man calleth Elias."

Again in Job 29:15, the obvious emphasis is on the merciful ministries performed by Job himself who is accused of wrongdoing: "Eyes to the blind, and feet to the lame, *became I*."

In Isaiah 53:4–6, the constant stress is upon "*our* griefs," "sorrows," "transgressions," "iniquities." He was not suffering for Himself but for us: the contrast is between "*we* and *Him*."

So important is this department of biblical study that Mr. Rotherham, the brilliant English scholar, has given many years to the preparation of an "emphasized" version in which he seeks to express and exhibit, by parallelism, arrangement and position of words, corresponding English idioms, and italics or capitals, the emphatic words in very sentence of both Testaments—and we must refer the reader to this colossal work of learning and painstaking care and ingenuity for further hints upon this engrossing subject. He shows in his introductory chapter, "Concerning Emphasis," how by position, repetition, formal expression, etc., the very word or words may be discovered upon which the Divine Revealer of truth would have the stress fall, and how we may thus discern the special point where the lesson is most to be found. Examples of this will frequently recur as we proceed to examine other laws and principles of Bible study: but we have here called attention to this matter as inseparable from the grammatical study of the Word.

A very important principle in grammatical structure is the relation of *primary* to *secondary* members of a sentence.

For example, the *imperative* and the *participle*.

Where in any injunction, an imperative is found with participles, the former represents the *main thought* and the participles the *subordinate one*, the latter often suggesting the means or helps to the carrying out of the main injunction. For this reason, it is to be regretted that the tenses and words of the original are not always faithfully reproduced in translation. A conspicuous example both of the principle advocated and the disregard of it in translation is found in 1 Peter 1:13–16. Here are three imperatives and three participles:

"Hope to the End."	"Girding up the loins," etc.
"Be Ye Holy"	"Being Sober."
(the latter repeated)	"Not fashioning yourselves," etc.

Here are two injunctions "Hope to the End," and "Be Ye Holy," and the participles indicate how the commands are to be obeyed; by disentangling the affections from worldly objects, by maintaining a holy sobriety and control over the flesh; and by keeping before us the divine model of holiness. It is more than a pity that such a homiletic and practical outline should be obscured by not adhering to the grammatic form of the original.

Another instance, where the structure is preserved, in Jude 1:20, 21.

Here the main member is:	The *helps* to this duty are three:
"Keep yourselves in the love of God."	"Building up yourselves."
	"Praying in the Holy Ghost."
	"Looking for the mercy," etc.

In other words, if we would *be* kept by God from stumbling, we must keep ourselves in His Love, we need to make ourselves more and more familiar with His Word and its teachings; to maintain habits of intimate prayer-fellowship; and to fix our gaze upon the great future reappearing of the Lord.

Similar instances of the relation of imperative and participle may be found in Matthew 27: 19, 20:

"Go ye,"　　　　　　　　　"Baptizing,"
"Disciple all nations,"　　　"Teaching."

Here the main thing is making disciples—the rest indicates how to train disciples as witnesses, and edify them as believers.

Again, in James 5:15:

"Let him call for the Elders, And let them pray over him";
"Anointing him with oil."

The prayer of faith is the main thing—the anointing with oil, a subsidiary, symbolic form. How different would be the impression of this passage if it read, "Let them anoint him with oil, praying over him," etc.

Thus, we have found grammatical study to serve a manifold end: first to show the construction of a sentence; then, the exact meaning of words, and the reason for their precise form, declension, conjugation, etc.; then their proper arrangement and comparative prominence; and finally the relation of the primary and secondary clauses, or the principal and subordinate members of a sentence. All this is but one more illustration of the duty and profit of searching the Scriptures, which like other workmanship of God, not only bear the most microscopic scrutiny, but only so disclose their perfection.

10

Bible Versions and Translations

WHILE ONLY SUCH APPROXIMATE ACCURACY can be claimed for even the most perfect rendering, it is remarkable how faithful all the standard translations are, and most remarkable how, amid all the thousands of doubtful disputed renderings, even of the most perplexing passages, not one affects a single vital doctrine of the Word of God. There are over 300 different expositions of Galatians 3:20; but, whichever be adopted, no essential truth is at risk. We cannot but believe that the God of the Bible has superintended the translation of the Book into more than 500 tongues, raising up men for this stupendous task and guiding them in it, so as to make their work practically unerring.

We advise every reader if possible to study the originals; if that is impracticable, to get the best helps to the understanding of them, in the way of literal renderings, such as that of Rotherham, Spurrell, Young, etc., and the most devout commentators. But it behooves us to remember that, though our great standard versions are only reflections of the originals, they are, like our own image in a mirror, which, though not the man himself is for all practical purposes his reproduction, sufficient guides in the understanding of God's Word, so that it is only the most captious who object to them because they are only translations.

There are some confessedly inexact and inadequate renderings, and whenever found, such should be carefully noted, and it is well to make the margin of one's own Bible the place of such record, indicating also the best possible rendering or paraphrase to convey the thoughts otherwise obscured.

Some inadequacies are inherent in the poverty of language and are unavoidable. Sometimes a word means too much, or again, too little; lacks definiteness and precision, or fails to express delicate shades of meaning.

For example, the English word, "World," is too comprehensive. It is used to render four or five Greek words, one of which means the earth; another, the cosmos, or created cosmic order; another, the age or indefinite time; and another, the world as the habitation of the human race. To discriminate these is difficult, yet often very necessary, for to confuse them is often to obscure or miss the meaning. This will clearly appear if the word, *aiōn*, or *eon*, be uniformly rendered "*age*," in which case the sense becomes not only luminous where now obscure, but sometimes wholly new. For instance, examine the following among many texts:

Matthew 12:32—"Shall not be forgiven, neither in this age nor in the age to come."

13:39—"Harvest in the end of the age."

28:20—"Unto the end of the age."

Romans 12:2—"Be not conformed to this age."

2 Corinthians 4:4—"The God of this age."

Galatians 1:4—"That He might deliver us from that present evil age."

Ephesians 1:21—"Not only in this age, but in the age to come" (2:7).

2 Timothy 4:10—Titus 2:12—"Present age."

Hebrews 6:5—"Tasted the powers of the age to come," etc.

There is an easy way to discriminate these kindred words, if we render *gē*, "matter-world," *kosmos*, "created-world," *aiōn*, "time-world," and *oikoumenē*, "inhabited world"; but in some way the reader should learn to distinguish them.

If the above cited passages, and others like them be carefully examined, and the context studied, it will be seen that the stress is upon the world-age, or period of time preceding the second appearing of the Lord. During this whole dispensation, Satan, as the god or prince of this world, is largely in control. He is seeking by masterly strategy and plausible subtlety, to draw away disciples into error both of doctrine and practice; to blind the eyes of men to the supreme beauty and value of what is immaterial, invisible and eternal by the transient and hollow baubles of the material, visible and temporal. He seeks also to impose upon even the believer by counterfeits of what is spiritual and divine. Hence the need of being perpetually on our guard against his sophistries and subtleties; of not being conformed to the notions and patterns of this present evil age. So perilous is this age in its temptations, and so awful in its coming judgments, that one grand object of our Lord's whole mission was to deliver us from it; and those who live in it but are not of it, are like travelers on a mountain top, or Moses upon Pisgah, they see things in their relations; they compare the desert with the land of promise, the present evil age with the coming age of glory, and so actually foretaste the age to come, and get a growing distaste of the age that now is.

Some such new views of biblical truth are the fruit of a searching study to "know the Scriptures and the power of God" in them, by ascertaining just what the language which they employ is meant to convey.

Psalm 26:1 reads in the authorized version:

"The transgression of the wicked saith within my heart, that there is no fear of God before his eyes."

This conveys no very clear, intelligible idea. Mrs. Spurrell translates: "The rebellion of the wicked causeth him to say within his heart: 'There is no fear!' God is not present to his sight." This is both intelligible and impressive.

Dr. John DeWitt paraphrases thus: "Sin's oracle voice possesses the wicked man's heart, and his eyes have before them no God to be feared." Similarly, Psalm 10:4 should be rendered:

> The wicked, in the height of his scorn:—
>   'God will not requite!
>   No God!'
> Such are all his thoughts.

Here the very abruptness of the transition expresses the haughty arrogance of the blasphemer. Sin is personified, assuring him that he may sin with impunity. Falsehood, like a lying spirit, a demon, possesses him and emboldens him to say, "There is no future judgment"—"no God to requite." The short, abrupt, fragmentary, exclamatory utterance is so far a part of the design that the supplying of extra words rather spoils the majestic brevity of the original. Sin is madness and strikes quick, sharp blows at God, and it is the manner of a madman to utter short and unfinished exclamations, like the mutterings of a wild beast.

So in Psalm 14:1—

"The fool [atheistic fool] hath said in his heart, 'NO GOD!' " i.e., "I would there were none!" This, or something like it, may be what is meant, as though he conspired to get God out of the way. An incomplete sentence leaves the imagination room to fill out the meaning. But the bottom idea in any case, is that sin hardens the heart, emboldens the sinner, and ends in his being given over to a reprobate mind (Rom. 1:28).

In the judgment of many scholarly exegetes no italics should be used in a translation. They represent words supplied by translators; if the original implies such words they need not be italicized; if it does not, to supply them is unwise, perhaps irreverent, for it may obscure and even pervert the sense. In Psalm 22, the whole of the opening verses is broken up into short ejaculations and exclamations, probably to make more vivid the dying agonies of the Sufferer, whose strength is gone and whose breath is too short to complete a single sentence. How pathetic if read as in the original,

"My God! My God! Why—forsaken Me?—far from helping Me!—words of My roaring!"

Psalm 99:1 reads:

"The Lord reigneth; let the people tremble! He sitteth between the cherubim; let the earth be moved."

Here, without doubt, the sense is *inverted;* it should read:

Jehovah is King, let the people be never so impatient: He sitteth between the cherubim, let the earth be never so unquiet" (English Psalter).

If the latter be the true rendering, the thought is, that, however men may be troubled by the course of events or tremble with fear, Jehovah is still Sovereign; and sits firm on His throne, however the earth shakes and is unsteady. Not only does this rendering completely invert the whole conception, but it supplies infinite encouragement to a believer, to look away from all earthly commotions and human disturbances to Him who is eternally calm and unmoved—immutable, while all else changes, the controller of all men and all events, without whose permission no disaster can occur, and who makes even the wrath of man to praise Him, and the uprisings of the people to prepare the way for His final triumph. Nothing takes place that is not part of His plan or in some way promotes it.

The Greek word in Galatians 4:16; Ephesians 4:15, means not only to speak, but to act, live the truth—to be true. It includes all, and is used but twice; in both cases how much clearer the meaning if literally translated:

"Am I become your enemy because I am *true to you*," or "deal truly with you," not only "speak the truth," but live it. "Truthing in love" means more than "speaking the truth in love"—it includes being true, wholly governed by what is sincere and genuine. The ideal character is one which thus combines truth and love, in which truth is always mingled with love, and love always faithful to truth.

The value of an exact rendering never perhaps more appears than in Romans 5:9, 10, where is a turning point of the whole New Testament.

"Much more being justified, we shall be saved from wrath."

"Much more being reconciled, we shall be saved by His life."

If reconciled and justified, we are already saved from wrath and from enmity; but the thought is that, being thus saved, we shall be *kept saved, kept safe in His life*, and not only so, but *kept always rejoicing*.* By his death we were delivered from judgment and reconciled to God. But He who died is risen no more to die, and in His undying life, the saved believer finds a sphere and atmosphere of eternal abiding and security, which assures him he shall never lapse into a condition of enmity and incur wrath anew. So important is this short sentence: "We shall be kept safe in His Life," that it first suggests that phrase which from this point on becomes the *dominant* phrase of the

---

* Dr. Moule on Romans.

inspired Word—recurring hundreds of times: "in Christ," or "in Christ Jesus," or its equivalents, "in Him," "in whom," etc. Compare Ephesians 1:3–13. In these ten verses we have "in Christ" or its equivalent at least *nine times, covering all God's gracious plans from His eternal choice* "in Him," to the obtaining of the inheritance "in Him."

Resemblances between words, both beautiful and instructive, are not always easily transferred to another tongue.

In 1 Timothy 3:11, "not slanderers" is in the original, "*not diabolic*" hinting at accusation in a malignant, devilish spirit.

4:5—"Sanctified by the Word of God and *prayer.*"

Here the last word means holy converse or communion with God, a personal meeting and conference with Him.

The word, *prokopē*, "advance," how like *proskopē*—"stumbling-block"? The close resemblance between the original words helps to hint the lesson, that a trifling difference may turn what would be progress into hindrance, both to self and others; and again, *prokrima*, "prejudice," how like *prosklisis*, "partiality—" "Without prejudice, doing nothing by partiality" (1 Tim. 5:21). May not the resemblance here hint kinship?

James uses two kindred words, both rendered "*gift*," 1:17; one means the act of giving—giving in its initiatory stage; the other the gift, as bestowed, the boon when perfected. "Every good giving and every perfect gift" (cf. Rotherham and Canon Fausset).

The best commentary on Scripture is Scripture itself—"comparing spiritual things with spiritual"—which yields a threefold result, interpretation, illustration, illumination. The Bible has its own lexicon, defining its terms; its own expositor, explaining its meaning; its own interpreter, unlocking its mysteries. Astonishing acquaintance with God and the things of God become possible through familiarity with this one Book, and surprising skill in handling and wielding his sword of the spirit, is attainable through practice in its use without recourse to outside aid.

11

Biblical Names and Titles

THE LEADING NAME, Jehovah, occurs 11,600 times, and it is a blemish, if not a blunder, that it finds its way into the English translation four times only (Ex. 6:3; Ps. 83:18; Is. 12:2; 26:4), shutting out the common reader from the full significance of hundreds of passages, such as Psalm 8:1, which should read, "O, Jehovah, our Lord."

The Jews, superstitiously fearful of needlessly pronouncing this august name, substituted for it when reading aloud, "Adhonai," "Lord"; and, so came in the Septuagint version, the Greek equivalent, "kurios," and in the English, which followed the Septuagint, "Lord," capitals indicating that the original is "Jehovah"; but, practically, this covenant name, upon which Jehovah himself laid such stress, is eliminated from both these versions.

The meaning of Jehovah is too complete to put into words. It seems a compound of the three tenses of the Hebrew verb, "to be," expanded in the familiar sentence, "Who *is* and *was* and *is to come*," conveying the idea of an existence to which past and future are also present, the "I AM," or the Everliving One (Ex. 3:14; Rev. 1:8).

As used, it suggests also the ever*loving* One, being connected with grace and salvation that have their origin in an eternal past, their outworking in progressive present, and their perfect goal in an eternal future. Jehovah, therefore, as the *covenant* name, conveys the conception of the Immutable One, whose purpose and promise are as unchanging as Himself, "the same yesterday and today and forever."

61

Were this great name always reproduced in the English, and especially in New Testament quotations from the Old, it would prove that our Lord Jesus Christ is absolutely equal and identical with the Father; for passages which, in the Old Testament contain the name, "Jehovah," are so quoted and applied to Him in the New as to demonstrate Him to be JEHOVAH-JESUS, one with the God of Eternal Past, Himself God manifested in the flesh, in the present, and the coming God of the Future. This is the climax of all arguments and evidences touching our Lord's Deity, for example:

Hebrews 1:10: "Thou, Jehovah, in the beginning hast laid the foundation of the Earth," etc. This is from Psalm 102:25–27, which whole psalm is addressed to Jehovah, whose name occurs *eight* times. Yet this magnificent tribute to the eternity and immutability of Jehovah, the Creator and Covenant God, is here applied to His Son.

"Prepare ye the way of Jehovah" (Matt. 3:3, from Is. 40:3).

"Jehovah, our Righteousness" (Jer. 23:6; Rom. 3; 1 Cor. 1:30).

Most complete and conclusive is Revelation 1:8, 1, 17, 18.

Taken together these passages present the Son of God in four aspects, any one alone proving His Deity: He is "the Alpha and Omega"; "The Beginning and the Ending"; "The First and the Last"; "The Lord, who is and was and is to come, the Almighty"—four descriptive phrases which are not mere repetitions of one idea in different words.

"Alpha and Omega," first and last letters of the Greek alphabet, suggest *literature*—the written Scriptures; "Beginning and Ending," the material creation; "First and Last," the Historic Ages, or Time-Worlds; "Who is and was and art to come," Jehovah's Eternity.

Thus He is here declared, declares Himself,

> The Subject Matter of all Scripture;
> The Creator of all worlds and creatures;
> The Controller of all History;
> The Eternal, unchangeable Jehovah.

Rabinowitz said: "What questioning and controversies the Jews have kept up over Zechariah 12:10: 'They shall look upon Me whom they pierced.' They will not admit that it is Jehovah whom they pierced, hence the dispute about the word 'whom' but this word is simply the first and last letters of the Hebrew alphabet—Aleph, Tav.

Filled with awe and astonishment, I open to Revelation 1:7 and 8, and read these words of Zachariah, as quoted by John: 'Behold, He cometh with clouds; and every eye shall see Him and they also that pierced Him'; and then heard the glorified Lord saying: '. . . I am the Alpha and Omega.' Jesus seemed to say: 'Do you doubt who it is *whom* you pierced? I am the Aleph, Tav—the Alpha and Omega—Jehovah the Almighty.' "

Three representative names are applied to the Son of God—"Jesus or Savior," "Christ" and "Lord."

Jesus (Savior) is the human name, linking Him with humanity whom He came to save; Christ (anointed), the messianic name, with prophecy which He came to fulfill; and Lord, the Jehovah name, with Deity, whom He came to represent and reveal. These three names have, when used, a definite *order*. The historic order is in the angelic announcement to the shepherds of Bethlehem—"a Savior Who is Christ, the Lord" (Luke 2:11). On the Day of Pentecost, "God hath made that same Jesus, both Lord and Christ" (Acts 2:36), Peter put last the name "Christ"—"the anointed One"—for it was on that day that, having received of the Father the promise of the Holy Spirit, He shed forth this anointing upon His people (v. 33). When Paul uses the three names (Phil. 2:11) "Jesus, Christ is Lord," he puts "Lord" last, emphasizing the fact that every tongue is to confess His divine Lordship.

These three names hint the historic development, for up to His crucifixion, He was conspicuous as Jesus—after His resurrection and ascension, preeminent as Christ, the anointed and anointing One; He will come again as Lord to reign.

These three names indicate also His threefold office and word—"Jesus," suggests His career as a prophet, teaching men the truth; "Christ," His priesthood, atoning for sin; "Lord," His kingship ruling over men. The priesthood came into full exercise where the prophetic work ended, and the kingly begins where the priestly terminates. These lines of separation are not absolute, yet they indicate general facts. These three names likewise suggest man's relation and responsibility—Obedience to Him as Prophet; Faith in Him as Priest; Surrender to Him as King.

It is very interesting to trace the *compound names* of Jehovah, such as "Jehovah-Elohim," "Jehovah-Jireh," "Jehovah-Rophi," "Jehovah-Nissi," "Jehovah-Shalom," "Jehovah-Tsidkenu," "Jehovah-Shammah" (cf. Gen. 1:4; 22:14; Ex. 15:26; 17:15; Judg. 6:24; Jer. 23:6; Ezek. 48:25).

The first of these seven compounds identifies Jehovah, God of the Covenant with the *Creator;* the second, with the *Provider;* the third, with the *Healer;* the fourth, with the *Victor;* the fifth, with the *Pacificator,* or *Reconciler;* the sixth, with the *Justifier;* the last, with the Indweller, the presiding center and absorbing charm of the heavenly city. It would seem as though there were not only a marvelous completeness here, but a designed order, the thought progressing toward a culmination and consummation.

"Jehovah" is compounded with Jah three times in Isaiah, so that, in one case, the names of God are duplicated and in another, triplicated!

The name "*Jah*" is probably not an abbreviation for *Jehovah,* but the *present* tense of the verb, *to be,* and suggests Jehovah as the PRESENT LIVING GOD. Though found but once in our English Bible it is in the Hebrew in *forty-nine* cases—seven times seven.

Exodus 15:2; 17:16; Psalms 68:4, 18; 77:11; 89:8; 94:7, 12; 102:18; 104:35; 105:45; 106:1, 48; 111:1; 112:1; 113:1, 9; 115:17, 18 (2); 116:19; 117:2; 118:5 (2), 14, 17, 18, 19; 122:4; 130:3; 135:1, 3, 4, 21; 146:1, 10; 147:1, 20; 148:1, 14; 149:1, 9; 150:1, 6 (2); Isaiah 12:2; 26:4; 38:11 (2).

Why JAH should be thus used, if only a contraction for Jehovah, cannot be seen. But if meant to emphasize Jehovah's *present* activity and oversight, the *Presence* of God in daily life, we can easily account for its use. In each case, there is some reason why this aspect of *present, living interposition is emphasized.* Canon Cook says it was doubtless chosen by Moses in the first instance of its use to draw attention to the promise ratified by the name, "*I am.*"

This name is first found in Exodus 15:2

> My strength and my song is Jah;
> He is become my Salvation.

Here, obviously, the stress is upon Jehovah's immediate interposition in appearing at the very instant of peril to overwhelm foes close on their heels, when delay would have made escapes impossible. Hence, this the first choral refrain of Miriam's triumphal hymn first uses the name Jah.

The name next occurs in connection with Moses' altar, called Jehovah Nissi—after the defeat of Amelek—when again Jehovah showed Himself a present deliverer.

In the first instance of Jah in the Psalms, Jah is extolled as One Who rideth upon the heavens, a father of the fatherless, and a judge of the widows, bending over us, as the overreaching skies, and to the destitute and desolate, an ever present Helper.

Again in Isaiah 12:2, when the refrain of Miriam's song is quoted, the same exact name is combined with Jehovah:

"My strength and my song is JAH JEHOVAH," for both present and future deliverances are celebrated. Again in 26:4, the Song of Salvation:

> Trust ye in Jehovah forever;
> For in JAH JEHOVAH is the Rock of Ages!

He is a present and a perpetual support and security. In the last instance of the use of Jah by Isaiah (38:11) it occurs twice, in Hezekiah's lament. Facing immediate death, he says,

"I shall not in the land of the living, see JAH JAH," that is, no more in the experiences of a present daily life is he to behold this present God.

The compounds of Jah are equally instructive:

"Hallelujah"—"praise ye Jah"—first occurring in Psalm 106:1: "Jehovah, the omnipotent God, reigneth"—a present ruler.

When the names of God are interwoven with human names, it is always with a particular purpose and meaning; including the exact name chosen in each case.

The name "Abram" was enlarged to "Abraham," and "Sarai" to "Sarah," by incorporating a syllable of Jehovah's name, as "Hoshea" was changed to "Jehoshua," or "Joshua," indicating in these parties a special property of Jehovah, a special relation to Him. "Jeconiah" and "Jehoiachin" differ only in the transposition of the two elements composing the names: both mean "Jehovah will establish." In Jeconiah, the sign of the future tense being cut off, the meaning becomes, "Jehovah establishes." Probably, originally called Jehoiachin (2 Sam. 7:12) when he ascended the throne, and required to take a new name, he chose simply to transpose the two parts of the old one so as to keep its good omen. But Jeremiah shortened this name to "Coniah" (Jer. 22:24, 28; 27:1), cutting off the notion of futurity, implying that Jehovah would *not* establish such a prince, as the events proved, for, after a reign of three months, he was carried captive to Babylon.

Jacob's name was changed to "Israel," not "Jehovah," but "*el*," being incorporated with the new name. "El" hints at Almighty *Power*, as specially manifested to Jacob, and is in all God's transactions with him, it is "el," not "Jah" that is memorialized. In Genesis 35:11, God said to him, "I am El Shaddai," the third instance in which these two names occur (Gen. 17:1; 28:3). Note the names "Beth-el," "Peni-el," "Isra-el," "El-elohe-Israel," meaning "House of El,' "Face of El," "Prince of El," etc. Jacob refers to God's revelation to him by this name. In Genesis 43:14, he says, as to Benjamin, "El Shaddai give you tender mercy before the man!" In his final, prophetic blessing of Joseph (49:25):

> From the El of thy father there shall help be to thee,
> And with Shaddai there might blessings be unto thee.

"El" set forth God's might, and *Shaddai* His exhaustless bounty, so that together they express The *All-bountiful One*.

Marked significance often attaches to human names such as "Adam," red earth; "Jacob," Supplanter; "Samuel," asked of El; "Micah," who is like Jah? "Malachi," my messenger.

Our Lord called James and John "Boanerges," sons of thunder, because of their impetuous temper; Simon He called Peter, etc.

12

Scripture Dialect and Self-Definition

SCRIPTURE DEFINITIONS form a distinct department of Bible study. When the Holy Spirit gives the equivalent of His own terms there is no room for conjecture; and, in all most important cases, we are taught in what sense Scripture words are employed. Where such equivalents are given, if substituted for the words or phrases they define, the sense is made clearer, and often erroneous notions corrected.

Hundreds of Scripture words are thus informed with a new significance. Though taken from terrestrial tongues they acquire a new celestial meaning by association with heavenly things; and as, in many cases, God has given us His own definitions, or equivalents, it is interesting to gather a sort of glossary of such terms, thus making a Bible lexicon. Probably no important word would be found undefined or without material for definition; and Bible definitions thus constructed, should be adhered to, as guides to the understanding of Scripture, for so, without outside help, the most unlettered may come to knowledge.

One prominent definition is that of *Faith*.

Hebrews 12:1—"Now, Faith is the substance of things hoped for; the evidence of things not seen."

This is probably less a definition of faith itself than a description of its *effects*, when it controls our experience, in giving, to what is future,

67

reality and verity, and, to what is unseen, substantial value and visibility. Two classes of objects are dreamy and shadowy; the invisible and the far-distant. Being so constituted as to be most influenced by sensible and present objects, what lies behind that double veil of invisibility and futurity, is proportionately unreal and uninfluential. Faith gives vividness and presentness to what is unseen and distant.

But faith has, in at least four cases, an indirect definition.

Luke 1:45—"Blessed is she that *believed that there shall be a performance* of those things which were told her from the Lord." (Marg.)

Acts 27:25—"I believe God that it shall be even as it was told me."

Romans 4:21—"Being fully persuaded that what He had promised He was able also to perform."

Hebrews 11:11—"Sarah judged Him faithful who had promised."

From such Scripture it is easy to frame a definition of Faith; it is belief, persuasion, judgment, that God is both able and faithful to perform what He has promised, and that there will be such performance.

A kindred definition is found in John 1:12: "To as many as *received Him* . . . even to them that *believe* on His name." Here *receiving* is the equivalent of *believing*; and believing, of receiving. The importance of this definition is immense, since the actual possession of Eternal Life depends upon it. In John 20:31, the object of the whole gospel record is stated to be that men might believe, and believing have life; and so, in the very beginning, it is made plain what it is to believe. In the narrative believing is referred to about 50 times; and in every case if *receiving* be substituted, the sense is perfect.

For example, 3:16: God so loved . . . that He gave His only begotten Son that whosoever receiveth Him might have Everlasting Life, etc.

Thus, no reader need lose the gift of God which is eternal life through Jesus Christ our Lord, by not understanding how to believe. He has only to receive him as God's gift, and receiving is so simple that it needs no defining.

Love is defined:

"Love is the fulfilling of the Law" (Rom. 13:10). "This is the Love of God that we keep His commandments" (1 John 5:3).

The former text defines Love to *Man* and the second, Love to *God*. Love to man is the principle that works no ill to one's neighbor; and Love to God, the kindred principle that yields obedience to all His commandments—benevolence, manward and obedience, Godward. How that lifts love above any mere sentiment, caprice, emotion or even affection, to the level of unchanging principle of life, what James calls the "Royal Law"!

Love, in that highest sense of *unselfish benevolence* is also a new term in Scripture. It is more than either the complacent affection that responds to worth in others, or the selfish principle that reciprocates favors or anticipates them (compare Matt. 5:14–18).

Sin is defined:

"Sin is the transgression of the Law" (1 John 3:4).

"To him that knoweth to do good and doeth it not, to him it is sin" (James 4:17).

"Sin that dwelleth in me" (Rom. 7:20).

Here the first definition includes all sins of *commission*—the second of *omission*; and so the Westminster divines got their definition: "Sin is any want of conformity unto, or transgression of, the Law of God." The last suggests a further idea of sin as an inborn, inbred, indwelling propensity and tendency.

Repentance is both defined and described in 2 Corinthians 7: 9–11. In its essence it is "sorrow after a godly manner"—literally, a sorrow *according to God*—a phrase thrice repeated here—and contrasted with a sorrow according to the world; one working life and salvation, the other death and condemnation. True repentance looks at sin as a crime against God primarily, in contrast with mere regret for consequences or remorse of conscience which drives to despair and sometimes suicide.

Among other valuable definitions, note the follow:

"The Carnal mind is enmity against God."

"To be Carnally minded is Death."

"To be Spiritually minded is Life and Peace" (Rom. 8:6, 7).

These definitions are doubly valuable: they give us the equivalents of the "Carnal mind" and the "Spiritual mind"; and, conversely, the equivalents of "life" and "death" in the spiritual realm. The only time *death* is defined in the Word of God it is made the equivalent of *minding the flesh*, which, again, is the equivalent of that enmity *against God*"which "is not subject to the Law of God neither indeed can be." Here then we learn that *Eternal Life* is equivalent to the *spiritual mind*—which is a supreme preference for God, and subjection to His Will; and spiritual death is a supreme preference for self with a corresponding enmity toward His Will. This we regard as one of the most noteworthy of all the biblical definitions of its own terms, and a light upon a mystery the wrong solution of which has misled many.

Here the habitual, engrossing preference of Carnal things, in a word the dominance of self life, is seen not only to *lead* to death but to *be* death; and the corresponding preference for spiritual things, the enthronement of God in place of self, as the equivalent of life and peace. No argument is so potent, as showing how baseless is the doctrine of "annihilation," so far as it rests on the statement that "when the Bible says 'death,' it *means* death." Certainly, but, according to this, death is not *the extinction of being*—not *destruction*, but *alienation*, putting self in the place of God, while life is not existence, but the supreme preference for God that evidences our oneness with Him by participation of His nature. Hence also Life may be "more abundant," as fellowship with God becomes more intimate and constant, increasing in power, wisdom and joy (John 10:10). Taken as a whole the Word of God reveals a present life, and beyond that another life, beyond which is no death; and a present death, and beyond that, a second death, and beyond that, no life (Dean Alford).

Hardness of heart is indirectly defined by close association with blindness, deafness, a conscience seared with a hot iron, a general condition of "being past feeling" (Eph. 4:19). It is in the *moral* nature what loss of sensation is in the physical, and suggests a kind of spiritual paralysis as when both sensor and motor nerves no longer act.

Changes of meaning of the same word must be traced by a careful comparison of its use and study of context. The word *diathēkē*, translated "covenant" and "Testament," is found thirty-three times in the New Testament. It always means a divine arrangement or disposition, something ordered and established by decree; sometimes a mutual arrangement, a compact between two or more contracting parties—a covenant; and at others a disposition by one party in favor of another—a testament. The former meaning easily passes into the latter, because man having broken all mutual covenants between himself and God, the Lord Jesus Christ becomes the contracting party in the new covenant on behalf of man. Now note (1) He cannot fail and hence the new covenant will never be forfeited; and (2) He makes provision for man's previous failure and forfeitures and by His death, as covenant Head, qualifies the body of heirs to receive the inheritance. Hence, the *covenant* becomes also a *Testament*, depending on the death of the testator. This progressive transition in meaning may be traced from Hebrews 7:22, through 8:6–10 to 9:15–17.

There is also a *Scripture dialect and usage.*

This is a sort of indirect definition. *Usus loquendi* is a technical term for usage in language, whether in speaking or writing. Every language has its idioms, peculiar meanings attaching to words, which undergo modifications in time, and change with periods. Individual authors also have their modes of expression so that to ascertain the sense in which words are used is often a necessary clue to style and sense. The Scriptures use words and phrases in a way of their own, and we must discern this to make interpretation accurate and authoritative.

The Word of God can be truly fathomed in its deeper teaching only by those who recognize this *Law of Higher Significance.*

Human writers have often shown marked individuality of expression as well as of thought, and use words and phrases in a characteristic way, exemplified in the case of such as Bunyan and Burke, Addison and Carlyle, Shakespeare and Bacon. One has to become familiar with their idiosyncrasies of style, to penetrate to the real inner chambers of their mind and meaning.

The Author of Scripture, having only the imperfect medium of human speech for conveyance of His thought, was compelled to invest many words with a new significance. Hence arose His scriptural *usus loquendi*—a peculiar and original sense, attaching to many words and phrases, due to their being vehicles for divine ideas. Phraseology became elastic, expanding to contain and convey larger conceptions than ever before.

Christianity has introduced among men not only new words but new ideas likewise, so that old words have become invested with new meanings.

Humanity is a word you look in vain for in Plato and Aristotle. The idea of mankind as one family, as the children of one God, is an idea of Christian growth, and the science of mankind without Christianity, would never have sprung into existence.

Take for example, *Humility*, in the New Testament. This word, borrowed from the Greek (*tapeinophrosynē*)—is used but four times, and literally means self-abasement, and suggests meanness of spirit. To the Greek, it suggested an outward prostration, a demeaning of oneself before another as a slave abases himself before his master. The Greek mind knew nothing of that voluntary laying aside of glory and excellency that leads even a master to become a slave, and prompted the Lord of Glory to humble Himself and become obedient unto death, even the death of the cross! John 13:4, 5 is a definition of humility *by action*, the Lord Jesus girding Himself with the slave's apron, to do for His disciples the most menial act of drudgery.

Christian humility is a virtue of so high an order that it may be doubted if any other outranks it. It is a noble condescension which in its very lowliness is lofty, and in its very loveliness unconscious, for it is not merely doing what is humble, but mot thinking of oneself more highly than one ought to think. It is at bottom not any form of outward demeanor but an inward habit of self-abasement and self-oblivion, that inner spirit, meek and quiet which is the one ornament, the hidden man of the heart which is in God's sight of great price.

To know in what specific sense words and terms are employed by any writer, is to have, so far, keys to unlock his meaning. It pleases the author of Holy Scripture to provide, in the Bible itself, the helps to its understanding and interpretation. If all doors to its secret chambers are not left open, the keys are to be found; and part of the object of leaving some things obscure, instead of obvious, is to incite and invite investigation, to prompt us to patient and prayerful search. Its obscurities awaken curiosity and inquiry, and study is rewarded by finding the clue to what was before a maze of perplexity.

13

Verbal Changes and Variations

IN PSALM 91, THERE ARE CHANGES IN THE USE of the personal pronoun which indicate a sort of dialogue:

"*He* that dwelleth" (v. 1).

"*I* will say of the Lord" (v. 2).

"Surely He shall deliver *thee*" (v. 3).

"Because He hath set His love upon *me*" (v. 14).

These changes of person and case divide the Psalm into four parts, and hint three separate speakers:

1. The Angel of the Lord, or a prophetic teacher, in verse one, announcing a benediction upon the believer who dwells in God.

2. The Believer, responding, and declaring Jehovah to be his refuge and fortress, his God in Whom he will trust.

3. Then again, the first speaker, expanding upon the blessing announced in the opening verses (vv. 3–13).

4. Jehovah Himself speaks, confirming all that the angel or prophet has said (vv. 14–16).

Some think this "Psalm of Life," like the previous "Psalm of Death," is by Moses, and may have been written to commemorate the deliverance at the time of the Passover to which it is so appropriate.

In Psalm 109, there is a most noticeable change of number and person. In verses 1 through 5 the plural "*they*" is prominent; and again, after verse 20. But from verse 6 to 19, the singular "he" and "his" and "him" is found thirty times. Here again this divides the psalm into three parts, and if the word "saying" be understood, at the close of verse 5, the whole imprecation that follows, down to verse 19, becomes *not the psalmist's prayer* for *vengeance on his adversaries* but *their imprecation of curses upon him*, and renders the whole psalm luminous. We then see a persecuted man of God, cursed by enemies, but giving himself unto prayer, and finally committing their whole judgment to Jehovah: "Let them curse, but do thou bless," etc. This relieves what is otherwise one of the bitterest of the imprecatory psalms of its character as such; and, instead of the psalmist dealing in cursing, and indulging a vindictive spirit, he is seen as a patient sufferer under reproach who answers not back; who, "when reviled, reviled not again; when he suffered threatened not, but committed himself to Him that judgeth righteously," like His Master after Him (1 Pet. 2:23).

In Isaiah 6:8, the voice of Jehovah asks, "Whom shall *I* send, and who will go for *us*?" a possible hint of the Trinity, as though Jehovah had inquired whom shall I, as God, commission, and who will accept the errand and offer to represent Father, Son and Spirit in the discharge of duty. This question, read in the light of the New Testament, is made most suggestive; for, after our Lord taught men more plainly of this commission, it began to be seen that we are not only witnesses to God the Father, but to God the Son, as the world's Redeemer, and co-witnesses with the Holy Spirit (cf. Is. 43:10; Acts 1:8; John 15:26, 27). It is as though, in a human firm, one of three partners acting in behalf of the other partners, calls for volunteers, who nevertheless represent the whole firm; or, as when a soldier accepting some special mission at the call of his general, serves the whole government that he represents.

In our Lord's primary lesson on alms-giving, prayer and fasting (Matt. 6:18), He uses very conspicuously the second personal pronoun, "thou," "thy," "thee." Although He begins with the plural, "Take heed that *ye* do not *your* righteousness before men to be seen of them," immediately after as He proceeds to details, He changes to the singular, "Therefore, when *thou* doest *thine* alms, do not sound a trumpet before *thee*." And in these three verses about almsgiving (2–4) this singular number occurs eight times. Again, in the two verses following about closet prayer, the singular is found expressed ten times; and again in the actions as to fasting (vv. 17, 18) eight times. Surely there is some great lesson here, for beside the express use of the singular, "thou" is implied in the verbs used also. Our Lord is impressing the need of *privacy* as in contrast with *publicity*. There is danger in display of giving, praying, fasting; the foremost necessity is to do all these as unto God—in His presence, with regard to His recognition, and solely for His glory. In almsgiving the great peril is the love of human probation; in prayer, undue attention to human hearers and observers; in fasting, desire to be conspicuous as humble and devoted to a religious life. The great Teacher impresses the need of what Jeremy Taylor calls, "the practice of the presence of God"; and insists upon the suppliant soul learning the great lesson of secret prayer, shut in with God alone. The presence of any third party prevents the highest success in the practice of the presence of God because it diverts the mind and divides the attention of the suppliant. And so, in other religious duties: to get sight of man is often to lose sight of God, and to seek human observation and approbation is absolutely fatal to all true acceptance, and forfeits God's observation and approbation altogether. Notably also our Lord returns to the plural "*ye*," in verses 7 and 8 because He is probably referring to collective prayer in public assemblies and not to private closet supplication.

In Luke 22:31, 32, our Lord first warns all the disciples of an evil design and device of the devil—"Behold, Satan hath desired to have *you*"—you all—"that he may sift you as wheat"; then, foreseeing that Peter, especially, would fall into his snare, and thrice deny Him, added, "But I have prayed for *thee*, that *thy* faith fail not," etc.

In Hosea 10:9, "O Israel, *thou* has sinned from the days of Gibeah! There *they* stood," etc.

The change of the third person and plural number removes them as to a greater distance. The singular "thou" is much more expressive of endearment and intimacy and harmony. A long course of sin has resulted in alienation. It reminds of the pathetic plea, "Only call *me* 'thou' again!"

In Isaiah 3:1, *Stay* and *Staff* are respectively masculine and feminine forms of the same word, an Arabic idiom for including everything of the nature of a support, as the succeeding verses show—whatever was their dependence—mighty man, warrior, judge or prophet—counselor, captain, artificer, orator—all, even Jehovah Himself, their only real stay or staff.

Hengstenberg calls attention to Ecclesiastes 7:23–29, where the whole passage turns upon a *feminine* verb, "Koheleth"—the "preacher," or "convener" or assembling one is conceived here as an ideal *female* and hence here only in the book is Koheleth connected with the feminine verb (v. 27). Solomon found no snare so ruinous as that of strange women—idolatrous women. And here earthly, sensual devilish wisdom is contrasted (as with James 3:15, 17) with the wisdom from above, answering to an ideal woman. Everywhere in this book, until now, Koheleth is *masculine*, but here the gender is changed. And here is the conclusion—"counting one by one," comparing or contrasting one with the other—among the thousand wives and concubines Solomon had not found one who was not a snare, certainly not one who could represent to him the Heavenly Wisdom. In the book of Revelation two women are again strongly in contrast—the harlot—an apostate church,—and the Bride—the church of the Redeemed.

A remarkable transition takes place at Isaiah 53:11. The word "servant" has always hitherto been in the *singular; but from that point on is in the plural*. Here it is "My righteous Servant"; but, in chapter 54, verse 17, "This is the heritage of the *servants* of the Lord," plural, and in chapter 65, seven times, "my servants"; always in the plural (cf. vv. 8, 9, 13, 15). Some find a hint in this "new name," the forecast that, in the latter days, disciples were to be called "Christians." The point of transition from singular to plural is this: "He shall see of the *travail of his soul*, and shall be satisfied." By his travail He is to become the parent of innumerable offspring, and the "Righteous Servant" of Jehovah is so identified with His spiritual seed that henceforth we read only of "the *servants* of Jehovah."

Mark the change of *pronoun* in Psalm 81:16, "*He* should have fed *them* also with the finest of wheat; And with honey out of the rock that *I* should have satisfied *thee*," as though Jehovah yearned to speak, not as a narrator, but as a covenant God, directly *to* them, one last word—"*I* would have satisfied *thee*."

One of the most noticeable changes of *gender* is found in John 6:37–40:

> All that the Father giveth Me, shall come to Me; and him that cometh to Me, I will in no wise cast out. For I came down from heaven, not to do Mine own will, but the will of Him that sent Me.
>
> And this is the Father's will which hath sent Me, that of all which He hath given Me, I should lose nothing, but should raise it up again at the last day. And this is the will of Him that sent Me, that every one which seeth the Son, and believeth on Him, may have everlasting life: and I will raise him up at the last day.

Notice the changes:

"*All that* the Father giveth Me."	"*Him* that cometh to Me."
"*All which* He hath given Me."	"That *every one*."
"I should raise *it* up."	"I will raise *him* up," etc.

A designed change of gender here runs throughout; and alongside of it, the conception of a sort of collective neuter mass—"all," "it"—resolved into masculine individuality—"every one," "him."

There is at first a general, abstract statement of a gift of the Father; then a concrete, individual statement of the effect and realization of it; first, an unredeemed body of humanity, like a dead mass of matter, without individual life or character—"As for all that which He hath given me I should not lose of it." Then this same dead mass of humanity, after the Son has vivified it, alive; it has developed individuality in developing vitality. Somewhat as a dead mass of matter takes form in living foliage, a million separated stalks and stems with endless variety of leaf, bloom fruit, so this mass of humanity is filled and thrilled with a new divine life, transformed, transfigured, glorified.

"O, the happiness of the man who walketh not," etc. (Ps. 1:1).

"Happiness" is found in the Hebrew, only in the *plural*, as though to indicate its manifold sides and aspects, or better still, that God's blessings never come singly or alone, but always in multitudes or companies. "*Goodness* and *mercy* shall follow me" (Ps. 23).

In Galatians 5:19–22, the *works* of the flesh are contrasted with the *fruit* of the Spirit. All these fleshly works may not and do not always appear in the same unregenerate man, but in every true child of God the fruit of the Spirit may be looked for, though not all in equal development, for these nine gracious characteristics all belong, like grapes, upon one cluster: the first three, "love, joy, peace," pertain especially to *God*; the next three, "long suffering, gentleness, goodness," to *man*; the last three, "fidelity, meekness, self-control," to *self*.

In 1 John 1:8, 9, "*Sin*" represents the depraved nature or tendency. "*Sins*," violations of law, outbreakings of sin.

14

Scriptural Precision and Discrimination

THE LAW OF CRITICAL THOROUGHNESS should govern all biblical study. Nothing should be deemed unimportant in the sacred narrative. To know the parties in a transaction, the place, time and circumstances, the causes and consequences of an occurrence—all are needful. "The historical *what*, its chronological *when*, and its geographical *where*, make history, chronology, and geography substantiate the truth of a statement" (Rev. G. L. Wilson).

Dr. Howard Osgood, a most thorough student, who searches the Scriptures with microscopic eyes, in the following summary gives an example of minute investigation:

Exclusive of proper names, the Hebrew Old Testament contains 6,413 different words, of these 1,798 are used but once; 724, twice; 448, thrice; 3,443, more than thrice. In the New Testament, Greek, there are 4,867 different words; of these, 1,654, used but once; 654, twice; 383 thrice; 2,176 more than thrice. Thus the Bible contains in its vocabulary only 11,280 different words. Isaiah uses altogether but 2,186 of which 1,924 are common, and only 262 unique—so brief is the Scripture vocabulary, and so simple its dialect.

Mr. Newberry reckons the names of God as found in the Old Testament, taken together, 10,900 times; Adhonai, 290; El, and Elohim, 2,833; Jehovah, 7,000, etc.

What an extraordinary book that must be that makes even such masters in literature feel compensated for such painstaking precision in examining into details! It is superficial acquaintance with the Holy Scripture that makes erroneous interpretations so easy and perilous.

It is the aggregation of the littles that makes the whole. *"Trifles make perfection, and perfection is no trifle,"* as said a great artist. As a great door swings on small hinges, a single adverb or preposition, article or even particle, may help to give definition or direction to a thought of God, or, like a delicate stroke of a pencil, assist in the delineation of a portrait. We are not competent to judge what is of little importance in the inspired Word of God, and nothing should be so deemed in such a study; we should mark minutely the force of particular words or phrases, believing that the Spirit of God selects words with full understanding of their meaning and chooses unerringly and with a reason. Those expressions should be specially noted which He uses to convey great leading thoughts and so lifts to a high level of importance.

Critical thoroughness is the only worthy way of studying the Word of God. The exact language of Scripture often proves a comment, if not a commentary, on the truth taught; indeed divine discrimination is the more needful because of the fixed ideas and associations connected with human speech, that men may not be misled into transferring to divine things the imperfection and infirmity inseparable from the human.

Some examples of scriptural precision may help to exhibit this exactness and illustrate its moral uses.

For instance, our Lord never addressed disciples as "brethren"—*adelphoi*—until after He had risen from the dead, who was Himself "the first born from the dead," "the first fruits of them that slept." Not till then were believers made "sons" and "heirs of God through Christ," and so prepared to claim full privileges of such sonship. Hence also the marked change of language from "children" to "sons," as in Galatians 54:5–7. In Psalm 22:22,—which Psalm He appropriates to Himself,—after He had been delivered from His sufferings, He claims the "great congregation"—the "many sons" of Hebrews 2:10

as His "brethren"; and, on that first Easter morning, for the first time, He says, "Go tell My *brethren*"—"go to My *brethren*, and say unto them, 'I ascend unto *My Father and your Father*'" (Matt. 28:10; John 20:17).

In 1 Corinthians 9:21, Paul describes himself as "not being without law to God, but under the law to Christ." Here the original words are *anomos* and *ennomos*—a delicate and designed contrast—literally, "not an outlaw but an inlaw." The two words convey the contrasted ideas of being outside of all legal restraints on the one hand, and voluntarily within them on the other.

Discrimination in terms is often very significant and important.

Lazarus, "the beggar, died and *was carried* by the angels to Abraham's bosom."

"The rich man also died and was *buried*" (Luke 16:22). No "burial" for the beggar, but a stately burial for the rich man—the pauper's body hustled into a hole without ceremony; the rich man's corpse attended to its costly sepulcher, by a funeral cortege and worldly display. But, beyond the earthly—what a contrast again—a convoy of angels for the beggar—but what of the other? Had our Lord no intention to suggest all the contrasts here so singularly exhibited?

The word in John 20:7, "Wrapped together," fails to convey the true significance. The original means *rolled up*, and suggests that these cloths were lying there *in their original convolutions*, as they had been tightly rolled up around our Lord's dead body. In chapter 19:40, it is recorded how they tightly wound—bound about—that body in the linen cloths—how tightly and rigidly may be inferred from the necessity of *loosing* Lazarus, even after miraculous power had raised up the dead body and given it life (11:44).

This explains verse 8, "And he, John, *saw* and *believed*." There was nothing in the mere fact of an empty tomb to compel belief in a miraculous resurrection; but, when John saw, on the floor of the sepulcher, the long linen wrappings that had been so tightly wound about the body and the head, lying there undisturbed, in those original convolutions, he knew nothing but a miracle could have made it possible.

Is there not an important moral and spiritual lesson here? Is not the believer to see here a type of his own deliverance in Christ, from the previous habits of sin which have so tightly wrapped their restraints about him that he is powerless to walk with God? They are to be regarded and treated as cerements of the sepulcher, what pertains to the old man, and left behind in the place of death—put off by divine power that the new man may put on the new garments of a resurrection life.

Delicate *shades of meaning*, often disclosed only by careful study, in many cases convey salutary suggestions in holy living.

In James 1:6, a wavering disciple is likened to "the surge of the sea, *driven with the wind and tossed.*" The sea, when agitated by the wind has two marked motions: one, to and fro, which is called "fluctuation"; and another, up and down, which is called "undulation." To both of these the writer refers. A sea wave cannot stay anywhere—if it is propelled forward, it recedes backward; if lifted upward, it sinks downward. And so a half-believing soul; whatever onward or upward impulse he gets he cannot retain. He relapses and returns to his former position and condition. He has no staying qualities. And it is the *surge* of the sea that is here referred to, the most frothy, the least substantial and stable, of anything about a wave. It is light, swept hither and thither by the wind, and forms and disappears again rapidly. What a simile to represent inconsistency and inconstancy in a praying soul, that can neither hold fast God's promise and faithfulness, nor maintain any advanced position of faith when once it is secured?

Words that seem unimportant, and even particles that appear insignificant, have their place and use. It is another disadvantage of not being familiar with the original that the force of many of these "jots and tittles" is not easily transferred to another tongue.

For instance, in Philippians 3:8, five small particles occur in succession—"but, indeed, therefore, even also do I." How hard to convey the significance of all these little words! Specially emphatic are two, "*en de,*" in verse 13, translated "but this one thing I do"; what Paul says is, "*but one.*" The very brevity of the phrase leaves no more room for the imagination to invest it with meaning: it suggests not only what he does, but what he desires, aims at, sets before him, as the all engrossing object and goal.

In Mark 13:4–32, two words continually recur (*tauta* and *ekeinos*), translated, "these," "those," "that." They indicate, however, two classes of events, one nearer at hand the other more remote, the former preparing for the latter.

When we read how "*The Lord* commended the unjust steward because he done sagaciously" (Luke 16:8)—it is not the Lord Jesus, but the *lord of the steward*—his master, that is meant. "Shall He find *the* faith on the earth?" (Luke 20:8). The definite article here must indicate definite faith—some think, the faith in a prayer hearing God; others, the faith in a divine avenger and retribution; others, the faith in the second advent. To make the faith specific and definite, not general, vague and indefinite, gives point to the parable.

Some scholarly student might do great service by a treatise on the use and force of such words as "wherefore" and "therefore," especially in Paul's epistles. They are the connecting links in argument; one connects it to something already stated or demonstrated; the other with what is to follow. The "Wherefore" in Hebrews 12:1 links the lesson on affliction with whole preceding history of triumphant faith: and in Romans 12:1, the "Therefore" sums up the whole argument of the eleven chapters that go before.

"The preposition, '*en*,' is applied to the Holy Spirit when it is about the *disciples* that the statement is made; but '*dia*,' when it is about Christ."

Individual words bear very close study. For example, in Hebrews 4:2, the word rendered "mixed," refers primarily to the process whereby, in the animal system, food taken into the body for nutritive purposes, is mixed with those secretions intended by nature for assimilation and appropriation to bodily wants, which is a threefold process: 1. Mastication, whereby food is mixed with saliva; 2. Digestion proper, whereby in the stomach it is mixed with bile and transformed into chyle; and 3. Absorption, whereby in its passage through the alimentary canals, it is taken up by the lacteal vessels and actually mixed with the blood, becoming a part of the body, displacing waste tissue by new material.

Upon this threefold process everything depends, strength and health, vigor and even vitality. And, in fact, if the aliment be not so mixed with ptyaline, bile, pancreatic juice, etc., it is harmful instead of profitable, a source of disease and death. How striking the lesson as to the need of mixing the word heard with meditation and prayer and holy examination of self, that it may be incorporated into practice, and affect our whole habit and frame of mind and heart and conscience and will, and reappear in our speech, conduct, frame of spirit, and whole life, becoming an integral part of ourselves! (See the Psalms.)

Another example of the need of observing the exact language of the inspired Word is found in the threefold parable of Luke 15. Usually even commentators fall into the error of reckoning here *three* parables, instead of *one in three parts*. But the record is explicit: "He spake *this parable* unto them" (v. 3).

The whole chapter is one parable: subject, "The Lost, found." There are three divisions, closely interrelated; the lost sheep, found by the shepherd; the lost silver piece, found by the woman; the lost son, found by the father. The point of unity is thus easily seen. But why the parable is threefold will appear on further examination.

In the finding of the lost there are *two* great aspects: first, the *divine* side, and second the *human*. The first and second parts show God seeking man, man being passive. The sheep is found and carried back by the shepherd; the silver piece is found and replaced on the woman's necklace. Did the parable end here, man might infer that he had nothing to do but wait for God to seek and find him. Hence a third part of threefold parable in which *man's* part in his recovery is seen. It is now God who is comparatively passive and man who is active—he who wanders from God, finds himself and goes back to the Father. It is only as *both* sides are seen that the whole truth is apprehended.

Possibly there is another reason for this *threefold* arrangement: the shepherd seeking the lost sheep may represent the Son of man seeking the lost sheep of the House of Israel; the woman, seeking her silver, the Spirit, in the church, recovering backslidden members; and the Father and Son may represent the wider relation of God the Father to His universal human family.

The exact order of words often contains in itself a valuable lesson.

It may seem unimportant whether we read 1 Thessalonians 5:23—"Your whole spirit, soul and body," or body, soul and spirit. But there is a reason—there may be many—for the inspired order. Not only is the spirit the highest part in man's complex being, but it is *here* that the God of Peace begins when He would sanctify us wholly. He illumines man's spiritual being with His Light of Truth, quickens it into new energy and vitality by His Eternal Life, and renews it by His Love. Then through the transformed spirit, He reaches the soul with its emotions, desires and propensities; and through that, reaches downward and outward to the body with its appetites and lusts. Man's mistaken method is too often the reverse. He begins with *body*, and hopes by improving the physical conditions and material surroundings to prepare the way for mental improvement and culture and so finally uplift and enlarge the spiritual being. God's way is to begin with the highest and work toward the lowest.

A Hebrew scholar, a Jewish Rabbi, has said that curiously enough, the names of the ten representative patriarchs of the first ten generations suggest a sort of redemptive sentence, scarce any word needing to be supplied to complete the sense, thus:

"Adam—'Red Earth,' Seth—'Hath appointed,' Enosh—(unto) 'mortal man,' Canaan—'Wailing-for-the-Dead,' Mahalaleel—'Why Praise God'? Jared—'He shall descend,' Enoch—A 'mortal man,' Methuseleh—'Dismissing Death,' Lamech—(bringing to) 'the Weary,' Noah—'Rest.' " Another similar sentence is suggested by the root significance of these words: "Man, placed in a fallen condition, the Ransomer, Light of God, descended, teaching his death brings the stricken, rest."

Here both the meaning of individual words and their order are essential to make this continuous redemptive sentence.

15

Similar and Equivalent Terms

SOUL" AND "SPIRIT" are carefully distinguished in both Testaments. *Nephesh* and *ruach* in Hebrew, *psyche* and *pneuma* in Greek (1 Thess. 5:23; Heb. 4:12). "Soul" is properly the animating principle of the body, and therefore common to the animal creation; it includes the appetites and desires both of flesh and mind, and the inclination and determination. The other words, properly meaning "spirit," originally signify breath or wind; but, in its higher application, a *breath from God* (Gen. 2); hence a mode of existence which is like His own shares His nature. God is never set forth in Scripture as *soul*, center of bodily life, animator of a physical organism and inspirer of its appetites; but as Spirit, independent of material conditions and limitations and having affections and emotions of His own. Spirit in man therefore represents that which no mere animal, as such, shares with him. While soul links him to the whole animal creation, spirit binds him to God, and makes possible a divine nature and life and participation in the holiness, happiness and glory of God.

Paul, in 1 Corinthians 2, 3 uses two words, both of which are rendered "carnal." Meyer, the commentator, sharply distinguishes *sarkinos* (3:1) as designating the unspiritual state of nature which the Corinthians still had in their early Christian minority, the Spirit having as yet so partially changed their character that they appeared still as fleshly; but *sarkikos* (v. 3) expresses a later ascendance over the divine principle of which they had been made partakers by progressive instruction; and this latter is here the main ground of reproach and rebuke. Some would distinguish by the terms "fleshy" and "fleshly"; the former denoting the carnality of the babe in whom the flesh as yet naturally predominates and preponderates, the mind being immature and undeveloped; the latter, denoting the carnality of the adult, full grown yet allowing the flesh to retain the ascendancy. The former word therefore carries rather the notion of tender pity for immaturity, while the latter is a term of reproach for inconsistency. This is a case in which not to grasp the delicate differences between words is to lose the point of a whole paragraph, and confound ideas which essentially differ.

In Galatians 6:2, 5, "burden" and "load" should be distinguished. We are to "bear one another's burdens," yet every "one should bear his own proper load." When his load is too heavy for him to bear alone, others are to put their shoulders beneath it, not to release him altogether, but to relieve him, not to shift it from his shoulders to their own, but to accept as a common burden for both. God would not have any one seek to be rid of his own responsibility or liability, nor have others encourage his idleness and selfishness, but we are all to do what we can to make others' loads tolerable and bearable by sympathetic help and support. What a valuable ethical lesson is lost if these kindred words are confused.

Four words are used to describe the relations of men to God as source of life and being. They are alike but by no means identical, and respectively rendered "offspring," "child," "son," etc. Compare John 13:33; Acts 17:28, 29, Romans 8:16, 17; Galatians 4:3, 5, etc. That they are not used indiscriminately will be plain from the passage in Galatians, already cited, where the argument turns upon the difference between a child—a minor, and a son, a child that has reached his majority.

The word "offspring"—*genos*—means literally *one who has come to be*—to exist, as a product of creative power, a human creature of God. "Child," *teknon, teknion,* suggests one born, brought forth, properly referring rather to the *mother,* suggesting the maternal relation, hinting parental love and care; or little child, as a term of endearment, fondly used by the Apostle John. *Nēpios* means literally one who does not yet talk—a mere babe, infant, hence one simple and unlearned (Matt. 11:25; 21:16). But *huios*, strongest of all, expressed the higher filial relationship and fellowship—a word worthy to be applied to the Son of God Himself.

How even so-called "synonyms" differ will be seen by comparing such English words as "enough" and "sufficient," "paternal" and "fatherly," "reputation" and "notoriety," or such kindred adjectives as "efficient," "effective," "effectual" and "efficacious," where the diversity of meaning behind the most similar terms is both instructive and suggestive.

The Old and New Testament synonyms have found volumes of treatment from such pens as those of Girdlestone and Trench. The various terms used to express forgiveness, salvation, punishment, vengeance; the four words that convey the idea of time—*aiōn*, time indefinite; *chronos*, time in actuality, making succession; *hōra*, a definite measure of time; *kairos*, a fit or appropriate time—how helpful to catch such distinctions and how hindering to overlook them.

Where one English word is used as the equivalent of two or more in the original, both beauty and force are sometimes sacrificed. In our Lord's last discourse (John 14, 15, 16), one root word is very prominent and constantly recurs—it is *menō*—which means to stay, remain, abide or continue. Its central sense is thus connected with something enduring and permanent as opposed to what is evanescent and transient, and hence unsatisfying because unenduring.

If this word and its derivatives are followed in that matchless discourse, the whole of it is lit up as with a celestial light. Our Lord is about to leave them: even *His* presence is to prove, like all else only for "a little while," and their hearts are "troubled." Hence He calls their thought away to what is to *last*. The "mansions" are *monai*, abiding places (v. 2); the Father *abides* in Him (v. 10), the Holy Spirit is the *abiding Spirit* in them (v. 17), the Godhead will come and in the believer make His *abode* (v. 23). The very key to the great last parable, the Vine and Branches, is this word *abide*—"Abide in Me, and I in you." And though translated "continue" (v. 9) and "remain" (v. 16) it is the same word throughout and should be uniformly rendered.

When believers are called "the *temple of God*" a peculiar word is used, one of two, both meaning "temple" (1 Cor. 3:16, 17, etc.). One, *hieron*, embraces the whole structure and its precincts, sometimes used for the courts alone; but the other, *naos*, of the fane itself, with its Holy of Holies and Shekinah flame of God's presence; and it is *this latter* which is used to describe a believer in whom dwells the Spirit of God. How marvelous this selection of the stronger and more hallowed term! The sacrifice was offered in the larger *hieron*, but the *naos* proper was the place where the blood was *applied*, where stood the furniture that represented the forms of communion and service, and the ideal of fellowship with God. The very word, therefore, hints that, while the believer has no part in the atoning work, with the blood from the altar he comes "to God's very mercy seat, and himself becomes His Shrine!"

Here spiritual truth is illuminated when the exact significance of one word is caught. The body of a believer becomes a shrine and the Spirit of God its inhabitant. While he has no share in the atoning work of the Lamb of God, he has a full enjoyment both of the access to God it secures, and the fellowship with God it makes possible. He learns also how precious in God's sight must be even the body of a disciple which is held sacred as His temple.

Canon Girdlestone calls attention to four principal words used as names of men, and which represent him in four apparently inconsistent aspects: as *Adam*, of the earth, earthy; as *Ish*, endowed with immaterial personal existence; as *Enosh*, weak and incurable; as *Gever*, mighty and noble (cf. Gen. 1:26; 2:23; 6:4; Ex. 10:11.)

How useful such distinctions are only investigation will show. For example, *Ish* first occurs in Genesis 2:23—"She shall be called *Ishah* because she is taken out of *Ish*." Here *ish* is first used when the man finds a second human being of his own kind and springing from him: hence it marks the man when first he sees himself as one of a kind and having his first fellow-feeling with another human being. *Ish* is therefore a human being, a husband as contrasted with a wife, and hints at a higher manhood connected with race origin, mastery and supremacy. This suffices to illustrate the importance of Old Testament synonymns. The Vulgate singularly keeps up the kinship of *Ish* and *Ishah* by rendering *vir* and *virago*.

Ten similar words occur as in Psalms 19, 119, etc., such as "Law," "Testimonies," "Ways," "precepts," "statutes," "commandments," "judgments," "Word," "counselors," "fear." All of these apply to the Scriptures as containing the Divine Code; but they present that code in ten different aspects, which together give a complete viewpoint.

First of all, it is a *Law*—that is, the expression of the mind of the Lord. Again, it is a *Testimony*, bearing witness to His character and will. Again, it is a *Way*, marking out a distinct path for man to walk in. Yet again, *precepts*, or definitely prescribed rules of duty. Again, *statutes*, which express permanent, unchangeable principles. Again, *Commandments*, having the authority of a legislator. Again, *judgments*, or laws having sanctions of reward and penalty. Again, they are the *Word* of God, or His expressed will in language. Again, they are *counselors*, or "men of counsel" advising in crises. And once more the Law of God is *"fear"*—i.e., fear producing—calculated to produce reverential awe.

Thus taking the ten words together, the Divine Code is seen at so many separate angles and aspects, all of which help to develop and exhibit its perfection.

A good concordance, in which the exact force of similar words is presented and the shades of meaning indicated, is of immense help to the studious reader. Such men as Cruden, Strong, Eadie, etc., have taken great pains to trace these exact differences of significance, and an examination of their work is often a most helpful commentary. Thus what variety of truth is suggested by such kindred words as "sin," "iniquity," "transgression," in Psalm 32, as also "forgiven," "not imputed," "covered," and "acknowledge," "confess" and "not hid," in the same psalm! Three aspects of evil doing, as transgression of law, sin against God, and essential iniquity; three aspects of divine grace, in forgiving, covering, not imputing; and three more, of man's acts, not hiding, confessing (to God), acknowledging (to man).

The changes of words, where at first no sufficient reason is apparent, are often due to the nice and delicate discrimination of the Spirit.

A noticeable example is Micah 7:20: "Thou wilt perform the *truth* to Jacob, the *mercy* to Abraham which Thou hast sworn unto our fathers from the days of old."

Jehovah was under no obligation to enter into Covenant with Abraham and promise blessings to his seed which He confirmed with an oath: but, having once made such covenant promise, He was under a self imposed obligation to keep it; hence what had originally been mercy to Abraham became *truth* to Jacob.

Precisely similar is the use of language in John 1:9. "If we confess our sins, He is *faithful* and *just* to forgive us our sins," etc. What have faithfulness and justice to do with forgiveness? It is rather the part of a faithful and just Judge and Ruler to punish and condemn, for loose clemency puts a premium on crime. But God had promised that "whoso confesseth and forsaketh his sins shall find mercy" (Prov. 28:13); and that if we "look up to Him" whom He hath lifted up on the cross, we shall "be saved." Therefore, what was originally merciful and gracious is now faithful and just—namely, to forgive and cleanse a penitent and believing sinner. For, having promised to forgive, His faithfulness is at stake; and having laid the load of guilt upon Another, justice forbids a second exaction of penalty.

So the change from "propitiation" to "Paraclete" (1 John 2:2) is necessary; for while He is the propitiation for the whole world, He is the advocate, or paraclete, only for those who are believers and whom as clients He represents in Court.

The word "fool" is used mainly in two senses—first of intellectual folly, or one destitute of understanding, perception or wisdom, as in Proverbs 15:21; 17:25; Ecclesiastes 1:17; 10:1; 2 Corinthians 11:1. And second, of *moral folly*, perverseness of heart, enmity against truth and God, as in Psalm 14:1; Proverbs 26:10; Joshua 7:15.

The two senses are not dissimilar but closely related: for nothing shows greater want of understanding than the commission of wickedness. The greater the value of virtue and the reward of piety, the greater the folly of vice and impiety: and the larger the endowments the more consummate the foolishness of misusing or abusing God's gifts in the service of sin.

16

Prominent and Dominant Words and Phrases

OF SUCH PROMINENT *words*, there are about 100, or more, which are so far essential to the substance of all biblical teaching that to understand them thoroughly and grasp their meaning and relation of the whole Word is to hold the secrets of its locked chambers. Their scriptural usage being often peculiar, must be apprehended, for it rarely if ever varies throughout; and, once mastered, goes far to unfold the entire ethical and spiritual contents of the Book. Sometimes a single word or phrase serves to illumine a whole chapter or even an epistle; and the leading words taken together help to interpret all Scripture.

Aside from the names and titles of the Deity, the following words bear this relation to the Word of God:

Righteousness, Justification, Salvation; Sanctification, Separation, Holiness; Sin, Condemnation, Judgment; Repentance, Believing, Faith, Obedience, Hope, Love, Works; World, Flesh, Devil, Self; Tongue, Walk, Life, Warfare, Witness; Pardon, Forgiveness, Reconciliation, Redemption; Temptation, Trial, Suffering; Blessedness, Victory, Glory; Light, Knowledge, Wisdom, Understanding; Law, Commandment; Word of God; Testimony; Revelation; Blood, Sacrifice, Offering. Worship, etc.

At some of these words we may well glance in passing. The word *truth* itself indicates stability. From the same root as a tree, it suggests the image of a huge oak deeply rooted in the soil—with its massive trunk and wide-spreading branches defying all the storms of heaven. The Hebrew word for truth is *Emeth*—the first and the last and the middlemost of the Hebrew letters of the alphabet, implying that truth is first and will be last, and combines all extremes and unites all ends. The Jews have often remarked that the quadrate, solid shape of the Hebrew letters of the word is significant of the firmness and steadfastness of truth. It is allied to the immortality of God, so that it is easier for heaven and earth to pass away than for one tittle of the truth to fail (Hugh McMillan, D.D.).

The *Blood* is very conspicuous. First mentioned in connection with Abel's murder, it is represented as crying from the ground to heaven for vengeance. Next, it appears as the *life*, and not to be eaten. Dr. Harvey, who discovered its "circulation," said, "The blood is the fountain of life, the first to live, the last to die, and the primary seat of the animal soul." What a comment of science upon Scripture! Then it appears as a token of salvation (Ex. 12:13). These three uses of the word interpret all Scripture. Blood stands for *guilt* and *death;* for *life* and for *salvation*.

WISDOM is very prominent and significant, and, though comparatively rare until Solomon's era, it then becomes one of the conspicuous words, occurring at least 300 times and in emphatic connections and relations.

It marks the Solomic Epoch, when a new class of men, known as "The Wise," as distinct from prophets and priests, suddenly seem to have appeared on the stage of action, henceforth constituting a class by themselves. What there was in the conditions then prevailing we imperfectly know—but there was a school of wisdom, headed by the King himself, specially given to studies, not of history only, but of philosophy and science, and ethical questions such as the relation of man to God, to himself and his fellow man and the world in which he lived; and the results of such reflections were embodied in proverbs or "wise sayings," framed in poetic parallelism. Some of these proverbial utterances are very deep and concern the laws of nature and of human nature, Divine Truth and order, virtue and duty. The mysteries of Providence occupied much thought.

The Books of Wisdom form a separate section of the Old Testament—and embrace Job, Psalms, Proverbs, Ecclesiastes, Solomon's Song, Lamentations. Not only was Hebrew wisdom far superior to that of other nations, but wisdom is often personified, and thus presented, is very nearly in the Old Testament what the *Logos* or Word Incarnate is, in the New.

To form an accurate conception of Wisdom, as presented, both in the Old Testament and in the New, where it is peculiarly the theme of the Epistle of James—is very needful. It represents Laws of Heaven for Life on Earth. It appears, first, as a *principle*. Hebrew wisdom is contrasted with the philosophy of all heathen peoples, in the point of its departure, not aiming at the discovery of an unknown god, but recognizing in all things a Known God, a God of providence, whose ways it seeks to justify and vindicate. Its fundamental idea is that of a *divinely constituted moral order*, under the phenomena of which, and within all human history, is the Living God, fulfilling Himself, His thoughts and will. The various ranks of society are the ordinance of God, to be observed with reverent feeling. Wisdom inculcates humility before God, gentleness and consideration toward men, gravity of deportment, thoughtful reflection, and slowness of speech. The mind of God is reflected in all things created and in the social order and moral career of man.

Wisdom appears also as a *person*, a principle personified, as in Proverbs 1:1–9, etc., at once projected out of the mind and being of God, and existing beside Him; (8:22–31); and finally, as God's Artificer in the creation and regulation of all things. This whole conception is connected with the *Word* of Wisdom—the inspired Scriptures; with the *Living Word*—Him who is called the "Wisdom from God," the Lord Jesus Christ; and with the "*Spirit* of Wisdom"—the Holy Ghost. The Son of God and Spirit of God are therefore the fullest impersonation and realization of all that is meant by "Wisdom."

Many aspects of *salvation* are found continuously in Matthew.

1. Preparation for salvation (Matt. 2, 3).

2. Person of the Savior; His obedience to the will of God, His words and works (Matt. 4–7).

3. Types of salvation as found in miracles (Matt. 8, 9).

4. Salvation, leading to service (9:35; 11:24).

5. Salvation revealed, received, rejected (11:25; 16:13).

6. Salvation from self (16:14; 20:28).

7. Salvation as connected with faith, obedience, and love (Matt. 20:29; 22:46).

8. Salvation and its consummation—duty of watchfulness (Matt. 23–25).

9. Salvation as connected with the death and resurrection of Christ (Matt. 26:28), etc.

The leading words of the first Epistle of John are three: LIFE, LIGHT, LOVE; and are singularly comprehensive: LIFE expresses the sum of all *Being*; LIGHT, the sum of all *intellectual excellence;* and LOVE, the sum of all moral excellence. To this brief category of the Divine Perfections nothing can be added. He is the Fountain of Life; He is Light; He is Love. These scriptural definitions of God leave nothing to be desired. They suggest not only completeness but a *unity*, which finds its finest natural illustration in the sunbeam, which at once contains and conveys Light, Heat and actinic Life.

These three words also beautifully express the threefold character and activity of the *Holy Spirit*. He is, at once,

The Spirit of LIGHT or TRUTH (John 14:17).

The Spirit of LIFE (Rom. 8:2).

The Spirit of LOVE (Rom. 5:5).

Curiously, also, the three great warnings as to our attitude toward the Spirit correspond to this threefold aspect of His character and work, RESIST NOT, GRIEVE NOT, QUENCH NOT.

Comparison of various passages, in the Epistles, referring to the *Body of Christ*, reveals a symmetric system of teaching (Rom. 12; 1 Cor. 12; Eph. 2, 4, etc.).

1. Unity and community of Life in its structure and interest.

2. Harmony of peace and love—Jew and Gentile, one new man.

3. Vitality and Energy through One indwelling Spirit.

4. Variety of Activity and Service.

5. Common responsibility, shared by all members.

6. Sanctity in the eyes, both of disciples and of God.

7. Authority, through association with the Head.

Such strikingly similar phrases as those used by Paul in Romans 7:17–20 and Galatians 2:20, cannot be without meaning. "It is no more I, but sin that dwelleth in me"; "Yet not I, but Christ liveth in me."

In both cases, two selves are contrasted—the carnal self and the spiritual self in the former; the human self and the divine self in the latter. On one hand, his higher personality is not absorbed and identified with sin, but with the will of God; on the other hand, even his better self is not his true life, but the Christ nature that is of God, and is His new creation. When the old sinful habits and tendencies re-assert themselves, and claim indulgence, he disowns them as not the voices and appeals of his truest self; but even when he feels the moving of his best spiritual life, he remembers that this is the voice of the Divine Christ who by the Holy Spirit dwells in him. In a sense, therefore, every disciple recognizing in himself a threefold personality, renounces the ego of his past unregenerate self; rejoices in the new ego that delights in the law of God after the inner man; but humbly remembers that even in this renewed inner man he cannot glory; for whatever in him responds to the Love of God he owes to the grace of Christ, and the power of the Spirit.

Key words may be found, unlocking the different books, such as:

Genesis:	"Beginning"
Exodus:	"Departure," "Passover"
Leviticus:	"Sacrifice," "Priesthood," "Atonement"
Numbers:	"Pilgrimage," "Sojourn"
Deuteronomy:	"Law," "Obedience"
Joshua:	"Possession," "Occupational"
Judges:	"Captivity," "Anarchy"
Ruth:	"Return," "Redeemer"
Samuel:	"Kingdom"
Kings:	"Royalty," "Division"
Chronicles:	"Theocracy"
Ezra:	"Temple," "Restoration"
Nehemiah:	"City-Rebuilding"
Esther:	"Providence," "Turned to the Contrary"

Job:	"Trial," "Discipline"
Psalms:	"Worship," "Devotion"
Proverbs:	"Wisdom"
Ecclesiastes:	"Vanity," "Vexation"
Canticles:	"Love," "Fidelity!"
Isaiah:	"Salvation"
Jeremiah:	"Warning"
Lamentations:	"Destruction," "Sorrow"
Ezekiel:	"Visions"
Daniel:	"Revelation," "Secret"
Hosea:	"Return"
Joel:	"Judgment"
Amos:	"Punishment"
Obadiah:	"Edom"
Jonah:	"Overthrow"
Micah:	"Controversy"
Nahum:	"Full-End"
Habakkuk:	"Faith"
Zephaniah:	"Remnant"
Haggai:	"Build"
Zechariah:	"Jealous"
Malachi:	"Robbery"
Matthew:	"Kingdom"
Mark:	"Service"
Luke:	"Son of Man," "Humanity"
John:	"Son of God," "Eternal Life"
Acts:	"Witness," "Power"
Romans:	"Righteousness"
1 Corinthians:	"Wisdom," "Temple"
2 Corinthians:	"Comfort"
Galatians:	"Walk"
Ephesians:	"Heavenlies"
Philippians:	"Gain," "Peace"
Colossians:	"Complete," "Filled"
1 Thessalonians:	"Waiting," "Coming"
2 Thessalonians:	"Man of Sin"
Timothy:	"Doctrine," "Sound Words"

Titus:	"Profitable"
Philemon:	"Receive"
Hebrews:	"Better," "Greater"
James:	"Good Works"
Peter:	"Precious"
John:	"Fellowship"
Jude:	"Kept," "Preserved," "Presented"
Revelation:	"Mystery"

Ordinarily, in each book itself, the word is suggested which is here given as a helpful key.

How significant the emphasis, in Mark 13:33, on that word—*"watch"*—which, with its Hebrew equivalents, is one of the emphatic words of all Scripture, the thought often recurring where the word does not (Prov. 4:23; Ps. 151:3). Out of the heart, primarily, and out of the mouth, secondarily, flow all life's issues and activities, never to be recalled, save for judgment; hence the duty of vigilance here.

To trace this emphatic word will show various motives and directions of watchfulness: forbidden and dangerous ground, as in Matthew 26:41; foes, many and mighty, as in 1 Peter 5:8, 9; thieves, as in Matthew 24:42–44; Luke 21:34–36; 1 Thess. 5:4–8; crises, as in 1 Peter 4:7; Mark 13:33–37; Matthew 25:13.

About three short and simple words, "Stand," "Walk," "Sit," all the practical truths of redemption, Christian privilege and duty cluster. "Stand" expresses a safe and sure *position* in contrast to an unsafe and unsound one, a judicial standing before God in Christ. "Walk" expresses conduct, the changing experience of passing from one duty, temptation and experience to another, but always in divine companionship.

"Sit" is expressive of a permanent cessation from effort and the quest of good, in an abiding rest and satisfaction in God. Compare Romans 5:1, 2; Galatians 5:16, 25; Colossians 3:1, 2.

17

Leading Paragraphs and Passages

THIS DESIGNED PROMINENCE is variously hinted, sometimes by the conspicuous place or position of a Scripture passage at the head of a discourse, or of a whole section.

In Exodus 20:1, 2, the authority of the whole Decalogue is made to rest upon one declaration:

"And God spake all these words, saying:"

And, further, that He who thus spake was the Jehovah of the Exodus, whose great deliverance of His people entitled Him to command, and obligated them to obey.

Psalm 81:9, 10 is very nearly the literal center of the whole inspired word; in Bagster's Teacher's Bible it holds the middle place. It certainly is one of the great leading passages of Scripture:

> Hear, O my people, and I will testify unto thee;
> O Israel, if thou wilt hearken unto me;
> There shall no strange gods be in thee;
> Neither shalt thou worship any strange god.
> I am the Lord thy God, which brought thee out of
> the land of Egypt:
> Open thy mouth wide, and I will fill it.

Here is another double *shema*—"Hear, O Israel!" Then follow two important double stanzas: the former an injunction against all idolatry; the latter an invitation to appropriate large blessing. The metaphor is drawn from the young fledglings that in the nest stretch

101

their beaks to the utmost capacity to take in the dainty morsel brought by the parent bird. Jehovah invites His people, shunning all worship of strange gods and compromise with them, to test to the utmost His power, wisdom and love. God's mercy is like water in a spring: man's supply is like the same water in a cup. How much each gets and drinks depends on the capacity of his vessel. To bring a large pitcher to be filled assumes both a large abundance in the spring, and a large confidence in the heart of him who brings the vessel.

Matthew 6:33 is one of the dominant tests, expounding a great law of life:

> Seek ye first the Kingdom of God and His Righteousness,
> And all these things shall be added unto you.

The substance of this is: Put first things in the first place; aim first of all to be like God and make others like Him, and He will take care of all lesser interests. The two great principles of God in His dealing with man are here indicated:

1. Whenever the primary things are put in the primary place, He adds the secondary things without their being sought at all;

2. Whenever the secondary things are put in the primary place, the primary are forfeited altogether and even the secondary may be. It is notable that "add" is a mathematical term, and implies something, already possessed—to be added to—and this implies that to seek the first things is to secure them, and it is to these that the secondary are added.

The whole context is dominated by this thought of putting first things in the first place—thought, affection, choice, being supremely fixed on the highest good, we shall not lay up treasures upon earth, nor lose singleness of aim, nor try to serve two masters, nor indulge anxious thought for the morrow.

Another dominant passage of Scripture is Matthew 16:13–28, and its two most important suggestions may be connected with two short leading words, "Rock" and "Rebuke": the rock is Peter's sublime confession of Christ; the rebuke if that evoked by his concession to Satan.

As to the rock, it is not the man but his message that is emphasized as the foundation upon which our Lord will build His church. *Petros* and *Petra* differ as a stone or piece of rock from the bedrock

Petros and *Petra* differ as a stone or piece of rock from the bedrock mass itself which alone furnishes a foundation. This interpretation is confirmed by the historic fact that upon the very confession of the divine character and mission of our Lord Jesus Christ, the church actually was built, and has ever since stood firm only upon that basis (Acts 8:37; Rom. 10; 1 Cor. 12:3; 1 John 4:15).

After the council at Jerusalem (Acts 15) Peter disappears from the church horizon and Paul becomes the prominent personage; and it is quite as true that the church was founded on Paul as on Peter. But, from Pentecost on, Peter's confession continued to be the church symbol, the heart of its creed, and the standard of discipleship and criterion of church membership.

As to our Lord's rebuke, the substance of the lesson is contained to the two short mottoes—"Spare thyself" and "Deny thyself"—the first was Peter's counsel to our Lord—the Devil's advice—and the second our Lord's counsel to Peter—the Savior's own motto.

Two texts, set side by side, are of paramount importance, John 6:28 and 29 and 16:9. The former shows the one saving work is believing on Jesus: the latter, the one damning sin is not believing. These brief sayings are meant to be dominant—and from them all may learn what is the one sin which incurs damnation—and what is the one and only good work which God either requires or accepts in order to salvation: "this is the work of God that ye believe on Him Whom God hath sent."

Seven words of our Lord—six in the original—are perhaps as significant in their bearing upon holy living, as any other equal number ever spoken:

"YE IN ME AND I IN YOU" (John 14:20).

This expression of mystic, corporate, double union between the disciple and his Lord was left to His last discourse before His crucifixion as the climax of all His teaching. What a paradox is here—a *mutual* abiding! For how can anything be at once *in* and *out*, contained and containing? His parable is His explanation. Botanically it is true, for the vine and branch grow into each other, their fibers interpenetrating and interlocking. Such language suggests an *element*, like air, fire, water, earth, of all which it is true that they are in what is in them, as the fire is in the iron when the iron is in the fire.

The *order* here is fixed: for He must be in us that we may be in Him, as the iron must first be in the fire if the fire is to be in the iron, or the bird in the air if the air is to be in the bird.

How comprehensive these few words! Here are the two sides or aspects of spiritual life: one concerns our being in Christ, accepted, forgiven, justified, reconciled—our *standing*; the other concerns His being in us, the power and secret of holy living—our *state*, and the standing in order to the state.

So important are these few words that they are the index to the contents of all the twenty-one Epistles, which may be classified according to their relations to this inspired motto, setting forth one or both sides of this double truth.

The sublime teachings of our Lord in His last discourse and prayer fall under one of these two heads, for example,

"YE IN ME"	"I IN YOU"
Access or approach to God 14:6	Abiding Life of God, 17:2, 3
Acquaintance with God. 14:7–9	Manifestation of God. 14:23
Acceptance in Prayer. "In my name."	Fruitfulness unto God. 15:4, 8, 16

Apply the same analysis to the *Epistles*:

Righteousness before God. Romans.	Sanctification by the Holy Spirit. Corinthians.
Exaltation to heavenly level. Ephesians.	Energy of transforming power. Galatians.
Completeness—filled with God. Colossians.	Satisfaction in God. Philippians.
Victory over Death and the Devil. Thessalonians.	Preservation or Presentation. Jude.

First Corinthians 3:14, 15 is a leading Scripture. Nowhere else are we so plainly taught the difference between the *salvation of the man, and the salvation of his work*. Every believer is a builder, and he cannot help it—and the great question is what sort of structure is the building. Even upon the one foundation which cannot be destroyed one may build worthless material—wood, hay, stubble, instead of gold, silver, precious stones. And when the fire tries every man's work, his work may be utterly burned while he himself escapes, so as by fire.

First Corinthians 16:17 says, "He that is joined to the Lord is one spirit" is a short sentence of ten English words. Yet it suggests to us the highest possible unity between the disciple and his Lord. Many other forms are used to express this identification, but none approach this in the conception of inseparable oneness. The sheep may wander from the shepherd, the branch be cut off from the vine; the member be severed from the body, the child alienated from the father, and even the wife from the husband; but when two spirits blend in one, what shall part them? No outward connection or union, even of wedlock, is so emphatically expressive of perfect merging of two lives in one.

Second Corinthians 5:7—"We walk by faith, not by sight," though printed as a parenthesis, in our English version, is one of the leading passages of the Scripture. It closes one paragraph and begins another, and interprets both. From chapter 4, verse 7, there has been a constant contrast presented between the seen and the unseen—the outward trials and the inward triumphs; the dying of the flesh and the life of the spirit; the affliction without, the compensation within; the dissolution of the body and the introduction to the presence of the Lord. The always confidence is due to the fact that the walk is by faith, not sight; looking at the unseen and eternal rather than the seen and temporal. To get a thorough conception of the meaning of those seven words is to comprehend all that precedes.

And so as to what follows. It has to do with the ministry of reconciliation, its motives, its dignity and its reward. To walk by faith is to "practice the presence of God," and to do everything as His ambassadors, under His instructions, in His stead, for His approval. It is to keep in mind not the superficial and indecisive judgment of men but the judgment seat of Christ; not the temporal success but the eternal reward. Thus this simple saying reflects light both ways, backward and forward, upon the context.

First Peter 1:10–12 is the leading Scripture upon the *purpose, character and limitations* of prophecy. From it we learn:

1. The prophets testified beforehand the sufferings of Christ and the glory that should follow.

2. They searched to find the meaning of their own predictions, uttering what was a mystery to themselves.

3. They were taught that it was mainly for future ages that they bore their testimony.

Here three great questions are settled: first, the Old Testament predictions are messianic; whatever their secondary reference, their primary application is to Jesus of Nazareth; second, so far were these predictions from being shrewd human conjectures that they were mysteries to those who spoke them; and, third, they could neither be understood nor fulfilled until after ages. What a number of mooted questions this one authoritative statement settles!

Whenever a circumstance or occurrence has a marked prominence in Scripture, and especially where it gives occasion for a new ordinance or signalizes a new departure it is to be very carefully noted. "As his part is that goeth down to the battle, so shall his part be that tarrieth by the stuff: they shall part alike. And it was so from that day forward, that he made it a statute and an ordinance for Israel unto this day" (1 Sam. 30:24, 25). Compare Numbers 31:11–27 and Joshua 22:8.

When the unexpected spoil nearly proved the pretext for a serious quarrel, the selfishness and sordidness of the children of Belial claiming it all for the actual warriors who had been in the battle, David decreed that the 200 whose faintness compelled them to tarry at the brook, Besor, should have a share of the booty. And this principle henceforth became *"a statute and an ordinance for Israel,"* for all time to come. It had been already done on previous occasions by Moses and Joshua; but it did not pass into the form of a stated and fixed decree until now. Its bearing is universal, and affects the whole work of the church of God. All cannot engage in the actual battle at the front, as in the great contests on the home mission borders and the foreign mission field; but those who at home tarry with the stuff and guard the base of supplies shall share alike.

18

Summaries of Biblical Truth

THE FIRST CONSPICUOUS SUMMARY is Deuteronomy 6:4, already referred to, as one of the leading passages of Scripture. It is not easy to translate so as to preserve the full force of the original. These words form the beginning of what in the Jewish services is termed the SHEMA ("Hear") and belong to the daily morning and evening services. They constitute the substance of the Jewish creed:

JEHOVAH, OUR ELOHIM—JEHOVAH ONE.

Here the brevity and terseness rather impart emphasis and suggest a broad, deep meaning, because capable of so many different constructions. The stress mainly falls upon the word *one*, which carries the idea of uniqueness as well as unity. Jehovah our God is the *alone* God—solitary, incomparable, unapproachable. This is not a statement of divine unity as against polytheism, nor of His revelation to Israel as contrasted with other manifestations of Himself; but it means that Jehovah is the one self-existent, independent God, the one Being that is the cause of all and the effect of none.

The last letters of the first and last words in this Hebrew sentence are "majascula"—that is written larger than the rest, and together spelling the word ED or "witness," and construed by the Jewish commentator as very significant, implying that this is in substance the witness borne by the faithful, and a challenge to Jehovah to bear His witness to them in turn. To convey some idea of the form in which

the scribes wrote this brief creedal declaration, a sort of paraphrase
may be given:

GivE heed, O Israel! Jehovah one, our GoD.

Hence not only the obligation to love such a God with the whole
being, but to teach these words unto their children, to bind them for
a sign upon the hand and as frontlets between the eyes; to write
them upon the door posts and gate posts, to be kept in sight and in
mind.

The Jews literally kept this command. A small square of parchment
inscribed with Deuteronomy 6:4–9, and 11:13–21, was rolled up, enclosed in a small cylinder of wood or metal, and affixed to the right-
hand post of every door in a Jewish house, a small hole being left in
the enclosing cylinder, so that as the pious believer passes, he may touch
the *mezuzah*, with his finger or kiss it with his lips, and say,

> The Lord shall preserve thy going out
> And thy coming in (Ps. 121:8).

Biblical summaries sometimes give the substance of a whole
book in one sentence:

"Let us hear the conclusion of the whole matter" (Eccl. 12:14).
Here the writer sums up his whole argument. "To fear God, and keep
His commandments," literally, "is *the whole man*," that is, here is the
secret of a complete, well-rounded, symmetrical character. In the previous chapters, the author records five successive experiments in the
search of the highest good. All have been failures. He has been looking "*under the sun*," and all that is earthly is temporal and human and
partial and imperfect. Only when he looked *beyond* the sun, at that
which is eternal, divine, perfect, did he find the missing hemisphere
which makes life, being, happiness, complete. Heaven is the complement of earth, the future, of the present; God, of man; the final
judgment, the corrective of all present inequalities and iniquities.

In the beginning of the Book of Proverbs we read that "the fear of
the Lord is the beginning of knowledge." Where we have the complementary truth, at the ending of Ecclesiastes—that this fear of
the Lord is the formative principle giving perfection to character. man,
as "a religious animal," demands God as his correlative, and without
faith toward God and holy obedience is forever incomplete.

Micah 7:18–20 is the grand summary of Divine Grace in the dealing with iniquity. It is at the conclusion of his prophecy, introduced by that august question which we have seen to be a sort of Scripture landmark, and an echo of the prophet's own name "Micah"—"who is Jah!"

This summary of Forgiving Grace is in three parts:
1. The grace that Pardons Iniquity; (v. 18)
2. The grace that subdues Iniquity; (v. 19)
3. The grace that performs what it promises (v. 20).

The comprehensiveness of this is apparent: the first is the assurance of mercy to the guilty instead of judgment; the second, of deliverance to the tempted when sins of the past pursue like malignant foes; and the third, of inheritance of covenant promise, when discouragements and difficulties suggest despair. And there is evidently a reference to the three typical stages of Hebrew history: the Passing by the Blood-stained doors; the Passing through the Red Sea; and the Passing over the Jordan. Isaiah 45:22:

> Look unto Me,
> And be ye Saved!
> All the ends of the Earth!
> For I am God:
> And there is none else.

This is one of the great Scripture landmarks, one of perhaps a score of texts that, like John 3:16, contain the essence of the gospel message in a few words. Here are only about twenty words, and yet they tell us all we need to know about God's Salvation.

For example:
1. It is simplicity: "Look."
2. Its Sufficiency: "Look unto *Me*."
3. Its Sublimity: "And be ye *Saved*."
4. Its Universality: "All the ends of the Earth."
5. Its Security: "For I am God."
6. Its Singularity: "And there is none Else."
7. Its Perpetuity: "An everlasting Salvation." Verse 17.

Or it may be put in another form:
1. The Greatest Good, "Salvation."

2. The Largest Number, "All."
3. The Surest Warrant, "I am God."
4. The Simplest Terms, "Look unto me."
5. The Farthest Reach, "Ends of earth."
6. The Narrowest Range, "There is none Else."
7. The Quickest Result, "Look and Live."
God offers Man Salvation, but He only can Save; and We need only to Look.

This text is linked with the conversion of C. H. Spurgeon. In the little primitive Methodist chapel at Colchester, he heard from an unknown and unlettered man this very message, and that morning he looked and lived.

John 3:16 is another similar summary, "the Gospel in miniature." Here are at least seven great truths, almost identical with those of Isaiah 45:22.

1. The greatest of gifts: "God gave His only begotten Son."
2. The greatest of numbers: "The world." Whosoever.
3. The greatest of blessings: "Everlasting life."
4. The greatest of deliverances: "Might not perish."
5. The greatest motive: "God so loved."
6. The greatest security: "God."
7. The greatest simplicity: Whosoever believeth.

Romans 5:1–5. Justification: its privileges and results.
1. Peace with God—the peace of reconciled relations.
2. A new standing before God—permanent acceptance.
3. A new access to God, by faith with freedom.
4. A new joy in God—rejoicing in hope.
5. A new glory—even in tribulation.
6. A new process of sanctification begun.
7. A new experience—patience, love, etc.

Another of these "little gospels" illustrates the summaries of truth. Romans 10:8–10. Paul calls it "the word of faith which we preach," that is its whole substance, and it includes two things: a heart belief and a mouth confession.

The belief centers on the resurrection, not the crucifixion, for a *dead* Christ could not save, and the stress of the New Testament is on the *risen* one (Rom. 4:15; 1 Cor. 15, etc.).

Note also that faith is unto righteousness, but confession is unto salvation, which includes more than justification. When we add testimony to belief, we rise to a higher plane: a faith that constrains to no witness finds no development. To suppress testimony by silence is to stifle the new life.

Observe also how the simple secret of worldwide missions is here hinted: the hearing ear prepares for the believing heart and the believing heart for the confessing mouth. Here is the hint of a true and endless "apostolic succession" of hearing, faith and testimony; and he who hears and believes not, or who believing, witnesses not, drops out of the succession and knows not the higher "Salvation."

Paul sums up the work of Christ in one brief sentence: "Who of God is made unto us Wisdom and Righteousness and Sanctification and Redemption" (1 Cor. 1:30).

Here at a glance we take in the fourfold work of our Lord for us. He is judicially "made," or constituted all that these words imply and in the order here given.

1. Wisdom from God—which is the preferable rendering. Paul writing to the Greeks who boasted of their wisdom, declares that Christ is wisdom from God, in comparison with whom the wisdom of this world is foolishness and the princes of this world, nought. He imparts to us knowledge of God and of self and is Himself the truth.

2. Righteousness. He becomes to us an all-sufficient righteousness, justification, giving us a new standing before God, and an imputed righteousness, which gives peace with Him, access to Him, and assurance of glory with Him.

3. Sanctification. In Christ we are assured of a holy State as well as a righteous standing. By the indwelling Spirit, every believer is constituted a temple of God and transformed from one degree of grace and glory to another.

4. Redemption. This expresses the final goal—a resurrection of the body, a complete deliverance of soul and spirit from all the power and presence of sin, and introduction of body and spirit, united, into the perfected home above.

The author of the Epistle to the Hebrews writes:

"Now of the things we have spoken, *this is the sum*"—"chief point," or "crowning point." He then proceeds to give in forty words the substance of all his argument. "We have a divine High Priest, now throned in Heaven, and ministering in our behalf in the true and Heavenly Tabernacle." The old priesthood was on earth, and the old tabernacle was for a season, but now the type is swallowed up in the antitype and prototype. And this summary comes about the middle of the Epistle, like the capstone of a pyramid with the lines slanting in both directions, toward the beginning and end.

Second Peter 1:16–21 is the grand summary of the evidences of Christianity, which prove to a believer that he has not "followed cunningly devised fables."

1. The testimony of the Transfiguration.
2. The witness of Prophetic Prediction.
3. The experimental proof, the day dawn in the heart.

These bear indefinite expansion and are all-comprehensive. The Old Testament portrait of our Lord Jesus Christ leaves no room for candid doubt, the word of prophecy, given as a light in the darkness. The New Testament manifestation of the Deity and glory of the Son of God culminates in the Transfiguration when for the first and only time Christ's glory was unveiled. Then when the day dawns in a conscious experience of Redemption in the heart, the Day Star rises, the last of the night, and the first of the morning, the darkness being past and the true light now shining. These three forms of proof are closely related: the first is God's witness to His Son; the second, the actual combined testimony of the Son to Himself and the Father to Him; and the last, the testimony of the believer's own personal life.

Such summaries have been called "little Bibles," or "little Gospels." And it is recommended to every reader to make his own selection and collection. A few more, beside those already mentioned, may be indicated as a guide.

Genesis 15:6. Believing, and Imputation of Righteousness.
Habakkuk 2:4. Faith and Justification.
Isaiah 53:6, 7. The Sole Source of Salvation.
John 3:36. Believing and Everlasting Life.
    14:23. Love, obedience and manifestation of God.
    15:7 Abiding in Christ and Power in Prayer.

Acts 2:38. The Pentecostal Gospel.

Romans 8:1, 2. In Christ Jesus justified and made free.

12:1, 2. The Self Presentation and Separation of the Believer.

2 Corinthians 7:1. The self-cleansing of flesh and spirit.

Galatians 2:20. Crucifixion with Christ and Life in Him.

Philippians 4:6, 7. The Refuge from care in prayer.

Titus 2:11–14. The grace that bringeth Salvation.

Hebrews 12:1, 2. The attitude of the Christian Racer.

1 John 3:2, 3. The now and hereafter of saints.

5:20. The Knowledge of God and Life Eternal.

19

Marked Recurrence of Like Language

W E SHOULD NOT ONLY NOTE what special words and terms the Spirit chooses and uses, but with what comparative frequency, whether once, twice, thrice or oftener. Especial meaning usually attaches to what is rare or exceptional, found but seldom and then in some conspicuous relation, or recurring at stated intervals like a refrain in a poem or a musical composition.

The *recurrence* of the noun "passover," or kindred verb, "pass over," is very significant. Compare Exodus 12:11, 12, 23, 27; 13:16, 22; 16:16; Hebrews 11:29, etc. The word, passover, first occurs in connection with Jacob's passing over the river Euphrates, in fleeing from Laban (Gen. 31:21), and recurs when he passed over Jordan; but its first highly significant use is when the Hebrews were exempted from death, in the last of the Egyptian plagues.

As the two previous instances suggest a *passing over from one place to another*, this is also the thought in Exodus 12:13; Jehovah, seeing the blood, *passing over the threshold into the house,* taking possession, becoming, as it were, the household Head, and a fellow pilgrim, stranger and sojourner with His people (Ps. 39:12). Hence His claim upon the first born as special heritage of the new Head of the house. It was more than passing *through* the land or passing *by* the blood sprinkled door posts, when Jehovah passed *over* the threshold *into* the house, in token of covenant relations and fellowship.

We have other significant passings over; as at the Red Sea, where Jehovah opened a path through the place of Death and Judgment, and Israel passed over from one side to the other, a type of passing over through Death into Resurrection—which the "Egyptians assaying to do were drowned" (Heb. 11:29), another very significant fact, for the unbeliever, passing indeed into death, passes not through and over into resurrection life, but is drowned in death. At the Jordan again Israel passes over from the Eastern and wilderness side into the Western or Canaan side—a type of consecration and separation in, and appropriation of the promises. Thus, the three Passovers stand respectively as types of emancipation and deliverance from Judgment penalty, identification with Christ in Death and Resurrection, and appropriation of the Promises of Grace; and, taken together, embrace the whole experience of the believer.

Thus the first Passover of the Exodus stands for Protection from the Destroyer, Jehovah's Proprietorship of the Redeemed, and their Fellowship with Him in Pilgrimage; the Passover at the Red Sea, for conquest over sinful habit and every foe, Death included; and the Passover at the Jordan, for full present Rest, and Possession of the Promises and privileges of the Believer.

There are three conspicuous references to the *vine* (Is. 5:1–7; Ps. 80:8–19; John 15:1–16). The first emphasizes God's care for His vine and His disappointment at its wild grapes; the second, its desolation under the ravages of foes; the third, the secrets of growth and fertility in union with Christ.

Mortify is found but twice (Rom. 8:13; Col. 3:15). It means *to make a corpse of*, implying that, having *judicially* died with Christ, all that pertains to the "old man"—the former sinful self and life—should be given over to death, *actually and practically* (Rom. 6:19; 7:5; Gal. 5:24, 25).

When the "members," so to be mortified, are specified, the first four of the five refer to various forms of *sensual appetite*, showing how hostile this is to spiritual life: impurity, with covetousness, thus cover nearly the whole array of carnal foes. And, if these members are not killed, they kill—if not put to death, they spread death; practically, therefore, it is a choice between living and dying unto God and holiness—death to the flesh or death to the spirit.

The word "panoply," translated "whole armor," or "all his armor," is found but twice (Luke 11:22; Eph. 6:11–13).

Further search shows a designed *contrast* in this case; in one case the panoply is that with which God clothes Saints, to resist the devil; in the other it is panoply with which the devil clothes the sinner, that he may fight against God; and further meditation will suggest something in each of the sinner's various pieces of armor that corresponds to those of the Saint:

The Helmet of Salvation is contrasted with a Delusive Hope.

The Breastplate of Righteousness is contrasted with a proud Self-righteousness.

The Girdle of Truth is contrasted with Lies, Deception.

The Sandals of Alacrity are contrasted with Procrastination.

The Shield of Faith is contrasted with Unbelief.

The Sword of the Spirit—the Word of God—is contrasted with the word of Man.

The word, "*centurion*," in the New Testament, occurs twenty-four times, and *always*, save in one case (Acts 27:11), *favorably*. Four centurions are conspicuous. He, whose faith the Lord so commended; he who, at the crucifixion, confessed to Christ's Deity; he, at whose palace occurred the Pentecostal outpouring; and he who was connected with the shipwreck, in the Mediterranean, and whose mediation saved Paul (cf. Matt. 8:5–13; 27:54; Acts 10:27).

Is there no practical lesson in all this? The Jews being under the Roman yoke, were tempted to despise and hate whatever was Roman. Yet, here were Rome's representatives, having authority over large hands of soldiers, to keep the Jews in subjection, yet showing real nobility, and shaming them by their treatment of the Messiah whom the Jews rejected and of the disciples whom they persecuted! One of them showed a great faith not found even in Israel; the alms and prayers of another went up for a memorial before God; the confession of another was boldly made to the fact that Christ was truly the Son of God, when even disciples forsook Him and fled and He hung upon a cross between thieves; and other centurions interposed to save Paul from the scourge, from conspiracies against his life and from death as a prisoner. How delicate the indirect rebuke of bigotry and racial hatred, and the lesson of tolerance and impartiality of judgment.

There is frequent and gracious mention of the *Samaritans.* Instance the good Samaritan, whose merciful ministry is contrasted with the apathy of priest and Levite; the Samaritan among the ten lepers, the only one who returned to give thanks; the Samaritan woman who found the Savior at the well and forgot her water pot in her zeal to save souls; the Samaritans who, in such throngs, welcomed the ministry and message of Philip (Luke 10:33; 17:16; John 4; Acts 8). Surely deep wells are here if one has something to draw with, a long enough rope of research, and a large enough vessel of charity!

Five times, in the Epistles of Peter, the word "End" recurs.

1 Peter 1:9: "Receiving the end of your faith, the salvation of your souls."

1 Peter 1:13: "Hope to the end for the grace that is to be brought," etc.

1 Peter 4:7: "The end of all things is at hand."

1 Peter 4:17: "What shall the end be of them that obey not the Gospel?"

2 Peter 2:20: "The latter end is worse with them than the beginning."

Around these uses of this one word, END, much of the teaching of these epistles gathers!

Toward one universal end moves the whole creation, physical and moral. Evil moves on toward its consummation in anti-christ, and good likewise to its consummation in Christ. The evil development includes some, from the nominal church of Christ, as well as the whole world of the ungodly that lieth in the wicked one, and all evil angels who are reserved unto the same final judgment of perdition. The good development includes all true believers, good angels and "the whole creation"; only that, while sinners among men and fallen angels are involved in the same condemnation, saints and angels do not share the same salvation or exaltation; for the saints, now "a little lower than angels," at the end rise higher than they, through their identification with the Lord Jesus Christ as Redeemer.

The phrase "Dead Works" occurs only twice, in both cases in the same Epistle (Heb. 6:1; 9:14); in the first instance, used of the unregenerate, in the second of the regenerate.

"Dead works" differ from either wicked works or good works, as "wild fruit" does from good fruit or bad fruit, as the wild fruit has the form and appearance of the good, without its flavor and savor, so dead works, while having more or less of the appearance of good works, *lack life*. Therefore even doling out goods to feed poverty and giving the body to the flames are pronounced unprofitable, because not prompted by that love which is the life of all true service (1 Cor. 13:1–3).

Dead works should be studied in connection with Numbers 19, where the ordinance of the red heifer is found, to which Hebrews 4:13 refers. The red heifer was the appointed remedy for contact with the dead or death, in every form. He that would serve the *living* God must not bring to Him *dead* works. "The body without the spirit is dead" (James 2:26). God cannot be imposed upon by externals.

The word, *kataphileō*, translated "kissed,"—meaning to kiss repeatedly and caressingly—is found but four times in the New Testament (Matt. 26:49; Luke 7:38; 15:20; Acts 20:37), and these instances are representative and exhaustive, the father's kiss of welcome, the penitent's kiss of gratitude, the friend's kiss of farewell, and the traitor's kiss of betrayal; in three cases Love's sign, and, in the fourth, its damnable prostitution.

Note the phrase "stand still." The earliest lesson on this subject: "Stand still and see the Salvation of the Lord," is in Exodus 14:13. For the first time men were taught the virtue of standing still in a great crisis of danger to witness the Lord's deliverance. But here a permanent lesson is taught, of which other representative and illustrative instances are found in subsequent times; indeed, to every great emergency, this policy is again inculcated, as for example, at Kadesh Barnea (Num. 14:9), and on the verge of entrance into Canaan (Deut. 20:1–4); and when the Syrians encompassed Elisha (2 Kgs. 6:16). To Jehoshaphat Jahaziel repeated these very words, when the Ammonites and Moabites massed their forces to drive the Jews out of their inheritance (2 Chr. 20:15–17), and when the Assyrians came against Hezekiah the lesson was repeated (2 Chr. 32:20, 21; Is. 37:14–37). The numerous instances in the apostolic age find their key here. The lesson is that in all such cases the Battle is not ours but God's.

We are not to depend upon ourselves nor on our fellow man, but "let God fight for us." "Our strength is to sit still" (Is. 30:7).

One of the foremost lessons of the New Testament, especially after the Day of Pentecost revealed man's complete dependence upon the Holy Spirit, is that in all matters pertaining to our witness, work and the warfare for God, we are to renounce all our own wisdom, strength and energy, and simply *let God have His way.*

Our Lord's last injunction was, "Tarry ye, until ye be endued with power from on high"; and ten days were spent in quietly waiting for God to work. At every succeeding crisis in the apostolic church, there was the same simple dependence upon Him. When the Sanhedrin forbade the disciples to speak at all or teach in the name of Jesus, under threat of persecution, they went to their own company, and with one accord committed to God the whole matter: "And now, Lord, behold their threatenings, and grant unto Thy servants that with all boldness they may speak Thy Word by stretching forth Thine hand to heal, and that signs and wonders may be done by the name of Jesus." And when they had prayed the very place of assembly was shaken (Acts 4:28, 30). And so in all that follows. The angel of the Lord opened prison doors, the Philippian jail was shaken by an earthquake; Herod, the persecutor, smitten with death, as Elymas, the Sorcerer, was with blindness; and in face of every danger and difficulty the infant church, standing still, saw God work in His might.

There are four or five special forms or phases of truth as to which men would crave and need instruction: Faith, Love, Hope, Good Works, and the danger of spiritual declension. Each of these has a prominent human exponent. Paul is especially the Apostle of Faith, Peter of Hope, John of Love, James of good works; and Jude warns against apostasy. Thus each follows his own natural bent, and in so doing fills out the design of the Holy Spirit, that each aspect of truth and duty shall have its presentation.

20

The Refrain and Chorus in Scripture

REFRAINS MAY BE DIVIDED into four main classes, of which a few examples follow:

1. *Choral*, dividing a poem into successive stanzas;
2. *Terminal*, indicating the division in a book;
3. *Ethical*, gathering up and repeating some moral lesson;
4. *Musical*, occurring at pauses in a sacred chant or song.

Sometimes a refrain serves more than one purpose at the same time, and there are some cases in which they rise to the level of the sublime. In a few instances, they form an introduction and conclusion to a section: at the beginning forecasting the object of what follows; then at the end reaffirming the principle or law stated, in view of the considerations presented.

In Exodus 8:10, Moses says to Pharaoh: "There is none like unto Jehovah, our God."

This grand, sententious declaration, here first made, is perhaps the leading refrain of all Scripture, and most frequently recurs in almost the same exact form.

For instance, it superbly reappears in that poem of victory, the triumphant chant of Miriam at the Red Sea;

> Who, O Jehovah, is like unto Thee among the gods!
> Who is like unto Thee!

Glorious in holiness,
Fearful in praises,
Doing wonders (Ex. 15:11)!

Here the august saying of Moses is repeated as an exclamation by Miriam, and its meaning expanded. There is none like Jehovah, in the Majesty of His Holiness, none so worthy of reverent worship and praise, none capable of such wonder working displays of power.

From time to time, that refrain recurs, and it is a lesson in grace to observe the great occasion when it is again heard, to study the connection, and to note the special divine attributes and aspects of the divine glory successively set forth.

For instance, in Psalm 35:10:

All my bones shall say,
        "Lord, who is like unto Thee!"

Here, the special reference is to His righteousness and greatness. Again, Psalm 113:5 and 6:

        Who is like unto the Lord, our God!

In this case, it is a tribute to His condescension in mercy and grace. In Isaiah 40:18 and 25:

        To whom, then, will ye liken God!

Here is a divine challenge to the heathen to produce any rival object of worship, or any thing worthy of comparison with Him, a rebuke of all idolatry and polytheism.

In Micah 7:18:

        Who is a god like unto Thee!

In this, the last recurrence of this exclamation, we may find its highest application. The question, "Who is like Jah?" is a play on the name *Micah*, which means this, as Malachi means "My Messenger."

Micah's interrogation plainly refers back to the wonders of the Exodus. He is exalting and extolling the wonders of Grace in forgiveness, in subduing the power of sin, and in keeping covenant (see vv. 18–20). Here are plain references to the passing over of the blood-sprinkled houses; then, the turning again of God, like a master general flinging his columns backward upon pursuing foes to overwhelm them with destruction at the Red Sea, and finally, to the covenant promises, sworn to Abraham and confirmed to Jacob, which explain Jehovah's subsequent dealings with His people.

If to these instances of the Interrogation, we add the numerous recurrences of the original affirmation, "There is none like unto Jehovah," we shall see, still more clearly, how important is that saying or the truth it embodies. Compare Deuteronomy 3:24; 33:26; 1 Samuel 2:2; 2 Samuel 7:22; 1 Kings 8:23; Psalm 86:6–8; Isaiah 46:8, 9; Jeremiah 10:6–16; 49:49, etc.)

Thus an exclamation twice found in the earliest of all Biblical Psalms—the Song of Moses at the Red Sea—echoes like a thunder peal among the mountain, at critical points in Old Testament history, only with this difference that, while echoes in nature become fainter with each new reverberation or repetition, the echoes in Scripture grow louder and clearer as they recur. And as we stand and listen to echo after echo, we feel more and more the incomparable majesty, infinity, holiness of Jehovah and are inspired with awe and adoration.

Another example of refrain is found first in Exodus 20:2:

> I am Jehovah, thy God,
> Which have brought thee out of the land of Egypt,
> Out of the house of bondage.

This connects the name of Jehovah with this signal act of deliverance which was the beginning of the national history as a redeemed and separate people. It conspicuously reappears in Leviticus 19:36; Numbers 15:41; Deuteronomy 5:6; Psalm 81:10, etc. In fact, it is the most frequently repeated of all Scripture sentences. It suggests what may be called the Old Testament *standard of measurement.* Whenever, in any emergency, the Lord would remind His people both of His power and love, He referred them back to the Exodus, so that this became a sort of secondary name of Jehovah, a historic designation, identifying the great Deliverer with the covenant God. This association of the name of Jehovah with the fame of the Exodus is found hundreds of times between the event and the end of the prophetic Scriptures: and at each new repetition serves some new purpose, to add sanction to God's law, majesty to His authority, terror to His judgments, grandeur to His covenant condescension, or glory to His gracious promises and invitations.

In the Psalms, each of the five books closes with a sort of terminal refrain.

> Blessed be Jehovah, God of Israel,
> From everlasting and to everlasting!
> Amen and amen! (41:13).

> Blessed be Jehovah, God, the God of Israel!
> Amen and amen! (72:18, 19).

> Blessed be Jehovah, for evermore!
> Amen and amen! (90:52).

> Blessed be Jehovah, God of Israel
> From everlasting to everlasting!
> And let all the people say Amen!
> Praise ye Jehovah! (106:48).

> Let every thing that hath breath
> Praise Jehovah.
> Praise ye Jehovah! (150:6).

Beside the recurrence of the refrain, there is a steady advance in thought, as seen in the changes and modifications in the refrain, and the expansion of its meaning and application.

From time to time, special local refrains occur, as in those companion Psalms, 42, 43, which open Book II.

"Why art thou cast down, O my soul?" etc.

This occurs thrice, at almost equal intervals (42:5, 11; 43:5).

And, when repeated, made more emphatic by considerations presented in the interval, and in the second and third cases adding "and any God."

Psalm 45 has its own refrain:

> Jehovah of hosts is with us,
> The God of Jacob is our refuge.
> Selah (vv. 7, 11).

Isaiah is rich in refrains:

> Jehovah alone shall be exalted in that day,
> For all this His anger is not turned away:
> But His hand is stretched out still
> (Is. 5:25; 9:12, 17, 21; 10:4)

These five repetitions indicate links of connection in his utterances. Each recurrence seems to hint that, notwithstanding all that has taken place, something more and greater is coming.

But Isaiah's most conspicuous refrain is that which occurs at the close of chapter 48:

There is no peace, saith Jehovah to the wicked!

This recurs at the close of chapter 57, "My God" being substituted for "Jehovah."

Then, in the closing chapter (66:24):

Their worm shall not die,
Neither shall their fire be quenched,

which expands and explains with awful emphasis the refrain. There is no peace to the wicked, for God's retributive fire is without and the undying worm of an accusing conscience within.

But further than this, these last twenty-seven chapters—the great Messianic poem of the Old Testament, are divided into three equal sections, of nine chapters each, by this refrain—one of the most remarkable instances in Scripture, where such a refrain serves all purposes at once, choral, musical, ethical, and terminal.

In Matthew 19:30, and 20:16 occurs a repetition of the same sentiment in almost the same words: "Many shall be last that are first, and first that are last." "So the last shall be first and the first last." The latter saying is exactly the former, only the order of words is inverted. This is one of the cases in which the refrain serves to show the proper bounds of the paragraph. There should be here no chapter division, for this proverbial utterance, immediately preceding and following the parable of the laborers in the vineyard, enunciates the principle of which that parable is the illustration, and, to make it the more emphatic, it both prefaces and concludes the parable. The connection is very striking.

After the rich young man, unwilling to leave all to follow Christ, turned away sorrowful, Peter, no doubt, in a self-complacent and somewhat boastful spirit, said, "Lo, we have left all and followed Thee; what shall we have therefore?" If we mistake not there was a little disposition both to brag and grab. And our Lord uses this parable as a gentle rebuke, reminding the disciples that some who are first in their own eyes may be last in His, and those who are last in expectation and conscious merit, may prove first in realization and reward. The consciousness of self-denial and the spirit that glories in it seriously impair its value. When we are absorbed in Him, years of toil and trial, for His sake seem as but a few days for the love we bear Him, as it was with Jacob when he served for Rachel. Self-surrender is close akin to self-oblivion, and a passion for God and souls leads us to a heroism that takes no count of its sacrifices. To impress this thought our Lord therefore first utters the proverb, then enforces it by a parable and then repeats it that the principle may get emphasis, and its setting may lend it impressivenss.

In John 14:1, 27, is perhaps the most significant illustration of the relation of these repetitions of language to the discourse which lies between. Our Lord, observing how at the hint of His withdrawal, sorrow has filled their heart, says to His disciples,

Let not your heart be troubled.

At the close of this section of His farewell address, exactly the same words are repeated: "Let not your heart be troubled," and in this case He adds, "neither let it be afraid." Between these two similar sayings, lie the reasons why thy should not be thus troubled. If the intermediate teaching be carefully followed, it will be seen that He hints at four classes of troubles and their remedies:

1. Problems of Creation and Providence. "Believe in God."

2. Problems of Sin and Salvation. "Believe in Me."

3. Problems of Death and the Hereafter. "Believe in the Father's House."

4. Problems of Present Daily Need. "Believe in the Holy Ghost."

Thus, having shown that faith has a solution and solace ready for every form of perplexity and anxiety, He not only repeats the words with which He began, but adds, "neither let your heart be apprehensive."

As the two verbs in the first verse are exactly the same in the original, nor reason is apparent why in one case they should be translated by an indicative and in the other by an imperative; in both cases, the imperative seems most natural. "Let not your heart be troubled. Believe in God; believe also in Me." To some heart anxieties, the Fatherhood of God is the answer; to others the mediation of the Son; to others, the fact that the whole universe is the Father's House, and that we are never out from under His roof; even death being only a moving from a lower to a higher mansion or abiding place in the same universal House. And, when to all other perplexities is added the anxiety as to our daily strength for duty and trial, our Lord reminds us that in the Indwelling Spirit we are to have Heaven brought down to earth, and earth brought in constant contact and communion with heaven—communion with both Father and Son, and supplies of all needed Grace, strength and consolation, while as yet sojourning here and awaiting His return to claim His own.

21

Thoughts Which Transcend All Speech

A FEW WORDS MAY BE CITED, in which these things, hard to be uttered, or understood, appear in Scripture:

1. Attempts to define or describe the Infinite God.
2. The use of words which are untranslatable.
3. The compound verbs, used of Christ's union with believers.
4. The superlatives and hyperboles employed.
5. The sublime climaxes which suggest the unspeakable.
6. The multiplication of figurative forms of speech.

There are six definitions of God, Who is so complex that no one definite can suffice.

Psalm 36:9—"With Thee, O God, is the *fountain of Life*."
James 1:17—"The *Father of Lights*."
1 John 1:5—"God is *love*."
1 John 4:8–16—"God is *love*."
John 4—"God is a *Spirit*."
Hebrews 12:9—"Father of Spirits."

Taking these passages together, He is Life, Light and Love—all in one—somewhat as the sun sends forth life in the blue ray, light in the yellow, heat in the red, but all united in the one sunbeam of glory. He is essentially a *Spirit*, invisible and disembodied, and the Father of all spiritual Being.

Some words are *untranslatable* and we have to resort to *transliter-*

ation, which is transferring the word as nearly as possible into another tongue, letter for letter, as for instance, "Abba," "Jehovah," "Hallelujah," "Selah," etc. *Sabbatismos* is one of these untranslatable words. It occurs but once (Heb. 4:9), and is translated "rest," and usually taken to mean an eternal rest, or Sabbath keeping with God, which is no doubt its highest sense. But, as used in this connection, it has a specific meaning. It occurs in the midst of an argument proving a *present rest, not in heaven, but on earth,* into which God would have all believers enter *now* by faith and of which Canaan, the earthly inheritance of His people, was a type and forecast. Into this rest believers enter by ceasing from their own works as God did from His.

Probably to render this word *Sabbatism* would be a great advance, transliterating instead of translating. There was among the Hebrews a most elaborate Sabbatic system, as may be seen by comparing Genesis 2, Numbers 25, Deuteronomy 15, Daniel 9, Revelation 20, etc.

It was built up in a sevenfold structure, which is embodied in the very framework of the Old Testament. There was first a seventh *day* of rest, then a rest of the seventh week, month, year, seven-times-seventh year, seventy-times-seventh, or four hundred and ninetieth year; and a dim forecast of a final Sabbatic thousand years—the Millennium. The "Sabbatism," here for the first and only time mentioned and represented by one word, probably included all these and what they separately and together signify and typify. Each seems to stand for some form of rest, from labor, care, selfish and sordid dispositions, exacting and vindictive tempers, and works of legalism, and together constitute the Sabbatism of God, the rest of subdued sin, banished anxiety, reconciled relations, peace with Him and fellowship with man, justification, sanctification, service, self-oblivious love; and in a word, the days of Heaven on earth.

Compound verbs, of uncommon force, are used to express *the believer's identity with his Lord.*

The plain design is to represent all His leading human experiences as *involving the disciple* in a joint relation and kindred experience. To convey this most vividly, some twenty-five different compounds are selected, most of which have no equivalents in single English words, so that we lose the close identity so expressed by these compounds.

For instance, there are eight words that convey the *fact* of this identity—translated, "Crucified with Him," "Die with Him," "Buried with Him," "Planted together," "Raised up together," "Sit together," "Reign with Him," "Glorified together," etc. (Gal. 2:20; 2 Tim. 2:11, 12; Rom. 6:4, 5; Eph. 2:6; Rom. 8:17).

There are other words referring to common intercourse, translated, "come together," "gather together," "assemble together," "sit together," "talk together," etc., and yet others referring to *results* of such identity, such as "live with Him," "suffer with Him," "work together," etc.

These are all compound words and not phrases in the original; and for only four or five are there any English equivalents. We can say "co-work," "convene," "consult," "co-heirs," etc., but not "co-die," "co-rise," "co-reign."

In some cases, superlatives are used, and even piled up like mountain upon mountain, in a vain attempt to express the inexpressible. This is one of the most fascinating departments of Bible study.

Paul's writings especially abound in these superlatives, and most of all, the Epistles to the Ephesians and Colossians, where are to be found the mountain peaks of the New Testament. It is here that we meet such expressions as "the exceeding greatness of his power"; "the working of the strength of His might"; "far above all rule, and authority and power and dominion, and every name that is named, not only in this age, but also in that which is to come; the exceeding riches of His Grace in His kindness toward us"; "the unsearchable riches of Christ"; "the manifold wisdom of God"; "to know the love of Christ which passeth knowledge, that ye may be filled with all the fullness of God"; "able to do exceeding abundantly above all we ask or think," etc.

It is very plain that the writer finds his theme too transcendently great to be crowded into the narrow compass of human words, and vainly seeks to stretch the meaning so as to make it more comprehensive by joining word to word, each of itself a superlative.

Man's superlatives are sometimes signs of weakness, carelessness, excitement. But God's superlatives, instead of going beyond, fall short of truth. They show both the poverty of earthly speech and the riches of heavenly thought, hinting an overflowing fullness of conception which no chalice of language can contain.

We give some biblical examples of superlatives:

The verb, *hyperballō* and the noun, *hyperbolē*, as applied to divine things and matters pertaining to redemption, are not easily translated. They really convey the idea of throwing or shooting beyond a given mark of limit, and hence the notion of surpassing excellence, a sort of excess; not exaggeration, like the English word, hyperbole, but rather something that passes the limit of language, defying description.

There are in all thirteen cases of the use of this verb or noun. 1. Romans 7:13, "That sin might become exceeding (or excessively) sinful." 2. Second Corinthians 11:31, "And yet show I unto you a more excellent way"—cultivate love. 3. Second Corinthians 1:8, "We were passed out of measure." 4. Second Corinthians 3:10, "By reason of the glory that excelleth." 5. Second Corinthians 4:7, "That the excellency of the Power may be of God." 6. Second Corinthians 4:17, "Worketh for us a far more exceeding weight of glory"—(here the word is twice used). 7. Second Corinthians 9:14, "The exceeding grace of God in you." 8. Second Corinthians 11:23, "In stripes above measure." 9. Second Corinthians 12:7, "Through the abundance of the revelations." 10. Galatians 1:13, "Beyond measure I persecuted the church of God." 11. Ephesians 1:19, "The exceeding greatness of His power." 12. Ephesians 2:7, "The exceeding riches of His grace." 13. Ephesians 3:19, "The love of Christ, which passeth knowledge."

Classifying these cases, we have the following significant result:

1. God's view of sin: It passes all description for its guilt, enormity, and deformity. And so does the enlightened soul see sin—as Paul saw his persecuting violence.

2. God's view of His own attributes and perfections: (1) His power, as exercised toward us; (2) His love in Christ; (3) His grace—and its riches; (4) His glory, the sum of all the rest.

3. God's view of man's highest excellence and ecstasy: (1) Love as the highest of graces; (2) Knowledge of Himself as the highest of Revelations; (3) Glory of His likeness as the highest result of affliction.

Again, the CLIMAXES IN SCRIPTURE suggest what defies description, leading from level to level of thought and revelation of truth, as, in ascending a mountain, the successive points of prospect command wider horizons and larger landscapes, one view preparing for another, and greater, till all the possibilities of present prospect are exhausted.

When King Amaziah remonstrated against the loss of money involved in a change of plan, the man of God replied: "The Lord is able to give thee *much more* than this" (2 Chr. 25:9).

In Romans 5:6–21, this phrase "much more" occurs five times and unlocks the whole passage (vv. 9, 10, 15, 17, 20), outlining what Christ does *beside dying* for us.

1. Justified by His blood—much more kept safe from wrath through Him.

2. Reconciled by His Death; much more kept safe in His Life.

3. Dead by offense of one. Much more Grace abounded in Righteousness.

4. Under the reign of Death. Much more made to reign in life.

5. Sin abounded in Ruin. Much more Grace abounded in Righteousness.

Here is a steady advance. We are saved from condemnation and kept safe; reconciled after alienation and kept reconciled; we died in consequence of Adam's sin, but are made alive in Christ, as the Second Adam or racial Head. Once, under the reign of sin and death, are made to reign over both; and all this is a triumph of grace through Righteousness, not a tame compromising laxity on the part of God; a forgiveness, purchased by atonement, and not at the expense of righteousness.

In Ephesians 3:14–21, Paul labors under a weight of conception that no powers of expression can sustain, praying that Ephesians may be able to comprehend dimensions which are infinite and take in a measureless immensity and an endless eternity; to know a love that "passeth knowledge," all it is possible to know of which is that it is an unfathomable depth. God, he adds, is able to do what we ask, what we think, all that we ask or think, above all, *abundantly* above all, EXCEEDING abundantly above all, that we ask or think, "unto all the *generations* of the AGE of the AGES."

Paul especially deals with these transcendent topics, probably because his rapture into the third heaven unveiled to him these unutterable wonders (2 Cor. 12).

22
Context and Connection

THERE IS A LAW of the *paragraph* which concerns this contextual study. Punctuation, with all the arrangement and division into chapter, paragraph and verse, are foreign to the original Scripture, and the work of uninspired men, mere devices of convenience of reference, and therefore open to criticism and modification. Punctuation points may often prove misleading, and these arbitrary divisions frequently interrupt continuity of thought and teaching, if they do not more seriously pervert the sense. It is only by much care that it is found where the pause occurs in the argument or narrative or discourse, and the paragraph is complete.

There is also a law of *connection* which demands that we observe words, sayings and sentences which are divinely linked together, since there can be no accidental or meaningless arrangement of terms or phrases when a divine Mind is at work. Patience will show both similarities and dissimilarities, unsuspected at first, and order of statement which significant and unalterable, because of a more important order of development in the truth set forth, or the experience of grace indicated.

Chapter divisions sometimes interrupt the progress of the narrative or discourse. A few prominent examples will illustrate this:

Matthew 9:38 and 10:1. Our Lord began to send forth laborers.

Matthew 16:28 and 17:1; Mark 8:38 and 9:1. The Transfiguration fulfills the promise.

Matthew 19:30 and 20:1. The parable illustrates the principle (cf. 20:16).

Mark 2:23–28, and 3:1–5. The miracle proves His lordship of the Sabbath.

Luke 20:45–47, and 21:1–4. Note in both passages the prominence of the poor *widow*.

Acts 7:60 and 8:1. Stephen's death led to Saul's conversion.

First Corinthians 10:33 and 11:1. Paul bids them follow him as an example of self-renunciation.

First Corinthians 12:31 and 13:1. Charity is the more excellent way.

Second Corinthians 4:18 and 5:1. The argument about the unseen and eternal continues.

Second Corinthians 6:18 and 7:1. This last verse sums up the previous argument.

Verse divisions often isolate a sentence from its surroundings, not only interrupting the sense, but very imperfectly presenting the truth. It is very unsafe to cite such broken and dismembered fragments of Scripture in support of any doctrinal position, as, so used, even "the devil can cite Scripture to his purpose," as he did in the temptation of Christ. A text is only a sure guide when it is taken in its surroundings and as a whole utterance.

Biblical punctuation is a human device and not authoritative. Sometimes it is no doubt misleading. A question mark might sometimes well displace a period.

Possibly in Romans 8:33, 34, we have a series of questions:

"Who shall lay any thing to the charge of God's elect? Shall God, Who justifieth? Who is he that condemneth? Shall Christ Who died, yea, rather is risen again?"

A recent writer quite insists on reading Ephesians 4:16,

"Can ye be angry and not sin?"

He feels a difficulty in reconciling a sanction of anger with the general tone of Scripture precepts, and especially with the command in verse 31, "Let all anger be put away from you." He would rather construe the apostle as asking, "Can you indulge anger and yet be sinless?" If his contention be true there may be ethics involved in a punctuation point.

Probably in Luke 13:24, a comma should displace a period: "Strive to enter in at the strait gate, for many, I say unto you, will seek to enter in and shall *not be able, when once the* master of the house hath risen up and hath shut to the doors," when it is too late (Matt. 25).

The illuminative force of context is illustrated by our Lord's great lesson on *almsgiving* (Matt. 6:1–4).

The greater lesson is on the *unseen world and the unseen God*. He has been showing how the unseen *in man* is the essential and true self—not the outer word, blow, act, but the inner thought, desire, disposition, will. And now He advances to a higher and more comprehensive conception; the greater *objective* as well as *subjective* reality is unseen. He would make the unseen in man responsive to the unseen in God and bring his unseen self into harmony with the whole realm of the invisible.

This may be illustrated by the "harp, the harper and the harmony," as the late Joseph Cook used to say. The main thing is not the beauty of the instrument nor the dress and appearance of the player, but the music evolved by his touch; and melody and harmony are inexplicable mysteries obedient to unseen forces. Imagination, memory, love, hope, faith, conscience, sensibility, all find expression in music which is their creation, and all these are unseen faculties and attributes. The soul of the harper must create the harmony. And so almsgiving is only music in God's ear when it is the outgoing and expression of an unseen spirit in man which is in accord with Himself, the response of what is best in us to what is best in Him; any lower motive spoils and degrades it as does a mere mercenary motive debase the musician's art.

In 1 Timothy 3:15, 16, the punctuation is probably misleading. It were better to read somewhat thus:

"That thou mayest know how thou oughtest to behave thyself in the house of God which is the church of the living God. The pillar and ground of the truth, and without controversy great, is the mystery of Godliness—namely," etc.

Thus read, we avoid a mixed and incongruous figure, at one instant comparing the church to a *house* and the next to a *pillar* in a house; but, according to this reading, the doctrine of the incarnation becomes the central pillar and pedestal of the church, upholding and sustaining it. A pillar consists of two parts—the upper and lower—one connects it with what is above, the other with what is below. Perhaps the thought is that the church, as the House or God, finds its central prop and pillar in the truth about the Lord Jesus Christ, Who as Son of God and son of man, related to both realms, links heaven and earth. By His humanity, Gospel, believing people, with earth; by His Deity, relation to angels, coronation as King, with Heaven. And so long as this pillar remains thus central in church life and doctrine, even the gates of hell shall not prevail against it (Matt. 16).

The two words together, "Life and Peace," (Rom. 8:6) describe the double result of the atoning work of Christ, and the order is unchangeable.

"Life" results from vital union with Him in whom is Life. It comes by simple acceptance of the Word of the Gospel as the incorruptible seed of God (1 Pet. 1:23) at once by believing we have the Son of God and have Life (1 John 5:12) and the Spirit of Life (Rom. 8:2).

"Peace" is the effect of His work, and faith in it as a finished work. It comes of minding the things of the Spirit, but is not to be confounded with Life, which precedes it and prepares for it.

Life does not always bring peace, but at first breaks up peace as a dead man raised to life like Lazarus would become conscious of sepulchral bonds.

Peace is threefold:

With God—reconciled relations (Rom. 5:1); with Men—new fellowship (Eph. 2); Peace *of* God—conscious indwelling (Phil. 4).

A child born to a king has his father's life in him from the first; but he has to be trained to know and understand all the duties and principles involved in being son and heir.

The one place where our Lord is expressly set before us as an *example* is 1 Peter 3:21–24. The exact word is writing-copy, as though the portrait of our Lord were put before us that we should study its exact lineaments and seek to reproduce them in our own character and conduct, speech, temper, will, and that inexpressible something which we call "spirit"—the inmost secret of the whole man which unconsciously molds all the rest.

Here we are commended to His example as our guide in all things: for our daily walk, abstinence from all known sin; in the truthfulness and self-restraint of the tongue, even under provocation; in the regulation of temper and disposition, forebearing threatening, and all retaliation and vindictiveness; in the great executive act of the will by which we commit ourselves to the keeping of a righteous God; and especially are we to imitate His self-sacrificing and self-oblivious spirit, which makes us ready to live and die for the salvation of others. What department of life is left untouched in this marvelously comprehensive example and ideal!

We have frequent occasions to refer to *verbal emphasis*, which is a science by itself, because emphasis is so often in effect exegesis. To find the word where the stress of a sentence falls is often to find the stress also of thought. Here again the study of context and connection is helpful, as showing the objective point toward which a whole discourse moves.

The emphatic word is often the pivot on which the meaning turns. When the anger of the Jews was aroused by the claim of our Lord that God was His Father, they retorted in almost insulting manner, "we be not born of fornication," by this stress upon the first personal pronoun, more than insinuating that *His* birth was unsanctified by wedlock, and a disgrace.

When our Lord says, "Take MY yoke upon you," the emphasis is on "my." In these few verses (Matt. 11:27–30), the emphasis seems throughout upon *Himself*. He alone has knowledge of the Father or power to reveal Him; He alone can give rest, teach lowliness and meekness, or impart the secret of rest even in toils and burden bearing. If the "I," "Me," "My," be uniformly emphasized the whole passage becomes luminous; the rest of salvation is *His* gift; the lesson of meekness is *His* lesson; the yoke that is easy is the yoke *He* makes, fits to us, and wears with us, and the burden in one which *He* lays on us and bears with us. What an example of the significance of emphasis!

If it be possible, "as much as lieth *in you*, live peaceably with all men" (Rom. 12:18), suggests that it may not always be possible with all men to live peaceably because they are not always pacifically inclined; but *so far as lies in us*, let there be peace. It takes but one to make an attack or *assault*, but it takes two to make a *quarrel*. There are some who are so contentious that the most peace-loving people cannot prevent the outbreaks of a wicked loquacity and pugnacity. But it is not necessary either to make angry reply or deal an angry blow. When slandered or struck we may remain passive and unresisting; or even return evil by good, and so quench the fires of strife.

In 1 Corinthians 7:40, the emphasis lies upon "I also"—"for I think that I also have the Spirit of God." This is usually taken to mean that Paul gives his private judgment, and thinks that he also has the Spirit's guidance. But, putting the emphasis where it belongs, he is confidently affirming that, whoever may claim to teach them as Spirit-led teachers, he, Paul, may also confidently claim the Holy Spirit's inspiration, as one specially commissioned to guide the churches.

In Hebrews 3:7 to 4:11, the context shows the emphatic word is *"Today."* It occurs three times, marking an intensive *present* and the accompanying tenses are all present, *"Exhort* one another *daily*, while it is called 'today ' ": *"Harden not* your heart"; *"Take heed"*; "We *are* made partakers of Christ, if *we* hold," etc. *"Let us*, therefore, *fear"*; "lest any of you should *seem to come short of it," "do enter into rest."* "There *remaineth* a Sabbatism"; "he that is *entered* into His rest," etc. To see where the emphasis lies prevents our mistaking the meaning; for the Sabbatic Rest here meant is not a future heaven, but a *present satisfaction in God*, corresponding to Canaan, which was the *earthly*, not *heavenly* inheritance promised to Israel. This present rest is entered into now, not by dying or ceasing from our earthly activities, but by believing and "ceasing from our own works."

Context and connection reveal *order*, which also often shows emphasis very plainly, as in Revelation 17:14, "called and *chosen* and FAITHFUL"—each successive term stronger than its predecessor; there are many "called," but few "chosen," and even out of the "chosen" comparatively few that are "faithful," "loving not their lives even unto death," the true martyr witnesses.

23

Recurrence of Thought and Idea

ONE OF THE MOST IMPORTANT and pervasive ideas of the Bible is the comparative unimportance of the *feelings* and the supreme importance of the *will* in the spiritual life; yet this is seldom referred to in explicit terms; it has to be discovered by the close study of the whole Word of God. Never once will it be found that the emphasis is laid upon what is merely emotional, because it is too uncertain and fluctuating. Feeling is capricious; it depends upon exciting or allaying causes, oftentimes beyond our control. Hence the Scriptures lay most stress upon *principles of living, fixed choices* of God and goodness which does not like a weather vane veer about with every change of wind.

All the great fundamental movements of the soul in the right direction are treated in reference to *volition* rather than *emotion*. Repentance is not so much a feeling of regret or sorrow over sin as a "change of mind," as the Greek word literally means, a new purpose to abandon sin, and embrace holiness; a new attitude of the whole being, in turning from evil and turning toward God.

Conversion is not a new state of feeling or even affection, so much as a "turning about," as the word hints, implying a new direction for the daily walk; and obedience is not an impulsive, capricious conformity to a command, but a self-surrender, a principle of submission to another's authority and control. Prayer is not an approach to God under the influence of warm sensibility and awakened feeling, but a deliberate habit of seeking after Him as the sole source of power and blessing. Faith is an executive act of the will, fixing upon one divine object of all confidence and trust; and even Love, which we most construe as an emotion or affection, is always regarded in the light of the Word as a principle of supreme loyalty toward God and preference for His will, and, subordinately, of unselfish service toward men.

So pervasive is this teaching in the Scripture that the reader may safely be challenged to find *one case* in which stress is laid upon mere feeling. These stirrings of our emotions and sensibilities are not under our control, being so often dependent on bodily health, mental condition, associations, surroundings, and even the changes of weather. God would have spiritual life built upon solid rock, not shifting quicksands.

The scriptural idea of *rewards* should be carefully studied in the light of the Inspired Word. The principles upon which they are administered by God are absolutely unique; and these alone suffice to accredit the Bible as divine. For example, mark the following laws which govern Rewards:

1. It is not the sphere that determines reward, but the spirit manifested in the sphere: not position but disposition. God Himself distributes the work as He will. Hence all spheres and forms of service are relatively equal in dignity and honor. What He asks is humble and constant obedience to His will wherever He put us.

2. It is therefore not the quantity but the quality of work done that measures reward—not how *much*, but how *well* (cf. Matt. 10:42 and the Widow's two mites).

3. The *will* to do, not the *ability* to accomplish is the determining factor. If there be first a willing mind it is accepted according to that a man hath, not according to what he hath not (2 Cor. 8).

4. Not *success* but *fidelity* is rewarded. We cannot always command success. A steward is required to be faithful and wise, not successful. Stephen yearned to evangelize but accepted stoning. Paul went to Macedonia because of a vision, but found scourging and a prison cell.

5. Not *endowment* but *improvement*. Compare the parables of Talents and Pounds. Taking the two together, we learn, first, that where

there is an unequal bestowment, but an equal or proportionate improvement, the reward is equal; second, that where there is equal bestowment but unequal improvement the reward is unequal.

6. The object ennobles the subject, the purpose sanctifies the offering, "The altar sanctifieth the gift."

The higher the aim and the more exalted the end the more valuable the offering. A deed is reckoned not by what is done but by the cause or object to which the service is rendered.

7. Not proud independence but humble dependence. Not the energy of the flesh but of the spirit. Hence all care savors of atheism. We are forbidden to worry: it is God's cause and service and he will take care of it.

8. God remembers and rewards service so small that we forget it and are unconscious of it (See Matt. 25).

He records and rewards what we regard as trifles, when the motive is holy, unselfish and spiritual. Nothing is insignificant done in His name.

These principles are wholly peculiar to the scriptural revelation of God's philosophy of rewards.

The conception of *covenant* is perpetually recurring, and is one of the controlling and interpreting ideas of all Scripture, but it is frequently suggested where other words are employed, such as "vow," "oath," "separation," "agreement," "fellowship," etc. The root idea from which all these kindred terms sprung is the same. A special relation between two parties, God and man, of which a vow is the expression and an oath the confirmation; agreement, the equivalent; separation, the condition, and fellowship the exhibition.

The God of the Bible is throughout a covenant God, and yet the word "covenant" has passed almost entirely out of Christian thinking. All true blessings God has covenanted to bestow on believers, and on the basis of the covenant, they may rest perfectly assured that all such promises can, must, and will be unfailingly fulfilled; God ever does what He has covenanted to do. There are two great covenants, and two parties, God and man. The Old Covenant shows what man could and could not do; the New Covenant manifests what God can and will do. "The two covenants represent two stages of God's education of man and of man's seeking of God." Many Christians continue to attempt to serve God under the Old Covenant; this results in weakness, doubt, discouragement and failure. It is the duty and privilege of believers to place themselves at once under the New Covenant. This is done by believing themselves in His sight judicially reckoned to be all that God wills them to be, and to receive all that He has promised in Christ. "A single decisive step," says Andrew Murray, gives the believer "full access into the immediate presence of God, and the full experience of the power of the Spirit."

The idea of *Salvation* is another of the recurring conceptions of Scripture, but its verbal equivalents are almost countless. Sometimes it appears under the guise of *pardon* and escape from judgment; again, of *justification* and acceptance in Christ; and again of *sanctification* and victory over sin, and deliverance from its power. Peter uses the word of the final consummation at the reappearing of our Lord Jesus Christ.

And so of *Holiness*. The word seldom appears in comparison to the thought which underlies it. But there are three great conceptions closely linked with it: separation from sin and unto God; spiritual health or wholeness, and conformity to the image of His Son.

So of *Service*. How seldom this word is found! In its proper and spiritual sense perhaps only ten times in all; yet the thought continually recurring in a variety of forms and figures. "Ministry," "good works" and "alms giving," "fruit," "seed sowing," "burden bearing," and almost a myriad of other forms. How could we learn the lesson of service if we were dependent on the mere recurrence of the word?

The word "*Faith*" is found but once in the Old Testament. "Children in whom is no faith" (Deut. 32:20), where it means faithfulness, or good faith. Yet the thought runs like a golden thread from Genesis 15:6, to the end. Even "believe," its nearest equivalent, is found only about thirty times, as applied to God, and yet the lesson is perpetually taught of confidence and trust, and associated with the whole history of the race. We might almost say that the two attitudes of believing and not believing are the explanation of all Old Testament history and doctrine. We may draw a line through the entire book, arrange on one side all those who had faith, and on the other, those who had not, and classify the entire contents of the Old Testament Scripture under the two heads of the rewards and results of faith, and penalties and consequences of unbelief. To get these great recurrent ideas of Scripture firmly in mind, and with them as guides search the Word, is to find many of the secrets of its unity and harmony.

Peace is another recurrent idea, and the word is found over 200 times. Yet the conception reappears a thousand, if the equivalent terms are consulted. One of the nearest is *rest*, which expresses both an aspect and a result of peace. *Safety* is another equivalent, so is security, quiet, firmness, courage. The thought is but the more eloquently impressive because so many ways are necessary to give it expression, like the faces into which a diamond is ground and polished, each of which adds to its brilliance and radiance.

How recurrent is the idea of *Power*—the power of God in man! Yet how seldom is it expressed as in Micah 3:8. "I am full of power by the Spirit of the Lord." Sometimes the thought is that of strength to do, courage to witness, patience to endure, boldness to rebuke; but to follow the thought throughout is not only to understand what the power of God in the believer is, but the hundred forms of its manifestation and directions of its utilization.

The Holy Indignation of God against sin must be understood only by knowing the whole Scripture. We must examine its whole testimony, under "anger," "wrath," "fury," "indignation," "displeasure," "jealousy," etc.; and all in the light of His immaculate Holiness, who is "of purer eyes than to behold evil and cannot look upon iniquity" (Hab. 1:13). Any one of these words might leave us with the false impression of a passionate being roused at times to a violent anger as terrible as His infinity. But a more general study will show wrath in God to be only another aspect of benevolence, as necessary to His perfections as Love, and itself only the other pole of love. For it is the same holiness that is attracted by the beauty of saintliness and as surely repelled by the deformity and corruption of sinfulness. To master the subject enables us to admire and adore God for the very wrath that at first made Him seem only too much like a man of undisciplined temper and ungoverned passions.

Inspiration is another and very important recurrent idea. It occurs but once in either Testament (Job 32:8, 2 Tim. 3:16). Yet is not the thought of a divine speaker behind all human tongues and pens, a dominant one in the Word of God? Is not the one idea that binds all Scripture in one, gives it uniform, divine authority, and constitutes it the final court of arbitration in all controversy as to truth or duty, the one consistent and all-controlling thought that in many ways, at many times, in many parts, and by many men, the one God spake unto the fathers; and that in these last days He spake finally and fully by His Son (Heb. 1:1, 2). Let that be the recurrent conception, and the whole Word is illumined. We see that each of these 66 books is a member of one organic body of Scripture, and each of the forty human writers a mouthpiece of one Divine speaker. We are not left without a sufficient guide in belief and practice, and, if we discover apparent inharmonies and discordances, are prepared to search more deeply for the secret of reconciliation and unity.

Here is another grand illustration of great underlying conceptions absolutely independent of explicit statement. Where in the Old Testament are "life and immortality brought to light" as in the New? David indeed said, "I shall go to him but he shall not return to me" (2 Sam. 12:23), but some think this only means that he shall go to the child in the grave. Job declared that his redeemer liveth, and that "in his flesh he shall see God," but some again think he refers to his confidence that he shall be restored from disease and in a recovered body be vindicated by Jehovah. The references to the future life are confessedly few and occult; yet if we once *assume* the doctrine, we shall find it everywhere implied and explanatory of otherwise obscure and enigmatical Scriptures. And so of the kindred idea of *resurrection* from the dead.

The word *"Discipline"* is found only in Job 36:10, and then it does not mean the beneficent influence of sorrow and suffering in educating character. Yet who would be willing to dismiss this ever-recurrent thought from the Holy Scripture, that, like as a father pitieth and loveth and chasteneth his children, so our Heavenly Father, because He loves and pities, afflicts. Let the student take this idea and trace its unfoldings, under such forms as: "chastening," "corruption," "affliction," "trial," "sorrow," "tribulation," "trouble," "rebuke," "reproach," etc., and see how rich is the body of instruction developed, that could never be gathered by simply following any one word.

The idea of *a life beyond death* is very seldom explicitly expressed in the Old Testament; yet the Lord Himself argues that an attentive reader may find it pervading it as well as the New (Matt. 22:32). The God of Abraham, Isaac and Jacob is the God not of the dead, but of the living, and He would not give Himself such a name as expressing His relation to corpses, rotting in their sepulchers, but to believers still living, though their bodies be sleeping.

24

Topical Methods of Study

S PECIAL THEMES NEED TO BE STUDIED in the light of the Word as a whole. Without being in form a philosophical or theological treatise, it contains sufficient guidance as to all truth and duty. To search out its witness wherever found, classify and combine it, yields such instruction that upon any needful question, the mind of God is disclosed in a remarkable manner and measure. Grand themes, that suffice for lifelong study, are found set like shining gems all along the circlet of the Scriptures, such as the following:

1. The Glory and Beauty of the Law of God (Ps. 119).
2. The Messiah as the Suffering Lamb of God (Is. 53).
3. The Four Successive World empires (Dan. 2:31–45).
4. Divine Forgiveness (Micah 7:15–20).
5. The Son of Covetousness (Luke 13:13–48).
6. The Antidote to Trouble (John 14:1–27).
7. The Righteousness which is by Faith (Rom. 3:9; 4:25).
8. The Message of Faith (Rom. 10).
9. The Body of Christ (1 Cor. 12).
10. Love as the "More Excellent Way" (1 Cor. 12:31—13:13).
11. The Resurrection from the Dead (1 Cor. 15:12–58).
12. The Law of Separation Unto God (2 Cor. 6:14—7:1).
13. The Peace of God (Phil. 4).
14. The Old and New Man (Eph. 4:22–32; Col. 3:1–17).
15. The Chorus of Virtues (2 Pet. 1:5–8).

16. The Perfect Deity and Humanity of our Lord (Heb. 1, 2).
17. The Great White Throne (Rev. 20:11–15).
18. The Final Perfection of Saints (Rev. 22:3–5).

Such *great* themes remind us of Kepler's exclamation when, after eighteen experiments, he found the key that unlocked astronomical problems: "O Almighty God! I am thinking Thy thoughts after Thee." Grattan said of Fox, "you must measure the magnitude of his mind by parallels of latitude"; but, in measuring the infinite mind, all such standards fail us; and, in research into the Scriptures, it is this constant recurrence of infinite ideas and ideals that transcend alike all human expression and conception that convinces us of their divine original- ity and authority. The level of the thinking which they suggest is so exalted as to be unapproachable.

We have instanced a score of subjects, treated in single passages; but in many cases for anything like a complete view, various Scrip- tures must be collated and compared, because in no one place are these themes fully presented. Sometimes different writers suggest various aspects of a common theme, or there is a historic development of it, in the succession of events, or ideas. A few of these may be likewise cited as examples of hundreds.

1. *The Fire of God*, represented in the Shekinah, the miraculous flamed kindled on His altars, the Pillar of Fire, etc., and above all, the Pentecostal Flame, and tongues of fire.

2. *The Angel of the Lord*, the constant wonder worker in all human history, the great Defender, Protector, Avenger, omniscient, om- nipotent, omnipresent, invisible, irresistible.

3. *The moral code of Jehovah*, embraced in the Decalogue, and modified and applied in the Sermon on the Mount—a complete and sublime ethical foundation for human character.

4. *The Spirit of God*, revealed officially and occasionally in the Old Testament, individually and perpetually in the New, as source of light, life, love and power to the human spirit.

5. *The God-Man*. A new order of Being, with divine and human natures perfectly combined in one personality—a mysterious blend- ing of the finite and the infinite.

6. *The Prophetic Vision*—divine sight, foresight and insight imparted to human agents so that they have a backward vision of prehistoric events and foreward vision of the future.

7. The conception of *substitutionary Sacrifice*—the obedience and suffering of a sinless being accepted in behalf of the sinner, so as to make pardon and reconciliation possible without sacrificing righteousness.

8. *Eternal Life through believing*, or the impartation of the nature of God to Man, through faith as a means of union and identification—the mystery of a perfect salvation through a new birth.

9. *The Rewards and Retributions of the Future State*, completing the partial administration of Justice in this age by the final awards of eternity and the settlement of destiny.

10. *The church of God*, as a called out body of believers and witnesses—indwelt by the Spirit of God, constituting one invisible organism of which Christ is Head.

11. *The World of Spirits*—invisible and innumerable—and divided into two great hosts—the unfallen and loyal, and the fallen and lost, with Satan at their head.

12. *The Whole Conception of the Godhead*—trinity yet unity—omnipresent yet not pantheistic; infinite and eternal, yet exercising providential care over all creatures however minute and events however trifling.

These are a few specimens of the wealth of the mines of thought which in the Holy Scriptures invite exploration and yet defy exhaustion. Not one of all these magnificent themes finds treatment in uninspired writings except as first suggested here, and therefore without this unique and unrivaled Book of God, the race would have been in midnight darkness as to these and all co-related truths. Who shall even glance at such topics and still say that no such revelation from God was needed!

In three Psalms, there is a singular tribute to "the Law of the Lord"—one title for Old Testament Scripture as a whole, naturally arising from the fact that of the three popular divisions of the Old Testament, the Law was first.

The Psalms are 1, 19, and 119, the second and third taking up the subject where the previous one left it, and no two covering the same ground. Psalm 1 depicts the blessedness of him whose delight is found in meditating upon Holy Scripture; Psalm 19 compares it with the Heavens as a field for the display of its author's glorious perfections; and Psalm 119 exhaustively presents its manifold attraction as a law of life, a counselor and guide. Comparison of these three Psalms is very suggestive. in the first the lover and doer of God's Word and the hater and scorner are contrasted in character, conduct and destiny. In the 19th, the heavens are compared in ten respects with as many of the perfections of Scripture; then in the 119th, every letter of the Hebrew alphabet heads an eightfold acrostic, as though to hint that if all possible combinations of letters are exhausted the excellence of the Holy Scriptures as a practical and personal guide to doctrine and duty cannot be expressed.

The *Putting Away of Sin* is one of the great conceptions of the whole Scripture. The goat that fell by lot to Jehovah as Lawgiver and Judge, presents that aspect of the work of Christ, according to which He by His shed blood expiates guilt, pays penalty and so vindicates the holiness and righteousness of God as expressed in His Law. It is expiatory. But the live goat presents and typifies that companion aspect of Christ's work which puts away sin by the sacrifice of Himself, securing for us not only exemption from judgment but justification before God, peace with God, access to God and finally glory in God (Rom. 5:1–4). This aspect is propitiatory. It is for us as though we had never sinned (Heb. 9:26; Rom. 8:33, 34).

The Word of God presents this great truth in many forms. The phrase, "put away sin," is very common and emphatic, as when Nathan said to the penitent David: "The Lord also hath put away thy sin" (2 Sam. 12:13). The same thought is otherwise expressed. The following are the main forms in which it is embodied:

1. The comprehensive expression "covered," as in Psalm 32:1, 2. "Blessed is he whose transgression is forgiven, whose sin is covered; blessed is the man unto whom the Lord imputeth not iniquity." Here, besides forgiveness, there is a covering of sin, a hiding of it beneath the blood, so that it is no more imputed or reckoned to the sinner as having been committed.

2. Hence the phrase "abundantly pardon," as found in Isaiah 55:7, where God is represented not only as having mercy upon a returning penitent, but as "multiplying to pardon"—an attempt to express by a sort of mathematical metaphor the thoroughness of forgiveness.

3. In Psalm 103:12 occurs the phrase "so far hath He removed our transgressions from us," where the immeasurable heights and breadths of infinite space are used to illustrate the distance to which forgiveness is banished.

4. Isaiah 38:17 conveys the thought by the phrase, "Thou hast cast all my sins behind Thy back"—drawn from human inability to see at all what is behind us.

5. Isaiah 44:22: "I have blotted out, as a thick cloud, thy transgressions"—another figure drawn from the utter dissipation and disappearance of a cloud that has obscured heaven's blue.

6. Micah 7:19 expresses the same thought by a reference to the drowning of Pharaoh's hosts in the Red Sea. "Thou will cast all their sins into the depth of the sea"—too deep for any dredging instrument to bring them up.

7. Jeremiah 31:34 touches the climax—"I will forgive their iniquity, and I will *remember their sin no more*"—a promise so remarkable that it becomes the leading mark of the New Covenant and is twice quoted as such in the Epistle to the Hebrews (8:12; 10:17).

This means practical annihilation of forgiven sins—and shows us how and why the pardoned, penitent, believing sinner has boldness and access with confidence by the faith of Him" (Eph. 3:12).

The word *Sanctification* is used of what is *separated* and of what is *subjugated*. The root idea is separation, from evil to good. It may be profitably studied under the following heads:

1. Its relations to the *Will of God*—His Eternal Purpose in Salvation (Rom. 8:29, 30; 1 Pet. 1:2).

This is *judicial* sanctification, immediate and complete from the first. It is sanctification as *God sees it*, in His purpose and plan, and determines the believer's *standing* in Christ.

2. Its relations to the *Blood of Christ* (Heb. 13:12; Lev. 27:32). Its *basis and ground* is identity with Him. We are sanctified in Him.

Hence that dominant phrase "in Christ," or "in Christ Jesus" that interprets every epistle.

3. Its relations to the *Truth*—the Word of God—which is largely its *instrument*—the means used for its accomplishment (John 17:17). It is a sort of atmosphere or element in which we live, move and have our being as saints.

4. Its relation to the *Holy Spirit* (1 Pet. 1:2), nothing is more important. The new life of God absolutely begins when He recreates us—Sin has made the spirit in man dead and He quickens it again. His double office is to show ourselves and God. He makes our *state consist* with our *standing*—the actual correspond with the judicial (cf. 1 Cor. 6:17; Gal. 5:16–25). This is like grafting a live nerve upon a dead one—that triumph of modern surgery.

5. Its relations to the *Example of Christ*—our model and standard of sanctification (John 17:19; 1 Pet. 2:21–23).

6. Its relations to *our own Will* (Rom. 6; 12:1, 2; 1 Pet. 1:1–16; 4:1–3; 2 Cor. 6:14; 7:1; Ex. 29). In this last chapter we have a fine illustration: What was first sanctified *to* God's glory He afterward sanctified *by* His glory? Three incentives are urged to promote voluntary separation unto God: His purchase of us, possession of us, and inhabitation in us.

7. Its relation to the *Glory of God* (Ex. 29).

Three stages: Separation and Self-presentation—our part. Consecration and Transformation—God's part.

The Scriptures suggest *four* conspicuous snares to sanctification:

1. False criteria: feelings and caprices—vs. faith and love.

2. Legalism and its bondage—and self-righteous spirit.

3. Antinomianism—or practical lawlessness.

4. Spiritual pride—self-confidence, loss of vigilance.

Again, notice the promises to prayer, and conditions of answer.

1. Faith in God—fundamental, rudimental (Heb. 11:6; James 1:5–7; Matt. 14:29, 30; 1 John 5:14, 15, the confidence).

2. Threefold condition—Asking, Seeking, Knocking (Matt. 7:7). Supplication, earnest desire, importunate continuance (Eph. 3:20; Heb. 4:13–16; Matt. 6:7, 8; Mark 10:51, 52; James 5:16–18; Hosea 12:4–6; Luke 11:5–10; 18:1–8).

3. Abandonment of Sin (Ps. 66:18, 19; Prov. 15:29; Is. 1:16; 59:2; John 9:31; 1 John 3:20–22).

4. Anticipating Answer (Mark 11:22–24). Such holding to the faith, or faithfulness of God, as to believe the blessing already received (Rom. 8:26, 27; Jude 1:20).

5. Boldness of Approach (1 John 5:14, 15; Heb. 4:16; John 15:7; 14:13, 14; 15:16; 16:23–26). In the Name of Jesus (Jer. 14:21; Ps. 78:41; Matt. 13:58).

6. Individual and Solitary Approach (Matt. 6:6). Secrecy, silence, solitude. Habit of closet communion. "Practice of the Presence of God" (Luke 6:12).

7. Collective, corporate prayer (Matt. 18:19, 20; 1 Chr. 17:1–4; Dan. 2:17–19; Acts 1:14; 2:1–4; 4:31; 12:5–17; 16:25, 26; Deut. 32:30).

The relation of *Believers to this world-age* can be fully seen only by a comparison of at least seven conspicuous passages of Scripture, where different phases of the subject appear: Matthew 6:19–34: Worldly avarice and anxiety, foes to faith. John 15:18–24; 17: Worldly hatred of our Lord and His disciples. Romans 12:1, 2: Duty of non-conformity to the world and its standards. Ephesians 2:1–7: The connection of the world with the flesh and the devil. James 4:4, 5: The friendship of the world enmity toward God. First John 2:15–17; 5:19: The love of the world forbidden, as not of God. Revelation 16:18: The greatness and glory and doom of the world.

When these Scriptures are compared there will be no mistaking the fact that, with singular uniformity, the world is held up as the foe of faith and Godliness. The Old Testament writes large the word *separation* over the very portals of a holy life; and the New Testament repeats it and forbids even conformity to the world's standards and methods.

Orcagna, in his great picture, in the Strozzi Chapel—The Last Judgment—represents Solomon, the worldly and idolatrous King, as rising out of his sepulcher in robe and crown, at the trump of the archangel, uncertain whether he is to turn to the right hand or to the left—a terrible satire on carnal discipleship.

25

The Totality of Scripture Testimony

OR EXAMPLE, THE DOCTRINE of *justification by works* might find seeming approval in James 2:14–26, which taken by itself would seem to teach that faith alone is insufficient. But, when compared with such Scripture as Romans 3:21; 4:25; Galatians 2:15; 3:14; etc., that is seen to be untenable error, and we are compelled to find some point of consistency and harmony which on further study proves to be this:

Paul is showing how a *sinner* is justified *before* God: James, how a *saint* is justified before *men*. Justification, in Romans, means imputed righteousness, reconciling a sinner to a righteous God; justification, in James, means actual rectitude, justifying the faith by proving it genuine, and reconciling confession of faith with consistency of conduct. Paul was rebuking and refuting pharisaic self-righteousness and formalism; James, antinomian license and lawlessness. Here it is the totality of Scripture testimony that saves us from the peril of both legalism on the one hand, and a liberty which is only freedom to sin, on the other.

The doctrine of sinless perfection finds apparent foundation in such texts as "he that is born of God doth not commit sin," etc. (1 John 3:3–9). In this passage, no room seems left for even an occasional lapse from duty, or stumble in the chosen path of obedience. "Whosoever abideth in Him sinneth not: whosoever sinneth hath not seen Him neither known Him." The seed of God is represented as so abiding in a disciple that he *cannot sin*.

This, however, is inconsistent alike with the experience of the most saintly souls and the testimony of the Scriptures. In fact, the writer of this Epistle, himself, says: "These things write I unto you that *ye sin not*; but, if *any man sin*, we have an *Advocate* with the father, Jesus Christ the righteous; and He is the *propitiation* for our sins, and not for ours only but for the whole world." Here he tells us that, while he is writing unto us in order to prevent our sinning, if we *do* fall into sin, we have a resort in the Advocacy and propitiation of our risen Lord: and it is the *disciple's* sins to which he refers, for he distinguishes between "*our* sins" and the *world's* needs. Here, again, it is the sum total of Scripture testimony that saves us from error, and compels us to seek some point of harmony. And we find that these verbs have *a continuous present* force—he that abideth in Him doth not *continue, or go on sinning*—sinning is not his *habit*, as with the devil who goes on sinning from the beginning. In this the children of God and the children of the devil are manifest. Saints habitually obey but occasionally sin: sinners habitually sin, even if occasionally they obey or conform to a right standard. It is a question of which way the face is turned and in what direction the main trend of life is. Thus we are not only saved from serious errors by referring to the totality of Scripture testimony, but we are forced to that deeper study which unveils a fuller truth and gives a wider vision.

Another example of the *corrective* value of comparative study of Scripture and the totality of its testimony may be found in 1 Samuel 15. Twice in this chapter, Jehovah is represented as repenting that He had made Saul king (vv. 11, 35), and yet it is positively affirmed: "The strength of Israel will not lie nor repent; for He is not a man that He should repent" (v. 29). The repentance attributed to God must, therefore, be explained and qualified by His own repudiation of all that is capricious, mutable and changeable as in human passions. When bad men break covenant with Him, and made void its provision, compelling Him to change His course toward them and His method of procedure, there is really *no change whatever in Him*—it is in *them*.

He is eternally and unchangeably the Lover of Good and the Hater of Evil. But when men instead of holding fast the good turn to the evil, by the same immutable law of His perfection, they incur His holy anger instead of favor. It is the same attribute of holiness which attracts or repels according to the character of that which approaches it. When God is said to repent, therefore, it is simply a face of *appearance*—a *relative* statement drawn from human usage and language, and strictly cannot be applied to Him in whom there is no variableness.

Comparative study of Scripture has often a high value as a *corrective* to false impressions, inferences and conclusions. For example, in 2 Samuel 24:1, we read that "the anger of the Lord was kindled against Israel, and He moved David against them, to say go, number Israel and Judah."

This seems unaccountable, since it was this very numbering which further kindled the anger of the Lord and brought one of His signal judgments upon both King and Kingdom. But when we turn to 1 Chronicles 21:1, we find the solution of our perplexity and the reconciliation of the discrepancy: "And *Satan* stood up against Israel, and provoked David to number Israel."

The two narratives are harmonized by making the former to read: "And *one* moved David to say, go number Israel and Judah."

Possibly in no one instance does a partial view of Scripture truth more mislead than in the difficult and perplexing doctrines of justification by Faith, and *Election* with its corresponding and correlated truths. Predestination has proved probably the greatest stumbling block of any doctrine taught in the Word, not only to unbelievers but to believers, and has been practically the wedge that split the whole church into two opposing bodies—"Arminians" and "Calvinists."

To most readers of Scripture, both Justification and Predestination are like the Domes of the Yosemite—while a few daring adventurers seek to scale their precipitous sides, most others can only look up with awe and despair of ever mounting to such summits. Yet, if studied in the light of the whole Word, there is seen to be a practical side from which the ascent is gradual and easy, and like those Domes, these truths are seen as half truths, united in God's mind, but rent asunder by man's controversies.

No doubt justification teaches acceptance with God on the ground of another's righteousness imputed to us; and predestination makes salvation primarily depend not on man's choice, but God's choice. Yet, when the entire testimony of Scripture is examined, we find that these statements are but partial and incomplete.

If on the one hand justification is by faith, the faith is not a mere acceptance of a doctrine, but a living bond of union with the risen Christ—a faith that must justify itself as genuine by works of obedience; and, if God elects a soul to salvation, so does that soul elect God as Savior and Sovereign.

Our Lord did not talk of justification through imputed righteousness, but told the parable of the prodigal son, who forfeited all claim to a father's love and care, went far from home, spent all his money, and, when he came back with only rags and wretchedness, the father's love and grace put on him a robe, shoes, and a ring and set him at his own banquet table.

From the first two parts of the threefold parable in Luke 15, it might be inferred that, in salvation, *God does all*; for the sheep is sought till found, and then neither driven nor led back but lifted and carried by the shepherd; and the lost piece of silver cannot recover itself and does not even know it is lost, but must be searched for, and found and restored to its place on the necklace of the woman.

Had we no other Scripture but 1 Corinthians 9:25–27, we might infer that life is a race course and heaven the goal and salvation the crown: and that Paul was keeping his body under and brining it into subjection, as a way of earning or winning heaven. But this will not stand the test of other Scripture, in which salvation is always represented as a *gift*, not *wages*, to be accepted nor merited. Thus we see clearly that the race course must *represent service*, and the crown, its *reward*; and that while Paul had not fear of failing of salvation, he was solicitous not to forfeit his reward.

Very important also is it to discriminate between the *terms of salvation* and the conditions of *sanctification* and *service*. We enter an emphatic protest against the current interpretation that the race we are called upon to run is a race in order that we might win heaven. As Dr. Campbell Morgan well says, "Here is one reason why the churches are half empty: men have been so long acting as if Christianity were a kind of fire insurance, which takes individuals and makes them safe so that they might never reach hell, but might reach heaven, and that all they had to do was to run as hard as they could to get out of the world into heaven. That is a false interpretation both of Christianity and of the passage. The race we are called to run is not in order that we might win heaven, but that God might win earth. The cities are hotbeds of iniquity, and our aim should be to make them cities of God. To run that race the weight which hinders progress, whatever it is, must be dropped, and each must find out what his is and drop it. The most comprehensive of all is unbelief. Many show a tendency to think their education not complete, unless they have a little unbelief in their Maker. The most crying sin is that Christian people do not believe, else fail to act as if they believed. It is one thing to sit at home and sing "Rescue the Perishing," and another to go down to the perishing and lift them up.

There are several other important themes upon which we need the verdict of the whole Scripture to prevent error, particularly the following:

1. The *Deity of our Lord Jesus Christ*, and His *equality with the Father*. Such sayings as "My Father is greater than I," need to be put side by side with "I and My Father are One"; and His utterances as a servant, during the period of His humiliation, with His language as a sovereign, after His glorification. Compare Hebrews 1:1–4, and Revelation 1, 2, 3.

2. The *Sleep of saints in Death*. Many passages give countenance to this idea that not only the body but the soul also sleeps in the grave till the resurrection. But other passages clearly show that while the body sleeps, the spirit is with Christ. Compare Luke 20:37, 38; 23:52, 43; 2 Corinthians 5:6–8; Philippians 1:23; Revelation 14:13, etc.

3. The *Personality of the Holy Spirit*. The word "spirit" being the equivalent of "wind," or "breath," some language of Scripture might imply that the Spirit of God is a mere influence; but other Scripture attributes to Him personal attributes and activities and precludes this notion. Compare John 14:16, 17; 16:8–10, 13, 14, etc. The same may be said of the *personality* of the devil.

THE FOUR JUDGMENTS
PAST

No.	Subject of Judgment	Period of Judgment	Place of Judgment	Bible References
I.	Of SIN, which has PASSED for the BELIEVER, *Christ*, having been judged for his sins, and he himself "crucified with Christ." Hence, "he that believeth . . . SHALL NOT COME INTO JUDGMENT."	When the Lord Jesus Christ died on the cross more than eighteen centuries ago.	On Calvary.	John 3:18; 5:24. Rom. 6:6; 8:1, 17. 2 Cor. 5:21. Gal. 2:20. Heb. 9:26; 10:14–17.

Many of God's dear children are kept from having "peace with God" through the supposition that they have yet to be judged for their sins. *Such is not the case, blessed be God!* for Christ has been judged in their place, "HAS APPEARED TO PUT AWAY SIN by the sacrifice of Himself"; and the Holy Ghost says: "Your sins and iniquities I will remember no more." Moreover, the believer is "PERFECTED FOREVER" and "SHALL NOT COME INTO JUDGMENT."

FUTURE

II.	Of the REDEEMED (of all ages), when each "shall receive his own REWARD according to his own labor."	After they have been "caught up" in glorified bodies to "meet the Lord in the air."	Before the "Judgment-Seat of Christ."	Rom. 14:10–12. 1 Cor. 3:8–15. 2 Cor. 5:10. Rev. 22:12.

But believers "must all appear before the Judgment-seat of Christ" to "receive REWARD" or "suffer LOSS," according to their works on earth. IT WILL NOT BE A QUESTION OF HEAVEN OR HELL (since they are all previously in heaven, in "bodies of glory").

☞ St. Paul has been "with Christ"—so has the thief—for hundreds of years. How absurd to suppose it has yet to be decided whether they are fit to be there!

III.	Of the LIVING "NATIONS" on the earth divided like sheep and goats, according to their treatment of the faithful Jewish "Remnant" (whom the Lord calls "my brethren").	At the commencement of the Millennium, or Christ's reign of 1,000 years.	In the "Valley of Jehoshaphat," at the base of the Mount of Olives.	Joel 3:3–16. Zech. 14:1–9. Matt. 25:31–46.

By a careful study of Matt. 25:31–46, and a comparison with Joel 3:3–16, and with Zech. 14:1–9, it will be seen that this judgment is confined to THE LIVING NATIONS (GENTILES) on the earth when the Lord Jesus returns to reign. This is important to seize, as it is generally confounded with No. IV judgment, which takes place at least 1,000 years later.

IV.	Of the UNCONVERTED "DEAD" of all ages, the only remaining class.	After the close of the Millennium of Christ's reign of 1,000 years.	Before the "Great White Throne," after heaven and earth have fled away.	Rev. 20:11–15.

The *Judgments of God* seem to be unintelligible unless we discriminate the *subjects, periods, places* and *times,* and *manner* of different judicial transactions. The old idea of one general and all comprehensive assize seems scarcely borne out by a careful comparative study. The preceding presentation of the subject may at least stimulate—study. It bears the initials, "J. C. T."

26

Analysis and Synthesis

IN ANY DEPARTMENT of study two processes are fundamental, the analytic and the synthetic, the former of which separates, and the latter combines. Both are needful. We take apart, to learn what are the component parts, the individual peculiarities and features; then we put together in new combinations based upon common characteristics and resemblances. In Scripture, as in nature, many things are grouped together which are not homogeneous, of like nature; though associated, not assimilated. Analysis discovers deeper affinities and adaptations and so prepares for new arrangement and combination founded on agreements and differences.

For example, we examine a narrative, prophecy, poem, discourse, or epistle, to learn its content; then rearrange that content according as we discover what belongs together historically, logically, doctrinally, practically. The order of thought is more important than the order of time; and logical connection and sequence, than that of occurrence and utterance.

The first illustration of this principle is found in the Bible as a whole. This "Volume of the Book" is an aggregate of over sixty, and these again have subdivisions, indicated or implied. What is nearby in the collection may be far apart in purpose and intent; and what is far apart may belong together. Only diligent search will find those subtle affinities and adaptations which guide to the higher unity and community of nature and design. Thus Bible study is constructive not destructive; it does not dissect the body of truth, to leave it in scattered and lifeless fragments, but coordinates its contents in a system, somewhat as bones, knit, bound, and compacted by ligaments and nerves, are formed into a living organism.

To discover essential likeness or substantial agreement is to find also mutual relation, and bring scattered facts and truths into unity and harmony; lesser factors are also seen to contribute to the completeness and symmetry of some larger fact and truth, somewhat as minute fragments combine in mosaic work or a stained glass window, evincing artistic design.

The Divine Author of Scripture evidently meant that only such meditative, comparative study should open up the hidden treasures of His Word. He might have made Holy Scripture a systematic treatise, but He chose rather to intersperse, throughout, hints upon all important practical subjects, inciting to search. If we would get the complete testimony of the inspired Word we must collate, compare, combine. How seldom all the particulars of the same event or occurrence are found in one place of continuous narrative. In all the historical books of the Old Testament, there is this interdependence. In the Pentateuch, the later books supplement the history of the earlier and supply additional facts. To understand the story of the kingdom we must compare the six historical books from 1 Samuel to 2 Chronicles. So Ezra, Nehemiah and Esther are interrelated as pictures of the captivity. In the four Gospel narratives, even when the same event is narrated or the same discourse recorded, each writer tells us what impressed his mind or memory most, or best suited his special province or purpose; and hence the help of a harmony of the Gospels, combining the four into one, so that we get all particulars at a single view. Paul's Epistles must be read side by side with the Acts, for each throws light upon the other. No words can do justice to the surprising wealth of instruction, information and suggestion which this double process of analysis and synthesis yields.

In this section we adduce some few examples of the results of such study in the illumination of Scripture topics.

First of all, as the Bible is the Book of Salvation, it is needful for us to know how salvation becomes ours. Here comparative study shows that it is by an act so simple as not to need definition. We find, scattered throughout the whole Scripture, a group of short and simple words, such as "look," "hear," "taste," "take," "come," "trust," "choose," etc. All of them are alike in this, that they refer to a *receptive* act or attitude, something by which we *take or receive or appropriate*. If something is to be seen we take it in with the eyes, by looking; if to be heard, with the ears, by hearing; food we take in with the mouth, by tasting; a gift we take with the hands; a walk, with the feet; a friend, with the heart; a choice, with the will. What no one of these words would fully convey, together they perfectly express; that *Salvation is God's gift*, and that what is needed and all that is needed is to *take* it; with the whole being in a receptive frame, eyes, ears, mouth, hands, feet, heart, will, ready to accept what He bestows. *All legalism is thus barred out.* Salvation is not a wage to be earned, a reward to be merited, a prize to be sought, or a crown to be won; but a gift to be taken.

The benefit of analytic study is very obvious in examining the various books of the Bible.

For example, how readily Genesis divides into three or four main parts, and under four representative heads: Adam, as head of the race; Noah, as its second father; Abram as the father of an elect family, and Jacob, as the progenitor of the twelve tribes.

The Books of the Kingdom, analyzed, suggest five main divisions: under *Samuel*, who marks the period of transition from patriarchal and judicial to regal; under *Saul, David* and *Solomon*, with a reign of forty years each, and very marked epochal eras; then the period of the rapture of the kingdom under *Rehoboam* and *Jeroboam*.

The Epistle to the Romans becomes a new book when the four main sections are clearly perceived: first, universal condemnation under law; second, free justification under grace; third, sanctification by the Spirit, and fourth, self-dedication as the outcome of all the mercies of God.

The help of analytic study is very obvious in homiletics, supplying the natural outline of discourse and developing the hidden beauty and riches of individual texts.

In John 5:31–47; 8:13–18; 15:26, 27, we find as nowhere else the complete statement of the *witnesses* to *our Lord Jesus Christ;* only as we rearrange them, in chronological order, do we see their completeness:

1. The written Scriptures, prophetic and historic.

2. John the Baptist, His forerunner.

3. The Father, in many ways, with many voices—preeminently at the Transfiguration.

4. His own witness, in His words and works.

5. The Witness of the Holy Spirit, first at His baptism, and conspicuously at Pentecost, etc.

6. His Resurrection.

7. The believers' testimony.

The Perversions of worship may be learned by a similar study.

Four Risks connected with worship are historically illustrated in the Old Testament, all teaching a different lesson and warning against a peculiar peril:

1. The gold calf at Sinai (Ex. 32). The risk of Symbolism—sensuous helps and visible representations of deity.

2. The Brazen serpent (Num. 21:1–9; 2 Kgs. 18:4). The danger of Sacramentalism, undue exaltation of the appointed means of Grace.

3. The Ephod of Gideon (Judg. 8:24–27). The peril of Sacerdotalism—or the magnifying of priestly robes, offices and functions.

4. The House of Micah (Judg. 17, 18). The snare of externalism and formalism, ceremonialism, irregularities tolerated because of outward conformity.

It cannot be accidental that all the prominent dangers, connected with religious worship, are thus hinted in these successive historic scenes. All visible helps in approaching God tend to idolatry, and endanger the purity, simplicity and spirituality of worship; we may unduly reverence the channels appointed to convey blessing, mistaking them for the grace they convey; we may pay homage to priestly pretensions and ceremonies; and substitute the mere machinery of worship for real conformity to the will of God.

Comparison and analysis of two passages on the Body of Christ, in Romans 12, and 1 Corinthians 12, likewise reveals the marked features of the duty and privilege of *service:*

1. No one has all gifts; therefore, there is no room for pride or boasting.

2. No one is without some gift; therefore, no room for idleness or despair.

3. Gifts differ; therefore no room for envy, jealousy or interference.

4. God Himself distributes; therefore, no room for complaint or discontent.

5. All gifts are needful; therefore no room for neglect or indifference.

6. All gifts derive power from the Giver; therefore, no room for weakness and inefficiency.

"Judas, by transgression fell, that he might *go to his own place*" (Acts 1:27), being analyzed, suggests:

1. As to sin: It is a fall downward, with increasing rapidity, with no power of self-recovery, and a gravitation toward hell.

2. As to penalty: Every man *has* his own place; largely *makes* his own place; ultimately *finds* his own place; consciously *feels* it to be his own place.

In Luke 9:46–62, there are six successive exhibitions of a *wrong temper or disposition*, with as many tender rebukes or admonitions of our Lord. It is very curious to observe also that these six are naturally divisible into two groups of three each; the former three being manifested by professed disciples, marring their character and conduct; and the latter three, by proposed disciples, hindering their acceptance and obedience. Furthermore, it would be difficult to find any form of such wrong or unseemly frame of mind, not here comprehended.

The first group have to do with disciples:

1. The ambitions, "reasoning which should be greatest."

2. The intolerant, "forbidding because he followeth not with us."

3. The vindictive, proposing to "command fire from heaven," etc.

The second group concerns candidates for discipleship:

1. The selfish, evidently seeking some temporal advantage.

2. The procrastinating: "Suffer me first to go and bury my father."

3. The vacillating: "Putting his hand to the plow," etc.

These morbid and misleading tempers must be studied in the light of our Lord's treatment of them.

To the ambitious, He commends the spirit that finds greatness in being least. To the intolerant, He answers that no man can at the same time do a miracle in His name and lightly speak evil of Him. To the vindictive, that they know not the malignity of their own spirit, nor the benignity of their Master's.

To the selfish, He refers to His own poverty and self-denial. To the procrastinating, He answers by the present and pressing need of a dead world, of the Word of Life. To the vacillating, He answers that a straight furrow needs in the plowman a steady eye on the goal.

This is but one example of the wealth discoverable in a single passage of Scripture by careful analysis and synthesis.

Where the inspiring Spirit Himself suggests an analysis, we may safely adhere both to His own divisions and order of thought. A conspicuous illustration is 1 Thessalonians 5:23:

"Your whole *spirit*, and *soul*, and *body*."

Here man's threefold constitution is hinted, and the order of rank. To keep this idea in mind solves many perplexities. The discrimination, for instance, between "soul" and "spirit" is most instructive. In dying, our Lord, and Stephen after Him, committed his "spirit" to the Divine keeping, and with uniformity the "spirit" is used of man's highest self (cf. Matt. 5:3; Luke 1:47; Rom. 1:9; 1 Cor. 7:17; Gal. 6:1; Eph. 1:17; 4:23, etc.).

So, likewise, the adjectives, formed respectively from these words, and so hard to render into English, as in 1 Corinthians 2, 3, 15, etc., where what is soulish or psychical is so distinct from what is pneumatical or spiritual.

27

Combination and Unification

A FINE RESISTANCE OF THE USE of combination of narratives may be found in the story of the woman with the "issue of blood." There are three records, each incomplete without the others: Matthew 9:20–22; Mark 5:25–34; Luke 8:43–48. We present them in combination:

But as he went, much people followed him, and thronged him. And, behold, a certain woman, which was diseased with an issue of blood twelve years, and had suffered many things of many physicians, neither could be healed of any, and had spent all that she had upon physicians, and was nothing bettered, but rather grew worse, when she had heard of Jesus, came in the press behind him and touched the hem of his garment. For she said within herself, "If I may touch but His clothes, I shall be whole." And the woman was made whole from that hour; and straightway her issue of blood staunched, and the fountain of her blood was dried up, and she felt in her body that she was healed of that plague. And Jesus, immediately knowing in Himself that virtue had gone out of Him, turned him about in the press, and said, "Who touched my clothes?" And when all denied, Peter and his disciples that were with him said unto him, "Master, the multitude throng thee and press thee, and thou seest the multitude thronging thee, and sayest thou, 'Who touched me?' " And Jesus said, "Somebody hath touched me: for I perceive that virtue is gone out of me." And he looked round about to see here that had done this thing. And when the woman saw that she was not hid, fearing and trembling, knowing what was done in her, she came and fell down before him, and told him all the truth, and declared unto him before all the people for what cause she had touched him and how she was healed immediately. And Jesus turned him about, and when he saw her, he said unto her, "Daughter, be of good comfort: thy faith hath made thee whole; go in peace, and be whole of thy plague."

Thus blended into one, there appears a *threefold classification*, and *seven particulars under each*.

1. Her *condition*: An infirmity—bloody flux—of twelve years standing—many physicians—all means exhausted—not healed but incurable—nothing bettered but rather worse, etc.

2. Her *course*: She heard of Jesus—came behind—said within herself—touched His garment—was made whole—and at once—and felt herself healed.

3. Her *confession*, etc.: Jesus knew in Himself—turned and asked 'Who touched me?'—declared virtue had gone out of Him—brought her to confession—comforted her—sent her away confirmed in her cure.

Taken thus together, we trace every step in her distress and extremity, inward perplexity and resolve, outward approach and act, His treatment of her and her final approval and dismissal.

Fragments of an ancient *Credal Hymn* seem found scattered through Paul's epistles—a possible primitive confession of faith framed in brief and striking parallelisms, and commonly called "faithful sayings," or utterances full of faith, embodying the tents of faith. These faithful sayings, collated and arranged, exhibit order, completeness and design, and, in the original, a beauty difficult to transfer into English. "This is a faithful saying and worthy of all acceptation"—naturally introduces a quotation from this early hymn or creed, and like phrases are used in other cases. To exhibit this hymn in its unity, we omit what serve as introductory clauses to the various parts, and cast the rest in a common mold, giving the various texts together at the close.

COMBINATION AND UNIFICATION

I.

"Christ Jesus came into the world to save sinners."

II.

"Pillar and mainstay of the truth,
   And, beyond dispute, great,
      Is the mystery of godliness:
He was manifested in the flesh,
   justified in the Spirit;
   revealed to messengers,
   preached among the nations;
   believed on in the world,
   received up into glory."

III.

"When the kindness of God, our Savior,
   And His love toward man appeared—
(Not by works of righteousness which we had done,
   but according to His mercy)
He saved us, through the washing of Regeneration,
   And renewing of the Holy Spirit,
Which He poured forth richly upon us,
   Through Jesus Christ, our Savior;
That, being justified by His grace,
We might become, according to hope,
   Heirs of Life Eternal."

IV.

"This is the *Word of faith:*
That if thou shalt, with thy mouth, confess
   That Jesus is Lord:
And shalt, in thine heart believe
   That God raised Him from the dead,
   Thou shalt be saved:
For with the heart man believeth unto righteousness;
And with the mouth is confession made unto Salvation."

V.

"For, if, together, we died
   Together shall we also live:

If together we endure,
   Together shall we also reign,
If we shall disown Him,
   He will also disown us;
If we are unfaithful,
   Faithful He abideth;
For disown Himself, He cannot."

VI.

"Bodily exercise profiteth a little;
   But godliness is profitable unto all things,
Having promise of the life that now is,
   And of that which is to come.
For to this end we labor and suffer reproach,
   Because we trust in the living God;
Who is the Savior of all men,
   Especially of those that believe."

VII.

"Sleeper, awake!
   And arise from the dead!
And upon thee Christ will shine."

VIII.

"If we believe that Jesus died and rose again,
   Even so them which sleep in Jesus
      Will God through Jesus bring with Him.
We who live and remain unto the coming of the Lord
   Shall not precede them who have fallen asleep.
For the Lord Himself from Heaven will descend,
   With a shout,
   With the voice of an archangel,
And with the trump of God!
   And, first, the dead in Christ will rise:
Then we, who live and remain,
   Shall be caught up together with them,
      In the clouds, in the air,
   To meet the Lord:
And so with the Lord shall we ever be!"

(See 1 Tim. 1:15; 3:15, 16; Titus 3:4–8; Rom. 10:8–10; 2 Tim. 2:11–13; 1 Tim. 4:8, 9; Eph. 5:14; 1 Thess. 4:14–17).

It is conjectured that these poetic fragments, and sayings of faith, counted worthy of all acceptation, are parts of some original credal hymn or hymnal creed; and they certainly contained a brief compendium of truth, such as:

The mission of Christ Jesus to this world—salvation for sinners;

The central truth of the Incarnation and its necessity to church life;

The doctrine of Justification by faith and Regeneration by the Spirit;

The terms of Salvation and Obedience: faith and confession;

The Identification of the believer with the Lord Jesus—in suffering and glory;

The double promise of blessing to the believer here and hereafter;

The duty of watchfulness—and the privilege of a life of resurrection power;

The blessed hope of Resurrection and glory at the Lord's coming.

We have one prominent case of Divine enumeration. Jehovah charges Israel with having "tempted" Him "now these ten times" (Num 14:22). Commonly reckoned as a round number, it suggests investigation, and, without counting the individual revolt of Miriam and Aaron against Moses, we trace ten prominent testings of God's patience and forbearance:

1. At the Red Sea (14:11, 12). Distrusting His power to help.

2. At Marah Spring (15:22–24). Doubting His provision for thirst.

3. At the Wilderness of Sin (16:1–3, 15, 20, 27). His Power to feed hunger.

4. At Rephidim (17:1–4). To supply water in drought.

5. At Sinai (32:1–6). By shameless idolatry.

6. At Mt. Horeb (33:1–5). By unwillingness to follow Him.

7. Revolt of Nadab and Abihu (Lev. 10:1–3). By the sin of profanation.

8. At Taberah (Num. 11:1–3). By complaint of the Way.

9. At Kirbroch Hataavah (11:4–35). By lusting after flesh.

10. At Kadesh Barnea (13, 14). By timidity and unbelief.

These ten examples exhibit all the forms of such "tempting" God, of which is professed followers could well be guilty, until at Kadesh all previous unbelief, distrust, disobedience and cowardice reached a climax and brought a crisis.

The Tenses of the Believer's Life.

If what is taught about *past, present,* and *future* facts in our experience is first gathered out, separated and then combined, we shall find, as to

I.   THE PAST.
     A completed Body of Scripture,
     A finished Atoning Work of Christ,
     An outpoured Pentecostal Spirit,
     A constituted Church of Christ.
II. THE PRESENT.
     A risen and exalted Savior and Intercessor,
     A full establishment of the "Means of Grace,"
     An appointed work of universal service,
     A perfecting process of disciplinary suffering.
III. THE FUTURE.
     Resurrection and translation at Christ's Coming,
     Perfected redemption, body, soul and spirit,
     Final glory with Christ in Heaven,
     New creation and consummation.

In Scripture classification, what Dr. A. J. Gordon used to call his "three pigeon holes," may be found very helpful. For example, label three such "pigeon holes" respectively with the words SALVATION, SANCTIFICATION, SERVICE. Then in each put the texts and teachings which belong there, carefully discriminating as to things that differ. Even intelligent believers are continually mixing and confusing what the Word of God never confounds. Salvation is God's *work for, and gift to us;* Sanctification, His *work in us;* Service, His work *through us.* In Salvation we do nothing but accept a free gift. In Sanctification we work with Him, as beautifully set forth in Philippians 2:12, 13. In Service we surrender ourselves as instruments and agents, for Him to work through us in accomplishing His purposes. To introduce the personal effort and warfare needful in Sanctification into the department of Salvation is to become legalists and turn free grace into self-righteousness. To confuse service with either of the others is to mistake what is to be accomplished for us and in us, with what is to be accomplished through us in others.

Let us try the pigeonhole device with mere catchwords to illustrate what belongs to each department.

In 2 Peter 1:5–8, we have the three all presented:

"Faith"—Salvation.

"Add to your faith, virtue, knowledge . . . charity"—Sanctification;

"If these things be in you and abound . . . neither *barren* nor *unfruitful* in the knowledge," etc.—Service.

Salvation	*Sanctification*	*Service*
Gift of God.	Work in us.	Work for God.
		Wages.
Received by faith.	Cooperation by us.	Fellowship with Him.
New Birth by Spirit.	Subject of grace.	Instrument of God.
Immediate.	Progressive.	Continual.
"Called."	"Chosen."	"Faithful."
Children of God.	Saints of God.	Stewards of God.
Cross borne for us.	Cross bearing.	"Corn or Wheat."
Purchase of God.	Temple of God.	Tool of God.
Accepted in Christ.	Battle of Victory.	Activity and Reward.
Believing.	Obeying, learning.	Witnessing.
Faith.	"Add to your faith," etc.	Fertility for God.
Blood shed for us.	Self-surrender.	"Salt, Light," etc.
Choosing foundation.	Building on it.	Leading others to build.
Born.	Growing.	Serving.
Discipleship.	Race.	Prize.
Espousing.	Enduring.	Cooperating.
Enlisting.	Overcoming.	Glorifying.

28

Classification and System

EXAMPLES OF CLASSIFICATION and its results in orderly system might be indefinitely multiplied. This method is mainly useful in the following directions, serving to group:

1. Facts or events having some common properties or characteristics.

2. Teachings or precepts which pertain to the same general subject.

3. Predictions which forecast the same person or occurrence.

4. Persons or characters that have similar qualities or relations.

5. Duties or dangers that have some natural connection or kinship.

Of classified facts and events we may find a leading example in the festivals of the Jews; in the great facts of Hebrew history, such as the passing out of Egypt, the passing through the sea, the passing into Canaan; or the prominent events of our Lord's career, His birth, baptism, temptation, transfiguration, crucifixion and resurrection and ascension.

Of grouped teachings and precepts, we may instance those which concern unselfish giving, secret praying, perpetual watching; or the various instructions scattered through Scripture upon such subjects as separation, service, and reward.

Of predictions, first of all, those which foretell the Messiah's first and second advents; then those that forecast Jewish history; then the destiny and doom of the nations of the world.

Of persons and characters, how naturally we group together Abraham, Moses, Aaron and Joshua; Ezra and Nehemiah; the various *women*, so conspicuous in the Bible: Miriam, Deborah, Esther, Mary of Bethlehem, Mary of Bethany, Mary of Magdala, Anna, Elizabeth, etc.

Of duties and dangers, praying, witnessing and giving; and the corresponding perils, carnality, unbelief and slothfulness.

This principle of classification, thoroughly carried out, would reduce the whole of Scripture to a consistent system of teaching, where one fact or truth offsets another and modifies and qualifies it.

To classify all the teachings of the Word of God on *affliction* would reveal a consistent body of truth of marvelous extent and value. For instance:

Afflictions are not accidental or incidental, but providential—of divine appointment (Ps. 66:11; 1 Thess. 3:3).

Not a mark of His anger, but of His love, and fatherly yearning for our profit (Heb. 12).

To be borne not only with patience, but with rejoicing on account of their results (Rom. 5:1–5).

To be abundantly recompensed in the future perfection and glory of the believer (2 Cor. 4).

Sometimes affording an opportunity for vindication of God, as in the case of Job 1, 2.

Always affording opportunity for the display of the supporting strength of God (2 Cor. 12).

The teachings of Scripture concerning *conscience* are well worthy of being classified:

Common to all men (Prov. 20:27; Rom. 2:14, 16).

A tender and weak conscience to be respected (Rom. 14:2).

The source of happiness and misery (Prov. 14:14; Acts 23:1).

To be kept void of offense, etc. (Gen. 42:21).

Capable of defilement (Titus 1:15).

Similarly, it is most useful to group and systematize Bible teachings on covetousness, discipleship, faith, forgiveness, grace, humility, idolatry, judgment, love, meekness, obedience, patience, peace, perseverance, praise, prayer, the promises, repentance, self-denial, sin, temptation, truth, unbelief, wisdom, worship, etc.

The full teaching of the Word upon *Righteousness*, and its relations to Law and Grace, may be found in Romans 3:9–28, where at least seven particulars are grouped together:

(1) By nature and habit, all men are without Righteousness.
(2) By Law, all Righteousness is impossible to a transgressor.
(3) Apart from Law, Righteousness is divinely provided.
(4) This Righteousness depends upon Faith in Jesus Christ.
(5) Righteousness is the free gift of Grace through Redemption.
(6) Righteousness involves the pretermission of past sins.
(7) The Righteousness of God is not imperiled in the sinner's Justification.

"*The Things of Christ*," form a special matter of revelation as to which our Lord promised that the Spirit would take and show them unto us (John 16:14, 15). Search will show what these things are, such as:

The Rest of Christ (Matt. 11:27–30).
The Divine Sonship (Matt. 17:16, 17).
The Perpetual Presence (Matt. 28:20; John 14:23).
The Peace of Christ (John 14:27).
The Knowledge of Christ (Phil. 3:10).
The Faith of Christ (Rom. 3:22; Gal. 2:20).
The Mind of Christ (Phil. 2:5; 1 Pet. 4:1).
The Intercession of Christ (Heb. 2:17, 18; 4:14, 16).
The Body of Christ (Rom. 12; 1 Cor. 12; Eph. 4:4–13).
The Cross of Christ (Gal. 6:14).
The Love of Christ (2 Cor. 5:14; Eph. 3:19).
The Power of Christ (2 Cor. 12:9)
The Life of Christ (Gal. 2:20).
The Law of Christ (Gal. 6:2).
The Stature of Christ (Eph. 4:13).
The Coming of Christ (2 Thess. 2:1).

"The Things of the Spirit" are also referred to in 1 Corinthians 2:14.

These concern His person and work, beautifully comprised under a threefold aspect, as the Spirit of *Life* (1 Cor. 3:6; Rom. 8:2); of *Light* (1 Cor. 4:6; Gen. 1:3), and of *Love* (Rom. 5:5; Eph. 4:23).

These three briefly comprehend all His offices and activities, imparting light upon truth and duty, communicating divine life, and shedding abroad in the heart the Love of God, so that we love both God and man.

Hence, the Things of the Spirit include our *attitude* toward Him, set forth under three main warnings; we are not to:

Resist Him, as the Spirit of Life (Acts 7:51; Heb. 10:29).

Quench Him, as the Spirit of Light (1 Thess. 5:19).

Grieve Him, as the Spirit of Love (Eph. 4:30).

The *figures* by which the Spirit's character and work are expressed are also very helpful.

Water, as diffused in the atmosphere, distilling in dew, descending in rain.

Oil, as connected with anointing.

Breath or *atmosphere*, the secret of vitality.

The *Dove*, the one bird that secrets no *gall*, etc.

Two prayers of Paul for the Ephesians are on record; they stand out prominent in that epistle and are the only prayers of any length which are found in his epistles. Carefully studied, they are seen to be companion prayers, singularly corresponding to each other, and obviously meant as mutually complementary. They are not only similar in length, but in structure; one of them emphasizes the exceeding greatness of the *Power* of God, and the other the exceeding abundance of His *Love*. In the former, Paul expresses his ceaseless yearning that Ephesian disciples may have the spirit of wisdom and revelation in the knowledge of Him, the eyes of their hearts being so enlightened as to know to what exalted destiny He calls and appoints them, and how immeasurable the power by which He perfects them for glory. In the latter, he shows like solicitude that they should be so strengthened in spirit as to be able, rooted and grounded in love, themselves to comprehend the infinite dimensions of God's gracious purpose toward them and know His unknowable love, if only by learning that it cannot be fully known but passeth understanding. Thus each prayer covers its own ground, but taken together they cover all that it is most desirable to know of God in Christ. Moreover, the *order* is important; they could not exchange places; the former is for a spiritual *vision*; the latter is for a spiritual *experience*. It is a greater thing to be so rooted and grounded in love as to know God's love by a like love, than to be so illumined as to know His power without possessing a like power. In one case we get a glimpse of what God can do; in the other we have a fellowship in His nature and interpret Him by a like experience. We are reminded of the order of *creation* first *light*, then *life*. Few things in the whole compass of Scripture yield richer results by comparison than these two prayers, where the order of the first and second could not be reversed.

The Biblical teaching as to *Satan, his wiles and assaults*, and how God *turns* his whole malignant testing and afflicting of saints into a blessing, can be seen only as we thus classify and systematize many different testimonies and historic examples. He appears in many aspects, characters and activities, such as the following:

1. A *fowler, spreading his snares*, to entice and entangle (Ps. 91:3). But God uses these to make us wary and watchful, like a bird (Prov. 1:17).

2. A *captor, binding and enslaving* (2 Tim. 2:26; Luke 13:11, 17). But again this makes God's unloosing and delivering the more conspicuous.

3. A *sower of tares in the field* (Matt. 13:39), designed to counterfeit discipleship. But the Lord uses this to show how dangerous it is to trust to outward appearance or venture on condemnatory judgments.

4. A *sifter with his sieve* (Luke 22:31–34). He would sift the chaff from the wheat, to let all the grain fall to the ground. But the Lord uses His sieve to reverse the process, and separates the chaff that He may gather and preserve the grain.

5. A *deceiver, deluding and blinding* his victims (1 Kgs. 22; Matt. 24:24; 2 Cor. 11:14). He means to deceive if possible the very elect. But God only uses him to compel His saints to test all teaching by the Word and the fruits in the life.

6. A *destroyer, with his scourge* and stake in the flesh (Job 1, 2; 2 Cor. 12:7–10). God uses him to develop patience, to exhibit His strength that is made perfect in weakness, and mature the martyr spirit.

7. A *warrior arming sinners* with his panoply, and carrying on war against God and saints (Rev. 20). God uses his worse assaults to make the final conquest of Christ the more glorious.

Further examination will reveal much more of this marvelous teaching, of which the above is a brief and partial outline.

A kindred subject, developed by such classification, is the *"Devices"* of the Devil, referred to in 2 Corinthians 2:11. This suggests his subtle inventions and machinations for betraying souls into error and evil. Comparative study shows the following as his main methods:

Diversion, turning the mind from things great to small, the unseen and eternal to the visible and temporal (2 Cor. 4:4).

Delusion, lies and wiles (2 Cor. 11:14; Eph. 6:11; 2 Thess. 2:11; Gen. 3:4; Ezek. 13:22); by denials, evasions, misrepresentations.

Doubt, inducing hesitation, by a "gospel of negation," leading to uncertainty, mental and moral (Rom. 14:23).

Double-mindedness, compromise, trying to serve God and mammon (Matt. 6:24; 2 Cor. 6:14; 7:1; Lev. 20:24–27).

Darkness, enveloping the soul in gloom, either of imaginary difficulty, alienation from God, or despair (Is. 50:10).

Deadness, substituting "dead works" for living, form of godliness without its power, ritualism, etc. (Heb. 6:1; 9:14).

Delay, procrastinating all that is good, leading men to put off the time of decision and action (Acts 22:25; 26:28).

Such comparison and classification of Scripture testimony has a *corrective* value. For example, there has always been a tendency to deny or evade the *personality of the devil*, and construe all references to Satan and satanic influence as referring to the working of the innate depravity of the human heart, or the subtle attraction of vicious surroundings and associations.

But when the various references to the devil in Scripture are compared and collated such views are corrected and are seen to be irreconcilable with the Scripture testimony.

1. First of all, *personal terms* and names and titles are repeatedly applied to Satan, as distinctly as to any historic personage or the incarnate Son of God.

2. Again, personal *utterances, plans and activities* are constantly ascribed to him, and particularly a superior subtlety and strategy to that of which man is capable.

3. Again, the *temptations* with which he assailed Adam in his innocence and our Lord in His sinlessness preclude the idea of a perverse human *self* as their source and suggestion.

4. *Again,* the devil is represented as *entering into* Judas, and *filling the heart* of Ananias and Sapphira to lie to the Holy Ghost—as beguiling Eve, etc.

5. Again, the devil is expressly *distinguished* from the world and the flesh in several passages of Scripture, notably Ephesians 2:2, 3; James 4; 1 John 2, 3, 4.

6. Yet again, our Lord's mission was and is to *destroy the devil* and his works, Him that had the power of death, etc., which is meaningless if he be not a personality separate from man.

7. Finally, his *doom is personal* and individual—and though man, if he persists in sin, is involved in it, it is a separate condemnation on separate grounds (Matt. 25).

29

Comparison and Contrast

AGAIN, WE REPEAT:
Scripture must be compared with itself, carefully and minutely. The comparative frequency with which words or phrases recur, and in what connection, is of the utmost significance and importance, suggesting singular confirmations of truth, progressive teaching and instructive variations and complementary ideas. The two Testaments will be seen as mutual counterparts and even their differences as not discordances but essential to correspondence and completeness.

Comparison often becomes contrast by revealing unlikeness as well as likeness. To observe wherein things differ is as important for classification as to discover wherein they agree. In the Scriptures, truth is often taught by placing side by side two or more precepts, persons, events or experiences which are opposite or apposite to each other, that attention may the more surely be called to their joint lesson.

The two narratives of blind Bartimeus and the publican Zaccheus, both men of Jericho, are companion accounts and should not be separated by chapter division. They illustrate three *diversities:* those of human need; of modes of approach to Christ; and of His dealing with souls; yet behind this diversity, the sublime unity of His love, compassion and power to save and help.

Bartimeus	*Zaccheus*
Poor beggar, blind, sitting by the wayside.	Rich publican climbing a tree.
Intent on asking alms.	Intent on seeing Jesus.
Hears the throng moving.	Sees the crowd passing.
Asks what it means.	Knows what it means.
Cries after Jesus.	Is called by Jesus.
Supplicates for mercy.	Is asked for hospitality.
The multitude rebuke him.	They murmur against Christ.
He persists in his prayer.	Our Lord, in His purpose.
Jesus stands and waits for him.	Zaccheus stands, announces his purpose.
Christ asks: What wilt thou?	Zaccheus asks himself as to duty.
He answers, "Sight."	Zaccheus answers, "Right."
Jesus says, Receive thy Sight.	Salvation is come, etc.
Immediate sight.	Immediate salvation.
Bartimeus follows Christ.	Zaccheus makes restitution, etc.

Law and grace are constantly held up in contrast:

The Law	*Grace*
Given by Moses.	And truth by Jesus Christ.
Graven on stone.	Fleshy tablets of the heart.
The letter killeth.	The Spirit quickeneth.
The glory fadeth.	The glory excelleth.
The veiled face.	The unveiled face.
Mt. Sinai and terrors.	Mt. Zion and attractions.
Emphasis on works.	Emphasis on faith.
Life by doing.	Life by believing.
Brings curse.	Brings blessings.
Commands but does not enable.	Enjoins and enables.
Leaves without excuse.	Supplies advocate.
Knows no pardon.	Reconciles and atones.
Knowledge of sin.	Knowledge of God.
Condemns.	Redeems, etc.

Similar contrasts are presented between the old and new, the former and latter things, the two Covenants, the present evil age and the age and ages to come, etc.

A most instructive contrast is suggested when we set, side by side, John 16:8–11, and Acts 24:25. In each case there is a threefold conviction of sin, righteousness and judgment; in one case wrought by the Spirit and gospel of grace in a penitent sinner; in the other, by conscience and the terrors of the law in an unrepenting evil doer. The Spirit leads to Salvation; the law and conscience only to despair and remorse. Dr. A. J. Gordon put the contrast very forcibly:

Legal Conviction	*Evangelical Conviction*
Of sin as committed.	Of sin as pardoned.
Of righteousness as impossible.	Of righteousness as imputed.
Of judgment, as impending.	Of judgment as abolished.

Worldly and Heavenly Wisdom are often contrasted, as in 1 Corinthians 1—3, and particularly in the following points:

Worldly Wisdom	*Heavenly Wisdom*
Weapons—Enticing, beguiling words.	Demonstration of Spirit.
Weakness—Unable to make faith stand.	Power of God.
Worldliness—Essential in spirit and method.	Of God.
Ignorance—Knowing nothing as it ought.	Knowledge and certainty.
Insufficiency—Eye, ear and heart cannot reveal.	Revelation of Spirit.
Limitations—Knowing only "spirit of Man."	Spirit of God.
Incapacity—To receive or perceive.	Illumination from God.

The contrast between the *use* and *abuse* of temporal possessions may be seen vividly by comparing Luke 12:33, 34 with 1 Timothy 6:17–19. "Sell that ye have and give alms."   "Charge them that are rich," etc.

Contrast is manifestly meant in 1 Corinthians 3:12:

"Gold, silver, precious stones"—"Wood, hay, stubble."

The former, advancing in value; the latter decreasing. Wood may be wrought, carved, polished into artistic beauty though still unable to endure the ordeal of fire; even hay, more inflammable, is useful for fodder: but stubble is mere refuse fit only for the fuel for flame. How delicately is here suggested that worldly wisdom, though it cannot stand God's searching tests, may present many beautiful forms in poetry, art and philosophy; and deceive by outward attractiveness. And there seems a designed descent from these highest forms of culture, toward the lower sensuous levels of worldliness and selfishness, and at last the most degrading and debasing sensuality and bestiality; on the other hand we may build upon the rock foundation a character and conduct, teaching and living, which will not only be as enduring as precious metals, surviving the fiery ordeal, but purified by it, and shining with the luster and radiance of gems.

Second Corinthians 4:7—5:9 is a paragraph of continuous contrasts, between what is seen and unseen, temporal and eternal, outward and inward, visible and invisible, material and spiritual, earthly and heavenly; between affliction and glory, being at home in the body and at home with the Lord, faith and sight, dying and living.

Of all these ten contrasts, the former members of each belong in one group and are akin; the latter members equally inseparable. What is seen, temporal, etc., belong to the realm of death; what is unseen and eternal to the realm of Life, and sight and faith are the respective organs of vision in the two realms; only sight which rightly sees in its own sphere, is blind to the other and cannot interpret the relation of the two; but faith not only sees its own realm, but all that sight sees beside, and is a true interpreter of both realms. Sight refuses what faith chooses and inversely, and knows only the present, while faith foretastes the future.

Satan as *Hinderer* is contrasted with the Holy Spirit as *Helper* (1 Thess. 3:18; Rom. 8:26, etc.). In these leading texts, the words are most meaningful. To "hinder" means to *cut into*, as a trench is dug to hinder an approaching foe; and "helpeth" hints at lending a hand, giving a lift with another. These two simple texts array the spirit of all evil and the Spirit of all good in opposition to each other: the one to obstruct our way and prevent progress; the other to take hold with us, helping us lift and carry our load, and urging us forward.

The *new man* and the *old man* or man of old—the former unregenerate self—(Rom. 6:5–14; Col. 3:5–14; Eph. 4:22–24). The metaphor—two men with all that pertains to a man—is consistently maintained; each is represented as having his own individual *image, members, attire, walk, standing* and *state,* and *master.*

The old man bears the image of the world, flesh, devil; and his fatherhood is of the devil; his members, the lusts of the flesh, and of the eyes and the pride of life, to be mortified—they are members of unrighteousness, used unto sin that leads to death and must be put to death to avoid incurring deeper death. The attire of the old man is his habits, to be put off as infected and defiling, unbecoming the new man, etc. He has his walk or manner of life, his path away from God, his standing—condemnation, and his state—corruption; dead in trespasses and sins, incapable of holy fellowship, his master is sin and Satan.

The new man is God's own Creation. His attire is supernatural and sevenfold, with love as the girdle about all the rest, his main ornament the meek and quiet spirit. His walk with God, his path onward and upward; His standing, acceptance in the beloved; his state, righteousness and holiness; complete in Christ, his Master the Lord Jesus Himself, etc.

The value of careful comparison is always found to be twofold; revealing both points of likeness and unlikeness, it teaches both by *resemblance* and by *contrast.*

For example, in Ephesians and Colossians are two passages of Scripture so strikingly alike as to suggest a designed parallelism; yet so far unlike as to suggest a designed appositeness, each complementing the other, and together exhibiting the complete truth. The double column will help in comparing the corresponding clauses and showing points of likeness and unlikeness.

These passages are obviously meant as companions—both a lesson on privilege and power of being filled, the first with the *Spirit,* and the second, with the *Word.* Both exhort children to obedience to parents: one because it is ethically right: the other, because it is spiritually well pleasing unto the Lord. One reminds us that for whatsoever good thing any one doeth he shall receive of the Lord; and the other that for whatsoever wrong, and in both cases without respect of persons. And so at every point the comparison and contrast both help to convey the complete conception and instruction designed. We put in capitals the leading injunctions, and change the punctuation to what seems the more correct.

EPHESIANS 5:18 TO 6:9	COLOSSIANS 3:16 TO 4:1
BE NOT DRUNK WITH WINE, WHEREIN IS EXCESS; BUT BE FILLED WITH THE SPIRIT;	LET THE WORD OF CHRIST DWELL IN YOU RICHLY IN ALL WISDOM;
Speaking to one another in psalms and hymns and spiritual songs, singing and making melody in your heart to the Lord;	Teaching and admonishing one another; In psalms and hymns and spiritual songs, singing with grace in your hearts to the Lord;
In the name of our Lord Jesus Christ, giving thanks always for all things unto God and the Father;	And whatsoever ye do in word or deed, do all in the name of the Lord Jesus, giving thanks to God and the Father by him.
Submitting yourselves one to another in the fear of God.	
Wives, submit yourselves unto your own husbands, as unto the Lord. . . .	Wives, submit yourselves unto your own husbands, as it is fit in the Lord.
Husbands, love your wives, even as Christ also loved the Church. . . .	Husbands, love your wives, and be not bitter against them.
Let every one of you in particular so love his wife even as himself; and the wife [see] that she reverence her husband.	
Children, obey your parents in the Lord: for this is right.	Children, obey your parents in all things: for this is well pleasing unto the Lord.
Honor thy father and mother . . . that it may be well with thee. . . .	
And, ye fathers, provoke not your children to wrath: but bring them up in the nurture and admonition of the Lord.	Fathers, provoke not your children to anger, lest they be discouraged.
Servants, be obedient to them that are your masters according to the flesh, with fear and trembling, in singleness of your heart, as unto Christ;	Servants, obey in all things your masters according to the flesh; not with eyeservice, as menpleasers; but in singleness of heart, fearing God:
Not with eyeservice, as menpleasers; but as the servants of Christ, doing the will of God from the heart; with good will doing service, as to the Lord, and not to men;	And whatsoever ye do, do it heartily, as to the Lord, and not unto men; knowing that of the Lord ye shall receive the reward of the inheritance; for ye serve the Lord Christ.
And, ye masters, do the same things unto them, forbearing threatening; knowing that your Master also is in heaven;	
Knowing that whatsoever good thing any man doeth, the same shall he receive of the Lord, whether he be bond or free.	But he that doeth wrong shall receive for the wrong which he hath done;
Neither is there any respect of persons with him.	And there is no respect of persons.

30

Systematic and Progressive Teaching

EVEN A CURSORY GLANCE SHOWS THAT, where forty writers jointly contribute to one volume, with no chance of conferring together, there can be no systematic development of truth; yet, in a book, meant primarily as a moral and spiritual guide, in knowledge of both truth and duty, such system is desirable and needful, for only so can two leading purposes be secured: first, that any important subject, needing to be unfolded, shall find adequate treatment; and second, that there shall be progressive and exhaustive teaching, without either deficiency in fullness, useless repetition, or conflict of opinion. This department of Bible study can have here only an outline, for lack of space; yet it is of too great importance to be altogether omitted, and the reader who desires to pursue the subject further may find whole volumes devoted to its ampler treatment.*

It is a literary miracle, to be accounted for only on a superhuman philosophy, that in a book where all such systematic unity is impracticable, in the nature of the case, such marvelous features are found as the following which surprise more and more as new study more perfectly reveals them:

1. There is, quite uniformly, a peculiar significance in *first mention.* Whenever any person, place, important word, or subject is first referred

---

* *God's Living Oracles,* and especially *The Bible and Spiritual Criticism,* by the same author, being *Exeter Hall Lectures,* published by Baker & Taylor.

to in Scripture, all subsequent recurrence of the same is forecast, or hinted; so that such first glimpse indicates its relation to the entire testimony and teaching of Scripture. The Spirit of God thus supplies in such primary mention a clue to all that follows on the same topic.

2. There is, again, a system of *illustrative mention*—an example or pattern of every important duty or danger, right or wrong principle or practice, once for all being provided. There is at least one such exhibition and exemplification of every form of virtue or vice, beauty or deformity, in character or conduct—a representative instance, with a corresponding example of God's method of dealing with it in judgment or approval.

3. There is, yet again, an *exhaustive* treatment of every leading subject. Scattered hints are found interspersed through Scripture; but, as though to aid even the simplest understanding and leave the most cursory reader without excuse, somewhere, from Genesis to Revelation, the mind of God is fully revealed on all major matters, the scattered rays of light being gathered up and focused at one point.

4. There is also *consecutive* and *progressive* teaching. If from the first to the last reference to a subject, the intermediate mention of it is traced, there will be found often, if not always, an advance from what is rudimental and fundamental to what is higher and completer, but which can only be understood when first principles have been taught; so that when the last mention is reached it is like placing the capstone upon a building.

Of each of these laws, a few representative instances are offered as examples.

1. Primary mention. The very first words of the Scripture: "In the Beginning, God," are a valuable first lesson. God is the universal Beginning of all truth and duty. Everything good finds in Him its source and its spring, alike the Author of Creation and the New Creation.

The first reference to the Holy Spirit is in verse 2: "And the Spirit of God moved upon the face of the waters." Thus our first glimpse of the Spirit is as a bird brooding over the abyss of chaos and brining forth from it, as by a process of divine incubation, order out of confusion and cosmos out of chaos—light out of darkness and life out of death. What a forecast of all the work of the Spirit in the realm of the moral chaos, developing cosmos and light, life and love.

Light is first mentioned in verse 3 and it is remarkable that it is not said like all that follows to be "formed," "made" or "created," but called forth—commanded to be—to shine. In the expressive original "God said: *'Let light be!' and light was!'* Another forecast. For, throughout Scripture light is the name and equivalent of God, the uncreated One, it is never regarded as a created substance, but as uncreated and a creative agency.

Thus the Spirit of God forecasts, at the beginning, what He is afterward to unfold more fully, imparting a prophetic quality to all Scripture by which a fragment serves to indicate the whole body of truth, as a single bone, to a comparative anatomist, hints the whole skeleton of an extinct species of animal, or to a botanist, one fossil leaf, the whole structure of a plant.

"I find in Scripture," wrote Benjamin Wills Newton, "a principle of interpretation which, I believe, if conscientiously adopted, will serve as an unfailing guide as to the mind of God, as contained therein; the very first words on any subject of which the Holy Ghost is going to treat are the keystone of the whole matter.

2. Illustrative mention (Gen. 4). Cain and Abel are the first representatives of unbelief and faith, disobedience and surrender, hate and love, murder and martyrdom; with corresponding examples of Jehovah's curse and blessing. If the whole body of Scripture be examined it will be found to contain one and generally only one, conspicuous, illustrative example of every type of both good and evil. Abraham is the typical man of faith; Moses, the representative leader, lawgiver and mediator; Aaron, the typical High Priest; Ahab, the idolatrous ruler; Elijah, the model reformer; David, the Psalmist-King; Abaslom, the demagogue; Daniel, the pattern exile and captive; Nebuchadnezzar, the example of self-glory; Isaiah, the Messianic seer; Peter, the model confessor; Paul, the pattern convert; Judas, the typical traitor, etc. And of each form of crime with God's abhorrence of it and judgment upon it, at least one summary instance is given, as in the case of the rebellion and profanation of Korah and his company; the hypocritical lie of Ananias and Sapphira; the smiting of the persecuting Herod, etc.

3. Exhaustive mention. James 1:18–25, covers the practical value and virtue of the Word of God: called "The Word of *Truth*"—the last of six instances where this phrase is found. It is the word of *Life*, the generative seed whereby God begat us (1 Pet. 1:23); "the *Engrafted* word," suggesting also lifegiving power. It is the Rule of Life, to be received with meekness, of which we are to be "doers," the measure and model of character and conduct. Last of all, it is the "Perfect Law of Liberty," a mirror for self-revelation and self-regulation, obedience to it being freedom not bondage. What a summary! The Word of God is to the doer, light, life, liberty; a revealer of God and self, truth and duty; it makes and molds character; our attitude is to be receptive, reflective, retentive, that precept may be turned into practice.

4. Of successive and progressive mention, we may instance "*the lamb*," or "*firstling of the flock*," first referred to in Genesis 4:4 and last, in Revelation 22:3 in connection with God's enthroned and glorified Lamb. Now, if between these two mentions, every intermediate reference be traced to the lamb as connected with sacrifice a remarkable succession and progression will be found, of which we here indicate a few prominent stages:

Genesis 22. A sacrificial lamb *provided* by Jehovah.

Exodus 12. A Paschal Lamb—the *sprinkled blood*.

Leviticus 16. A *double* offering; for *Expiation* and *Removal*.

Isaiah 53. The Paschal Lamb—a *type* of *Messiah*.

John 1. *Jesus* of Nazareth *identified as God's Lamb*.

1 Peter 1. The slain Lamb, *raised* and *glorified*.

Revelation 5. The Lamb identified with the *Lion* and the *Book*.

Here it will be seen that, in every new reference something is added not taught before—and that when we reach the closing book of the whole collection we have learned that the firstling of the flock offered by Abel was the first forecast and type of Him whom God Himself provides for His altar, whose blood is the refuge of sinners, who both expiates guilt and takes it away; who is the vicarious Savior, now raised, glorified, enthroned, etc. This is the more surprising inasmuch as the books which compose the Bible are not in chronological order; and yet, as they stand, truth generally is found unfolded in logical order, as though the Author of Scripture had not been indifferent even to the arrangement of books in the canon.

Another striking instance of progressive teaching is John 1—11. Taking chapter 1:4 as the key: "In Him was Life," these 11 chapters progressively unveil the meaning of these four words:

1. The human condition of His imparting Life—receiving by believing (1:12, 13).

2. The Divine condition of such impartation—the new birth from above (v. 3).

3. The gift of Life for the asking and its immediate reception (4:10–29).

4. The Life giving power of Christ, illustrated in physical healing.

5. The Bread of Life, imparting and sustaining life (v. 6).

6. The Believer receiving and transmitting Life (7:37–39; 8:12).

7. The Light of Life—a new vision of God implied in Life (v. 9).

8. The Life more abundant found in the Good Shepherd (v. 10).

9. The Life including the Body in Resurrection (v. 11).

There is, even to the concluding chapter, a continuous unfolding of Eternal Life as the gift of God in Christ, received by faith, realized in regeneration, satisfying spiritual craving, feeding and nourishing the soul, and culminating in resurrection triumph over death.

The Death of our Lord Jesus Christ is the theme of progressive teaching. In the New Testament there are no less than 100 references in the twenty-one epistles to its bearings upon, and relations to, both God and man, with no real repetition, but a steady development of doctrine, every successive mention being an addition and advance upon previous teaching.

In the Epistles to the Romans is laid the great foundation: His death, the ground of pardon and Justification, reconciliation, and preservation in His life. In Corinthians there is an advance to the conception of Identification with Him in death and resurrection and the indwelling of the Holy Spirit. In Galatians we are seen to have been crucified in Him and with Him and to live by His life, walking with Him in newness of life. In Ephesians we are exalted with Him to the Heavenlies, etc. And so on to the end, each epistle carrying us further in the conception of, incorporation into, and identification with, the crucified and Risen Christ.

Such *successive* and *progressive* mention of truth might be expected if there is a divine method; it follows as a natural sequence. This is properly called a *"structured law"*; for it reminds us of a building process, the first mention being as the cornerstone and the last the capstone, and all between, the structure of truth resting on the first and reaching toward the last. Mr. Newton says, "the only unfailing method of interpreting Scripture is the structural."

All effective teaching follows a process of development, corresponding to the development of those taught, one lesson preparing the next; learning advances by successive stages from the lower to the higher.

Our Lord Himself foretells a period of revelation in the economy of the Spirit, surpassing even His own in fullness and clearness.

"I have yet many things to say unto you, but ye cannot bear them now; howbeit, when He, the Spirit of Truth is come, He will guide you into all truth," etc. (John 16:12, 13).

In three respects at least this was true:

1. He would enlarge their capacity to understand truth.
2. He would amplify and apply the teachings of Christ.
3. He would reveal truth not before ready for its unveiling.
4. He would present old truths in new forms and illustrations.
5. He would magnify and glorify the Person of Christ.

All this and more marked the era of Pentecostal outpouring. At once truth, previously revealed, became plain and new truth was unveiled. Disciples now found the deeper meaning of our Lord's utterances and had new apprehension of Him in all His offices as Prophet, Priest and King.

One striking example of the *new forms* in which even our Lord's teachings might be presented after the Spirit was outpoured is seen by comparing the parable of the vine and the branches in John 15, with the teaching of the same essential truth in Romans 12, 1 Corinthians 12, Ephesians 4, etc.

If we compare the two metaphors—the Vine and the Body—we detect striking resemblances and correspondences:

The vine and branches	The body and members
The sap	The blood
The vegetable life	The animal soul
The leaves as breathing organs	The lungs and respiration

The interlocking fibers	The interwoven muscles
The circulation of the sap	The circulation of the blood
The growth of the vine	The growth of the body
The reproductive power	The reproductive power
The excision of dead branches	The excision of diseased limbs
Vegetable exudiations	Animal perspiration
Branches apart from the vine.	Limbs sundered from the body.

And so in other respects, singular correspondences. Yet our Lord left this higher method of conveying the same truth till the Spirit forming the body of Christ and pervading it with the breath of His divine life should thus supply a key to this new metaphor, unintelligible before.

If the teaching of truth, after Pentecost, is examined and compared with that previously taught, this additional amplitude of scope and transparency of meaning will appear, in scores, if not hundreds, of particulars, such as the vital relation of the believer to Christ; his identity with Him in death, burial, resurrection, ascension, session at the right hand of God and second appearing in glory; the new application of the Gospel of Grace to all nations and the new man made by the union of Jew and Gentile; the church as a called-out body, and its mission to and separation from the world; the man of sin and the final apostasy; the consummation of salvation in the city of God and new creation. These and much more waited for their fuller presentation in doctrinal form, until He the Spirit of Truth was come. We must therefore *count Pentecost as opening a new and final era* in the revelation of the highest spiritual truth.

This general progress of thought reminds us of a pyramid, where all lines and angles meet in the top stone which is itself the whole pyramid in miniature—a model of the entire structure. In the Apocalypse all the leading thoughts, prophecies, promises and warnings of the rest of Scripture, and all the leading metaphors and symbols and figures of speech, previously used, reappear. We might say that it is a sort of compendium of the whole Bible. Whatever the date of its composition it could find but one place in the structure of the Word—it must be the closing book, the capstone of the whole; and in the last chapters we find exactly what we first found in the first of Genesis—

the paradise with its river, tree of life, and Tabernacle of God with men—only with one difference—there shall be no more curse. Creation is displaced by the new creation and death and the grave, sin and Satan, are no more. Thus the whole Bible exhibits consecutive thought, progressive teaching; from cornerstone to capstone there is a constant ascent, advance and development toward ultimate completion and perfection.

Not less conspicuous are some other features of the Bible as a whole, in its capacity as a moral and spiritual counselor:

1. *Its silence and reserve*, as marvelous for what it does not contain as for what it does. Its Divine Author knows where to advance and where to arrest revelation, where silence is better than speech and where curiosity becomes intrusive and irreverent. We are not told whether there are "few that be saved," or when moral responsibility begins in a child, or just when the end of the age will come. Some things are left wisely under a veil.

2. *Its Individual Fitness*. Here is a magic mirror where every man may see himself, and find the thoughts of his heart revealed. Here is a universal oracle where every inquirer may find response to his own question and need, and as close fitting a guidance as though he were the only one requiring counsel. It is not like an armory with one style of armor, but one where each man finds his own coat of mail and weapons that fit him and no one else.

Such are some of the evidences that in the construction of the Bible there has been a Divine Designer and Builder at work.

31

Poetic Parallelism

ALL THE POETIC PORTIONS OF THE BIBLE are arranged in corresponding sentences, a sort of thought meter and melody. This is a remarkable provision for translation, since such parallelism of thought can be reproduced in any other language without sacrificing its beauty or pertinency, whereas verbal rhythm and rhyme might be difficult to transfer to a new tongue.

Parallelism is of five kinds: Apposite, Opposite, Synonymous, Synthetic, Inverted.

1. *Apposite:* where two or more parallel sentences are arranged so as to present the same or closely related thoughts, by way of correspondence or comparison. Thus Proverbs 3:5:

> Trust in the Lord with all thine heart;
> And lean not unto thine own understanding.

Here is one thought, *trusting in Jehovah*, is presented in both members, first positively, then negatively. The truly wise man trusts in God, and not in himself.

2. *Opposite:* where exactly opposite thoughts are contrasted. Thus Proverbs 10:7:

> The memory of the just is blessed;
> But the name of the wicked shall rot.

Here the sharp antithesis extends to all prominent words in both members.

3. *Synonymous*: where the same thought is repeated in equivalent terms and phrases. Thus Proverbs 1:4:

> To give subtlety to the simple;
> To the young man, knowledge and discretion.

4. *Synthetic*: where thoughts are built up into structural forms, like block upon block, cumulatively and often climactrically; before the whole idea is complete, several successive pairs of parallels may enter into the construction. Thus Proverbs 30:17:

> The eye that mocketh at his father,
> And despiseth to obey his mother:
> The ravens of the valley shall pick it out,
> And the young eagles [vultures] shall eat it.

Here two synonymous parallels are built up into one synthetic. Agur's Prayer, Proverbs 30: 7–9, and the passage from verses 24 to 28, are examples of still more complex synthetic parallelism. Some are very complicated; the correspondence between the various propositions reaches even to minor details; and the whole paragraph with its constructive parts crystallizes about one dominant idea (cf. Ps. 148:7–13; 19:7–11).

5. *Inverted*: where stanzas are so framed that, to perceive the true relations of the sentences we must begin at the extremes and move toward the center. Bishop Jebb calls this "Introverted." Thus Psalm 135:5–18:

> The idols of the heath are silver and gold,
> The work of men's hand;
>> They have mouths, but they speak not;
>> They have eyes, but they see not;
>> They have ears, but they hear not;
>> Neither is there any breath in their mouths.
> They who make them are like unto them;
> So are all they who put their trust in them.

The relation of the various lines and members will appear in the above arrangement, where correspondent clauses are placed directly in line with each other vertically.

To master this symmetric structure of poetic parts of the Bible is, as has been hinted, a help to intelligent *exposition* and *exegesis*. The mutual relation of the words and thoughts will not appear until we discover what phrases or sentences are parallel, and detect the thought-rhythm. Thus Psalm 10:4, reads, translating literally:

> The wicked in the height of his scorn:
>   "He will not require it
>   "There is no God!"
> *These* are all his thoughts.

Here the wicked is represented at the very apex and climax of daring impiety and blasphemy. His secret thought is: "God will not requite my sin," and from this denial of judgment the step is easy to the last and worst thought: "There is no God!"

Once more. Matthew 7:6:

> Give not that which is holy unto the dogs;
>   Neither cast ye your pearls before swine,
>   Lest they trample them under their feet,
> And turn again and rend you.

At first glance, all the latter half of this stanza would be referred to the swine. But every part of such a stanza demands its parallel, and the law of thought-rhyme leads us to construe the last line as the correspondent and complement of the first.

> Give not that which is holy unto the dogs,
> Lest they turn again and rend you.
> Neither cast ye your pearls before swine,
> Lest they trample them under their feet.

Parallelism is best and most fully exhibited in the books of Proverbs and Ecclesiastes.

Thus,

> A wise son maketh a glad father:
> But a foolish son is the heaviness of his mother.

Here the "wise son" corresponds to the "foolish," "gladness" to "heaviness," and "father" to "mother." The same parallelism of thought, with the addition of verbal rhyme and rhythm, would read somewhat thus:

> A son by wisdom makes his father glad,
> But he that's foolish makes his mother sad.

But nothing is here gained, thought-wise, and, in translation, it might much increase the difficulty, were it needful to find words in another tongue which would reproduce the metrical measures and the rhyme. But, where only the correspondence of ideas is to be preserved, the task is greatly simplified, and this illustrates one reason already assigned for the use of parallel structure in Hebrew poetry, that, in translating the Word of God into all other tongues, there might be no loss of force and beauty.

This matter, though having mainly to do with literary form and structure, sometimes concerns the thought and substance also, and should therefore be studied. A considerable portion of Holy Scripture is framed in parallelism, and, in many cases, this is not obvious as in the book of Proverbs, but concealed as in some discourses of our Lord. In the "Blackader Bible" the editor has discovered and exhibited many of these hidden beauties as in the Gospel according to John:

> In the beginning was the Word;
>> And the Word was with God,
>> And the Word was God;
> The same was in the beginning with God.

And, again:

> Let not your heart be troubled!
>> Ye believe in God,
>> Believe also in Me.
> In My Father's house are many mansions;
>> If it were not so I would have told you.
> I go to prepare a place for you,
> And if I go and prepare a place for you,
>> I will come again,
>> And receive you unto Myself;
> That, where I am, ye may be also, etc.

Matthew 11:28–30 is perhaps the best example of a concealed parallel structure, where the omission of one member must be supplied to complete the poetic stanza. Here are three injunctions, each enforced by two considerations; there should therefore be three promises, though only two are expressed; but, when the parallel structure is seen, the lacking member is easily suggested: Here the italics show the substance of the obvious missing member of this complex threefold parallelism, which has thus in all twelve members.

Injunction	Consideration	Promise
"Come unto Me."	"Labor, Heavy laden."	"I will give you Rest."
"Learn of Me."	"Meek, Lowly in heart."	"Ye shall find Rest unto your souls.
"Take My yoke."	"Easy, Light."	*"Ye shall rest even in your toils."*

Parallel structure is often hidden under the continuity of a paragraph, but is detected by close study, and when the grammatical and rhetorical members are seen in their relation, a passage takes on a crystalline beauty.

Thus, in Romans 10:8–10:

1. "The Word is nigh thee;
2.   Even in thy mouth,
3.   And in thy heart;
4. That is, the Word of Faith,
5.   Which we preach:
6. That, if thou shalt confess with thy mouth
7.   That Jesus is Lord;
8.   And shalt believe in thine heart,
9.   That God hath raised Him from the dead,
10. Thou shalt be saved;
11.   For, with the heart man believeth
12.   Unto righteousness;
13.   And with the mouth confession is made
14.   Unto Salvation."

By comparison, it at once appears that the following members, as above arranged, closely correspond, namely: 1 and 4; 2, 6, and 13; 3, 8, and 11; 10 and 14, etc. If, in all cases, this hidden parallelism were thus exhibited by an arrangement of clauses, much of what seems prose would be found to be poetry. Countless new beauties of correspondence would be disclosed that otherwise escape us, and, behind these verbal responses of thought or truth to one another, would be found not a few helps to the understanding of the substance of Scripture teaching.

In some cases, there is in the original both rhythm and rhyme, which it is not easy to convey in English.

Thus Isaiah said to Ahaz,

> If ye will not believe
> Surely ye shall not be established.

We might paraphrase this somewhat thus:

> If to believe ye are not able,
> Surely ye shall not be made stable;

or

> If in the Lord there is no confiding;
> Surely in strength there is no abiding.

The most conspicuous instance of rhythm and rhyme of words is in the original Greek of John 3:36:

> *Ho pistueōn eis ton Huion,*
> *Echei zōēn aiōnion.*
>> "Whoso doth on the Son believe
>> Doth Everlasting Life receive."

Here is a perfect Iambic couplet, with rhyme.

There are not a few other cases in which a student of the original finds almost as perfect versification. In Hebrews 12:12–15, the whole structure is beautifully metrical. One line is a perfect dactylic hexameter; another, a rough, irregular Iambic trimeter, and the last two lines are strictly metrical.

In 1 Thessalonians 4:16 is a marked example, in the Greek, of both metrical melody and onomatopoeia, or the expression of sense by sound. When intelligently read aloud, with proper taste, and appreciation of the force of vowels and consonants, it is as though we heard the blast and clang of the archangel's trumpet. Perhaps some idea of the rhetorical beauty of this passage might be conveyed by a paraphrase:

> For the Lord Himself shall from Heaven come down!
> And Archangel's voice, and God's trump shall sound;
> And the dead in Christ
> Shall first arise, etc.

But no English rendering can convey the awe-inspiring music of the original, where trumpets, cornets and clanging cymbals seem sounding all at once.

The introduction of such occasional metrical passages into the Word of God cannot be without design. We have given four conspicuous instances. In the first, we have a permanent lesson on faith as the basis of all fidelity and stability; in the second, on faith as the condition of salvation, the immediate gift of eternal life which is the central lesson of John's Gospel; in the third, we have the grand conclusion of the exhortation to faith in the Fatherhood of God in disciplinary correction; and, in the last, faith looks far into the future to the consummation of all things. These poetic passages seem meant to arrest attention, and emphasize a great truth by a unique form of statement.

Careful students discover whole epistles to be built up on a basis or plan of parallelism. Thus one writer suggests that the First Epistle to Timothy is so constructed.

A|1:1, 2. Benediction.
  B|3–20. Doctrine.
    C|2—3:13. Discipline.
      D|14, 15. Intended visit and interval.
       E|16. The mystery of godliness.
       E|4:1–12. The mystery of iniquity.
      D|13–16. Intended visit and interval.
    C|5—6:2. Discipline.
  B|3–21. Doctrine.
A|21. Benediction.
  The expansion of B (1:3–20):—
F|a|3, 4. The charge.
  b|5. Faith and a good conscience (defined).
    c|6–10. The shipwreck of "some."
      G|11. The glory of God in His Gospel.
       H|12. Paul, the "faithful" minister of Christ Jesus.
        J|13. Paul, the chief of sinners (unsaved).
         K|14. The abounding grace of our Lord.
         K|15. His mission of grace to sinners.
        J|15. Paul, the chief of sinners (saved).
       H|16. Paul, the "pattern" believer in Jesus Christ.
      G|17. The glory of God in Himself.

F|a|18. The charge.

   b|19. Faith and a good conscience (to be held fast).

      c|19, 20. The shipwreck of "some."*

Another writer finds a more comprehensive correspondence still, and traces the order of God's work in the light of the parallel arrangement of Scripture.

A. The Original Creation, Genesis 1:1 ("Heavens and earth").

  B. Ruin. Genesis 1:2 (Is. 45:18, Heb.) Cause: Satan's *first* rebellion.

    C. Earth blessed, but cursed because of sin.

      D. Mankind dealt with as a whole (Adam to Abram).

        E. Chosen Nation blessed.

          F. First appearing of Christ. Hebrews 9:26.

            G. Church (taken *out).* Acts 15:14.

When the Church is completed (Rom. 11:25) and "He returns for restitution of all things" (Acts 3:21), He will follow *reverse* order.

            G. Church (taken *up*). 1 Thessalonians 4:16, 17.

          F. Second appearing on earth. Heb. 9:28; Zech. 14:4.

        E. Chosen Nation blessed. Romans 11:25.

      D. Mankind as a whole ("All Gentiles") blessed. Acts 15:16.

    C. Curse removed and earth blessed and beautified. (Amos 9:13–15; Is. 35:1; Ps. 67:6).

  B. Satan's *final* rebellion. Revelation 20:7.

A. "New heavens and new earth," Revelation 21:1.

"Known unto God are all His works from 'the *beginning*' of the world" (Acts 15:18).**

---

* Geo. F. Trench.
** Morton W. Plummer.

32
The Scattered Proverbs of Scripture

THIS DEPARTMENT OF STUDY is quite apart from that of professed collections and arrangements of such wise sayings like the "books of wisdom." Dispersed throughout the whole Word of God are these occasional sententious utterances, brief maxims, part of whose beauty and value depends on the fact that a few well chosen words are used in which great truth is condensed. In many cases *antithesis* is designedly used, the opposing points of a contrasted statement serving, like the opposite sides of a forceps, to hold firmly and present boldly an ethical or spiritual truth. A great service would be done to Bible readers if some collection of these scattered axioms or maxims could be carefully arranged. We give a few examples, partly to stimulate such further study. There are not less than 500 of these scattered axioms and proverbs, having singular brevity and beauty, variety and pertinency; some of them have so intimate a bearing on the immediate context as to be the text of which it is the discourse, as in Luke 12:15.

"Take heed and beware of covetousness; For a man's life consisteth not in the abundance of things which he possesseth."

Here, in the entire teaching that follows (vv. 16–59), there are only amplification and illustration of these three truths: first, the danger of covetousness; second the dignity and value of life; and third, false estimates or riches and the true estimate of treasure.

"Keep thee far from a false matter" (Ex. 23:7).

This is a representative injunction, the importance of which does not at first appear. The original words hint at a *painted sham* or *gilded counterfeit*. So understood, here is a warning for all time to come. It is a historical fact that the most subtle errors and evils, both in doctrine and practice, have been counterfeits and imitations of what is good, where, the closer the resemblance, the greater the risk. Satan's age-long business has been that of a counterfeiter: his worse snares are not found in systems openly antagonistic to God and truth, but in things half good and half evil, in half truths mixed with half lies, a skillful combination of what is attractive and what is repulsive, where all that is lawful or commendable is adulterated and corrupted by such mixture with its opposite. For example, false doctrine, corrupted worship, formal godliness, a Satanic synagogue, antichrist, lying wonders and miracles of falsehood, a false civilization or commonwealth, and the mystery of lawlessness. Whatever God gives to man as a blessing, Satan thus perverts into a curse, by devising something so like it as to deceive the unwary and if possible the very elect; and yet so unlike it as to be in fact antagonistic to it in spirit and in tendency. Compare Acts 20:30; James 2:26; 2 Timothy 3:5; Revelation 17; Matthew 24:4, 5; 2 Thessalonians 2:9; Revelation 17:8; 20:1, with 1:4.

In some cases in the original the contrast is marvelously conveyed, as in the following case, suggested in the apocalypse:

> *hē nymphē kai to arnion;*
> *hē pornē kai to thērion.*

This parallel and contrast cannot easily be conveyed in English. "The bride and the lamb"; "the harlot and the beast."

Thus, as far back as the giving of the Sinaitic Code of Law, God gave a brief caution, which has a vital bearing upon the whole future history of the race, warning men against the risk of being imposed upon by deceptive appearances and imitations of truth and goodness.

Sometimes such proverbs interpret the entire body of scriptural truth or serve to hint the whole secret of the contrasted experience of saints and sinners, as in our Lord's maxim:

> He that saveth his life shall lose it;
> But he that loseth his life for My sake, the
>   same shall save it.

This is the only such proverbial saying of our Lord which is substantially repeated in all four Gospel narratives (Matt. 10:39; 16:25; Mark 8:35; Luke 9:24; 17:33; John 12:25); and manifestly because it embodies a fundamental law both of redemptive blessing and redemptive service. "Life" here stands for self-interest and advantage: to save one's self is ultimate self loss; and to sacrifice self is ultimate self gain. Life, is the first of all the possessions that men value; because, without life, there can be nothing else possessed or enjoyed. Hence, life naturally stands for what men most value as the highest form of self-interest. And our Lord here contrasts those who put self life with all self-interest, foremost, with those who put God's interest foremost and for that surrender and sacrifice all that is dearest to self. He declares that those who thus give God preference over self shall find ultimately that they have only advanced and promoted their own highest interest; while those who for the time now present put self before God and jealously guard their own advancement will ultimately find that they have lost even the advantage they seemed to secure.

The universal hearing of such a proverbial precept as this, no words can convey. It interprets life, duty, sacrifice, service, reward; it shows self-denial to be not a final forfeiture but a temporary postponement. It links the temporal and the eternal and reveals their mutual relations, and it hints the essential law both of the worldly life and the saintly. The proverb takes the form of the paradox, purposely, that attention may be arrested by the contradiction in terms which covers perfect accord of sentiment.

Sometimes from a single book may be culled a whole body of brief and telling *maxims*. Of all the examples of this none surpass the Book of Daniel in the Old Testament and of Hebrews in the New, except those which, like the books of Psalms and Proverbs, naturally take the form of maxims, or are professedly collections and arrangements of wise sayings. In Daniel, we meet with a series of maxims, especially suitable to young men, for example:

"He purposed in his heart that he would not defile himself" (1:8).
"God revealeth the deep and secret things" (2:22).
"Those that walk in pride He is able to abase" (4:37).
"Thou art weighted in the balances and found wanting" (5:27).

"An excellent spirit was in him" (6:3).

"He believed in his God" (23).

"I kept the matter in my heart" (7:28).

"I had seen the vision, and sought for the meaning" (8:15).

"I set my face unto the Lord God to seek by prayer" (9:3).

"My comeliness was turned in me into corruption" (10:8).

"The people that do know their God shall be strong and do exploits" (11:32).

"They that be teachers shall shine as the brightness of the firmament; And they that turn many to righteousness as the stars forever and ever" (12:3).

"Stand in thy lot" (13).

In the Epistle to the Hebrews may be found between thirty and forty maxims, of which the following are examples:

Take heed (2:1; 3:12).

Lay aside (12:1).

Lay hold (6:18).

Hold fast (3:6, 14; 4:14; 10:23).

Consider Him (3:1; 12:3).

Harden not your hearts (3:8, 13, 15; 4:7).

Hear His voice (3:7, 15; 4:7).

Let us fear (4:1).

Labor to enter in (4:11).

Come boldly (4:16).

Draw nigh or near (7:19; 10:22).

Look for Him (9:28).

Look unto Him (12:2).

Look diligently (12:15).

Show diligence

Refuse not (12:25).

Despise not (12:5).

Faint not (12:5).

Cast not away (10:35).

Go on to perfection (6:1).

Go forth unto Him

Whose faith follow (13:7).

There are many more such maxims in this one epistle.

Several examples have already been cited and dwelt upon in this and former sections; but we instance some twenty or more from each Testament, culled almost at random, which serve to show how rich the Word of God is in these scattered sayings of wisdom, meant to be maxims and axioms for our guidance. Found at various points in the inspired Scriptures, they strike the mind at once as marvelously comprehensive, and sometimes as exhaustive of ethical and spiritual truth.

Be ye holy, for I the Lord your God, am holy (Lev. 19:2).

Be sure your sin will find you out (Num. 32:23).

Be strong and of good courage (Josh. 1:6).

The Lord recompense thy work (Ruth 2:12).

Thou, Thou only knowest the hearts (1 Kgs. 8:39).

Jeroboam sinned and made Israel to sin (1 Kgs. 15:30).

They feared Jehovah and served their own gods (2 Kgs. 17:33).

As the duty of every day required (Ezra 3:4).

The hand of our God is upon all them for good that seek Him (8:22).

Arise; for this matter belongeth unto thee!

We also will be with thee:

Be of good courage and do it (10:4).

The God of Heaven, He will prosper us.

Therefore we, His servants will arise and build (Neh. 2:20).

"Every one, over against his house" (3:28).

The builders, every one had his sword girded by his side (4:18).

The heathen perceived that this work was wrought of our God (6:16).

Cease to do evil

Learn to do well (Is. 1:16, 17).

The Lord alone shall be exalted;

And the idols He shall utterly abolish (2:17, 18).

Return unto me and I will return unto you (Mal. 3:7).

Bring ye all the tithes into the storehouse (10).

They that feared the Lord spake often one to another

And the Lord hearkened and heard it (16).

Abide in Me and I in you (John 15:4).

Whatsoever is not of faith is sin (Rom. 14:23).
He that is joined unto the Lord is one spirit (1 Cor. 6:17).
Not I but Christ (Gal. 2:20).
By love serve one another (Shaftesbury's coat-of-arms) (13).
Walk in the Spirit,
And ye shall not fulfill the lusts of the flesh (5:16).
Bear ye one another's burdens (6:2).
Every man shall bear his own burden (5).
Whatsoever a man soweth that shall he also reap (7).
Be filled with the Spirit (Eph. 5:19).
One thing I do (Phil. 3:13).
Our citizenship is in Heaven (20).
Be careful for nothing (4:6).
Ye are complete in Him (Col. 2:20).
Let the Word of Christ dwell in you richly in all wisdom (3:16).
Serve and wait (1 Thess. 1:9, 10).
Adorn the doctrine (Titus 2:10).
Be content with such things as ye have (Heb. 13:5).
We have here no continuing city (14).
The body with the spirit is dead (James 2:26).
Hope to the end (1 Pet. 1:13).
Keep yourselves in the love of God (Jude 1:21).
Hold fast till I come (Rev. 2:25).

A few of these scattered sayings should have a word of comment by the way:

"The Lord is with you while ye be with Him." Already referred to as the unique maxim of Azariah, this is the explanation of a thousand successes and disappointments of life (2 Chr. 15:2).

"The Lord is a God of knowledge;
By Him actions are weighed" (1 Sam. 2:3).

This probably suggested the awful metaphor "Tekel" in the writing on the wall (Dan. 5:27).

"Quit you like men, be strong" (1 Sam. 4:9; 1 Cor. 16:13).

This is specially remarkable as a maxim, originating with Philistine enemies of Israel, and addressed to the warriors of their own army, but adopted by the apostle and addressed to fellow disciples.

"Every man did that which was right in his own eyes" (Judg. 21:25). What a brief compendium of a state of anarchy!

"To obey is better than sacrifice" (1 Sam. 15:22).

Here is the great principle, illustrating such other utterances as Psalm 40:6–8; 51:16, 17, which it may have suggested:

"The Lord seeth not as man seeth: For man looketh on the outward appearance; but the Lord looketh upon the heart" (1 Sam. 16:7).

This remarkable saying might be written over the whole volume of Scripture, as the principle of all divine judgments.

"For we must needs die, and be as water spilt upon the ground, which cannot be gathered up again. Neither doth God respect any person. Yet doth He devise means that His banished be not expelled from Him" (2 Sam. 14:14).

This short poetic outburst of the woman of Tekoah has almost the ring of inspiration. What a view of the human side of death, its wastefulness and hopelessness! What a sublime view of God's impartiality and absolute rectitude! And what a marvelously condensed compendium of His redemptive scheme.

"We do not well: This day is a day of good tidings, and we hold our peace! Come—that we may go and tell" (2 Kgs. 7:9).

Can there be found a more beautiful lesson on missions than this from the lepers of Samaria? And how close the analogy! A world famine—abundance of supply—the guilt of selfish monopoly—the blessed privilege of going and telling the good news!

"So they read in the book of the law of God distinctly:
And gave the sense;
And caused them to understand the reading" (Neh. 8:8).

We suggest this as a motto for a church Bible school.

"Our God turned the curse into a blessing" (Neh. 13:2).

"I will curse your blessings" (Mal. 2:2).

How obviously these two sayings are mutually counterparts, presenting the two aspects of God's dealing, making the curse of foes and enemies a blessing to His own obedient friends and allies; but turning even outward blessing into a curse when received in unthankfulness and perverted by disobedience!

33

Divine Patterns and Encomiums

S O COMPREHENSIVE AND COMPLETE is this practical exhibit of doctrine and duty that probably there is no important precept or idea presented in Scripture without its corresponding pattern or ideal. This accomplishes two main results; first, it illustrates and incarnates truth in example; and, second, it brings what might be vague or obscure within the apprehension and comprehension of the simplest and humblest.

Already, in another connection, we have glanced at the Tent of meeting, and its counterpart, the Temple, as a pattern of a building for worship; but many other equally instructive models are supplied, of which the following may be cited as a few examples of divine patterns for human guidance:

1. First, we instance the pattern of *liberal giving*, on the part of His people, toward the making and furnishing of His sanctuary; an example without a parallel for universal participation, variety of offering, and liberal spirit (Ex. 35:5; 36:8).

One New Testament example of liberal giving to the necessities of saints is its counterpart (2 Cor. 8, 9).

2. Of a *moral code*, in the Decalogue, or Ten Words of Jehovah twice written by Him upon Tables of Stone (Ex. 20).

Its counterpart in the New Testament may be found in the sermon on the mount, where they may be traced some ten corresponding commands for human guidance, based on higher ethics (Matt. 5—7).

3. Of *acceptable prayer*, in the model furnished by our Lord to His disciples, singularly brief yet as singularly full and comprehensive: three petitions as to God, Himself—His name, kingdom, will; four, as to man—his wants, sins, leadership and deliverances. "After this manner therefore pray ye" (Matt. 6:9–13; Luke 11:2–4).

4. Of *holy living and loving*, obedience and suffering, in the supreme "example left us that we should follow His steps" (1 Pet. 2:21). Other minor examples are furnished of particular virtues as in Abraham, Daniel, Nehemiah; but in Him all virtues combine, and in perfection.

5. Of a *forgiven sinner*, in Saul of Tarsus, outwardly righteous, yet chief of sinners of his own sight, and who himself declared that he "obtained mercy that in him first Jesus Christ might show forth all long suffering for a *pattern* to them which should hereafter believe on Him to life everlasting" (1 Tim. 1:16).

6. Of a *church assembly*, presided over by the Holy Spirit, indwelt by Him, witnessing, working and warring for God, cemented by mutual love, pervaded by common self-sacrifice, and daily having additions of saved souls. Never before nor since has there been any such church pattern (Acts 2:4).

7. Of the *City of God*, the final community of the Redeemed, when all things are become new, where nothing enters that defiles, works abomination or makes a lie, and where all sin and sickness, sorrow and pain, darkness and death are forever banished (Rev. 21—22).

Upon some of these divine patterns, it may be well to dilate, that we may catch their inspiration.

Macedonian benevolence is a noble example and illustration of New Testament principles. How cramped and uninviting does the mere legal "tithing system" appear in comparison with this wholehearted devotion to God!

In 2 Corinthians 8 and 9 is the one discourse on "giving" that makes needless all other treatment of this great theme. The two chapters not only present every grand principle and motive of consecrated giving, but they present seven paradoxes that are very remarkable. These Macedonians seem to have furnished the most singular example of Christian benevolence to be found anywhere in sacred Scripture; their giving was a sort of reversal of all ordinary experience.

1. They gave out of the abundance of their poverty, not out of the plenitude of wealth.

2. Their willingness exceeded their ability, instead of their ability exceeding their willingness.

3. They were urgent to be allowed to give rather than reluctant, while those who received the gift were reluctant to take it, knowing how deep was their poverty.

4. They made the greater gift first (of themselves), and the latter gift was the less (their money). Usually people give the least they can, to begin with, and have to be educated up to giving themselves at the very last.

5. In these chapters value of gifts is reckoned, not by the amount given, but by the degree of willingness and cheerfulness exhibited.

6. We are here taught that increase comes not by keeping, but by giving; that the way to get more is to give more, and the way to lose is to keep.

7. And the crowning lesson of all is that they regarded giving, not as a privation to be evaded and avoided, but as a privilege and a blessing to be courted and cultivated.

The Life of Christ which is held up as a "writing copy" for our close imitation is presented.

First in its practical sinlessness—"who did no sin."

Second, its faultless speech—"in whose mouth no guile."

Third, its perfect self-control—"when He was reviled," etc.

Fourth, its faultless temper—"when He suffered, threatened not."

Fifth, its absolute committal to the Father—"but committed Himself," etc.

Sixth, its self-sacrifice for human salvation—"who His own self bare our sins," etc.

What is further to be desired in an example for imitation?

Disciples may here see a pattern of faultless conduct, speech, disposition and even manners; with a will full of energy in all self-government, yet in all things surrendered to the will of God, and, to crown all the rest, sublime self-oblivion for the sake of others.

The pattern of a church assembly in the Acts of Apostles is very instructive, and in the following particulars:

1. A holy unity and community—not a breath of discord or division until the murmurings were heard (chap. 6).

2. A universal participation in witnessing—no line between "clergy" and "laity" yet appearing, to limit or restrain testimony.

3. Constant spiritual fellowship and growth—accessions from without and increase of life and power within.

4. Unselfish benevolence to a remarkable degree—those who had possessions turning them into a central fund for redistribution.

5. Bold and uncompromising witness to the Lord, amid great and growing opposition and persecution.

6. Presence and presidency of the Holy Spirit, so that His personal control was more absorbing and actual than even apostolic guidance.

7. And consequently superhuman power in prayer and the continual working of miracles.

These are some of the marks of the church of apostolic days as seen in the first five chapters of the Acts, and there has been nothing like it before or since.

Paul is a pattern for all penitent believers in at least eight respects:

1. He was a self-righteous sinner—a Pharisee, and therefore very difficult to reach.

2. He was a persecuting sinner, full of antagonism to the church and Christ.

3. He was a conscientious sinner—he had the highest human authority back of him in his career.

5. He was a successful sinner—his whole course was one that tempted him to continue in it.

6. And yet he was a thoroughly penitent sinner—and saw himself as guilty of an almost unpardonable crime.

7. And he was an instantly converted sinner—proving the possibility of an immediate radical change.

8. And finally, he was a thoroughly transformed sinner, becoming at once a disciple and evangelist, a witness and an apostle; and from that moment completely dedicated to the service of God.

Subordinate patterns may be traced in the Word, exhibiting, in an inferior degree, individual traits, imitatible but imperfect human examples of fidelity, faith and virtue. In compassion for human infirmity, God records a few cases of His *Encomiums*, to help us to see what He approves, and how, even amid most hostile surroundings, men and women have attained lofty heights of holy living and serving. He rarely deals in praise, and for the obvious reason, that, were He lavish of His approval, He would both lessen its value, and lower its standard. But, when God does deign to commend, and especially in strong terms, His words of praise reveal deep secrets of what is well pleasing in His sight. To know what He approves must be of transcendent value in one who seeks to be well pleasing in His sight. While we may not hope here to reach perfection, we may "stand complete in all the will of God," "blameless and harmless," if not "faultless." We therefore call attention to a few of these lesser patterns for imitation.

1. *Abel*, the first who offered acceptable sacrifice, God bearing witness of his gifts (Heb. 11:4).

2. *Noah*, preacher of righteousness, witnessing to a world of ungodly (Heb. 11:7; 2 Pet. 2:5).

3. *Enoch*, example of an intercessor, in the midst of a godless, prayerless world (Heb. 11:5, 6).

4. *Job*, one who feared God and eschewed evil, and patiently endured (Job 1:2; James 5:11).

5. *Abram*, as a friend of God, who believed against human hope and obeyed sometimes against reason (Gen. 15:6; Rom. 4:1–22; James 2:21–23).

6. *Moses* as renouncing pleasure and treasure for the sake of Jehovah and His people (Heb. 11:23–29).

7. *Caleb*, as one who followed the Lord wholly and fully and dared to be in a minority (Deut. 1:36; Josh. 14:8, 9–14).

8. *Elijah*, as a reformer, separate from idolatry and the corruptions of a wicked court, mighty in prayer (James 5:17, 18).

9. *Nehemiah*, as a zealous, prayerful, self-denying governor in the days of reconstruction.

10. *Daniel*, on the whole the most faultless example of godliness in all Old Testament history (Dan. 6:4, 5; 10:11).

God's special commendation is recorded of the youthful Solomon's prayer (1 Kgs. 3:5–15; 1 Chr. 1:7–12), for "an understanding heart to judge the people." "And the speech pleased the Lord that Solomon had asked this thing." Manifestly, no greater quality in a ruler of a great nation could be desired than a true wisdom in administration; and what pleased the Lord was that, instead of asking anything that terminated on himself, personally and individually, he had sought that which would insure his being a capable, faithful, efficient *ruler*. Thus having first sought the higher good for the greater number, God added the lesser good for himself that he had not even asked (cf. Matt. 6:33).

Proverbs 31:10–31. Who can find a virtuous woman?

This is apparently a product of the pen of that same mother of King Lemuel, whose wise words on the virtues of a true king occupy the first third of this closing chapter. Here is an alphabetic and acrostic poem, meant to outline the portrait of an *ideal woman*. Much in it is local and exceptional, for it is associated with a *royal* writer, but aside from all this, there are a great many features of universal application and from these we select the following:

First of all, a true woman is *trustworthy*. At the bottom of every noble character lies truth, without which nothing else is *true* or genuine.

Then she is *industrious*—no idler, and not ashamed of any honest toil. She does not stand aloof from what to some is drudgery, but worketh willingly with her hands.

Again she is *unselfish*. Those same hands that handle the spindle and distaff, the needle and the shuttle, reach forth to the poor and needy.

Again, she is *domestic*. She is not impatient of the narrow sphere of home, of which she is the radiant center, most loved and honored of those who know her best.

Again, she is *self-controlled*. Her mouth is opened only to utter wisdom, and in her tongue is the *law* of kindness. Whatever her natural tempter, it is under *discipline*, and obeys the law of love.

Again, she wears the rare clothing of strength and honor. "If you *honor* be clothing, the suit will wear a lifetime; if your clothing be your honor, it will soon be threadbare"—Arnot.

And once more, her *beauty* is that of character. Other charms soon fade, but this never loses its attraction.

Thus, in this brief eulogy of womanhood, we learn what are the qualities of her heart, her hands, her tongue; what is her true clothing, her riches, her beauty, and what is the sphere where she most shines.

Turning to the New Testament, two examples of faith conspicuously confront us—the only occasions when our Lord attributed to any human being "*great faith*"—the centurion of Capernaum, and the woman of Canaan (Matt. 8:5–10; 15:22–28).

Conspicuous also is His condemnation of Peter's grand confession: "Thou art the Christ, the Son of the living God." He immediately followed this fearless declaration of His Messiahship and divine Sonship by a special word of blessing, affirming that such confession was both a result of divine supernatural revelation, and that it would prove the impregnable rock basis upon which the church should be built, and which should assure the church's absolute triumph over even diabolical assault.

34

Legal and Ethical Standards

S O GREAT PROMINENCE is given to the *Legal* element that not only was one of the three recognized divisions of the Old Testament "The Law," but the whole book was often known as "The Law of the Lord."

The Ten Commandments were twice graven on stone tablets, by God; this fact serving to separate them as eternal ethical principles from the code generally, many of whose features were ceremonial and temporal; and to indicate their peculiar obligation, supremacy and perpetuity.

The Decalogue is a specimen of singular symmetry and system. It is in two parts: four commands pertaining to God, and six pertaining to man. In the first four there is a regular progress of thought; first as to God as the sole object of all worship and obedience; then as to the spirituality of the mode of His worship; then as to reverence for His *name*, and finally for His *day*.

The latter six precepts show a similar progress of thought. Duty to parents leads the way as the first form of obligation and obedience, then follow five things to be protected and guarded, and in the order of their importance: first life, then purity, then property, then reputation, and finally secret desires and dispositions.

Careful examination and analysis resolve the law into *three* codes. There is clearly, first of all, the *moral*, then one that is mainly *ceremonial*, and finally another which constituted the common *civil* and

223

criminal code for the Hebrews. Some have thought that "command-ments" stand for the moral, "statutes" for the ceremonial, and "judg-ments" for the civil and criminal. But this distinction is not easy to maintain.

The principle that God is to be worshiped, loved and served su-premely is properly a moral one, and the ten commandments all rep-resent a moral code, the last being solely moral as it has reference to the heart and motive which man cannot see or judge and of which courts cannot take cognizance. Some of the ten, such as concern out-ward acts, sins of the tongue and conduct, may belong both to the moral and civil or criminal codes, since they may be judged in human courts.

Enactments relating to the priesthood, and the whole service of of-ferings and sacrifices, observance of fasts and feasts, are mainly cer-emonial, as they refer to an order which, however permanent, was not perpetual and has now passed away. There was little inherently right or wrong in a priest's dress, form of consecration, or acts of media-tion. These all acquired their moral force from their typical bearings, and no one would for a moment lift to the same rank of obligation the injunction not to go up by steps to God's Altar, or not to wear a garment of mixed woolen and linen, with such commands as not to worship a graven image, or not to kill, steal, or bear false witness.

It is equally plain that such portions of the code as cover misde-meanors, disputes between man and man, etc., constitute a distinct civil and criminal code to be enforced by judges in courts.

The ceremonial code is doubtless meant in Hebrews 8:7 as "the first covenant," described as decaying, waxing old, and ready to vanish away (13). Hence the apostles refused to impose it on new Christian con-verts (Acts 15:23–29, etc.). Its function was fulfilled when Christ, the great antitype, came and fulfilled its forecasts, and the substance was given of which its provisions were passing shadows.

Underneath all that is local, temporal and occasional, careful search will detect a deeper meaning:

1. A *sanitary* purpose, in guarding physical health.
2. A *salutary* object, in separating from surrounding heathenism.
3. A *typical* value, in exhibiting and illustrating moral distinc-tions.

4. A *practical* effect in abating carnal and sensual tendencies.

5. A *sacrificial* significance in connection with God's Altar.

6. A *spiritual* purport in antagonizing prevailing idolatry and immorality.

7. A *prophetical* forecast, in foreshadowing the Great Sacrifice.*
The more carefully this whole code is studied the wiser it appears. Some facts, never known until modern medical and sanitary science disclosed them, are giving new reason and significance to its provisions, justifying even what before seemed to be trivial or trifling, and vindicating its divine wisdom.

The idea of a *Decalogue*, or system of Ten Words of God, or divine decrees, may be traced in other departments beside the moral, or ethical.

There is, for instance, the *Creative* Decalogue, or Code of Natural Laws prevailing in Creation and hinted in the Creative decrees in Genesis 1.**

1. "Let Light be!" Very noticeable as not created but commanded to shine.

2. "Let there be an expanse." An ordinance of atmospheric separation.

3. "Let the waters be gathered together." An ordinance of segregation and aggregation.

4. "Let the earth bring forth grass," etc. A decree of vegetable origins.

5. "Let there be lights in the expanse." A decree of astronomical illumination.

6. "Let them be for signs and seasons." A decree of natural succession of seasons.

7. "Let the waters bring forth the living creature." A decree of animal beginnings.

8. "Let us make man." The great ordinance of human creation.

9. "Let them have dominion." The decree of sovereignty of higher life over lower.

10. "Be fruitful and multiply." The ordinance of propagation.

---

* *The Sanitary Code of the Pentateuch.* Rev. C. G. Gillespie. *The Wonderful Law.* H. L. Hastings. *Code of Health.* Whitelaw.
** Dr. Payne Smith.

The enumeration and classification are unimportant to settle, but a progressive series of decrees is manifest, forming a code of natural laws for the material creation, such as the following:

Chemical combustion and combination developing the original cosmic heat and light.

Condensation, segregation and aggregation, with affinity and cohesion, producing a body of waters.

Vegetation, with cellular structure, growth and the phenomena of fertility and reproduction.

Planetary and stellar motion, axial and orbital, with centripetal and centrifugal forces, gravitation, etc. Illumination.

Duration and succession, the establishment of a temporal order with succession of day and night, times and seasons.

Elemental animal life, conscious, sentient, voluntary, with motion and reproduction.

Higher animal life, with advance in complexity of structure, organization, intelligence and rank of being—mammalia.

Humanity—the last and highest—with the divine image, independence, conscience, intelligence, the spirit of life, etc.

Dominion—the highest forms of life subjecting and controlling the lower, and maintaining supremacy.

There is here both a manifest completeness and a steady advance from lower to higher, simple to complex, from matter to mind, etc.

The sermon on the mount gives us a *modified moral* Decalogue, which is easily traceable—the new laws of the Kingdom singularly correspondent with the old, such as:

"Seek first the Kingdom of God and His Righteousness."

"Swear not at all."

"Be not angry."

"Resist not evil." [Turn the other cheek.]

"Thou shalt not lust."

"Lay not up for yourselves treasures upon earth."

"Judge not."

"Love your enemies."

"Do unto others as you would that others should do unto you," etc.

A whole system of moral precepts may be gleaned here, which, being carefully arranged, singularly match and modify the ten commandments, and lift all ethical duties to the higher plane of loyalty to God and love to man—a sort of new decalogue, modified to suit the dispensation of grace, and the increased revelation of truth and man's relation to his fellow man. The correspondences and the differences are alike instructive.

The old Decalogue opened by an assertion of the supremacy of Jehovah and the duty of giving Him the primary and solitary place in worship. The new Decalogue correspondingly insists upon giving Him the first rank in all things, seeking His righteousness and Kingdom as the foremost object and aim, and not allowing even right and lawful things which are secondary to hold the primary place. This injunction is the equivalent of the whole first table, as it puts God first and foremost. But the prohibition, "Swear not at all," etc., expands the third commandment and applies its principle in several practical directions, giving it also wider scope as affecting all that in man deserves honor and reverence. The command, "Resist not evil," with the rebuke of causeless and unjustifiable anger and insolent speech, expands the second table—and applies its principles. Obviously there will be no disobedience to parents, no murder, and no kindred acts of violence, if there be no disposition to retaliate injury, indulge wrong tempers, or permit unbridled speech.

When we are forbidden even to lust after what is another's, it covers all impure and unholy envy and jealousy, as well as sensuality. And if there be no avaricious greed, no lust of accumulation, there will be no stealing, or indirect robbery through unjust and dishonest dealing.

When bidden to judge no one unjustly or harshly, and to love even our enemies, the sin of bearing false witness is nipped in the bud, for behind a lying and slanderous tongue, lies hatred or at least unjust judgment.

These considerations at least illustrate the fact that, in this sermon on the mount, our Lord is promulgating a sort of Christian Decalogue; He is interpreting the true sense of the original "Ten Words" of Jehovah, cleansing them from the corruption of traditionalism and the perversions of pharisaic formalism, giving them a deeper and more spiritual meaning and application, and teaching disciples a practically new code without destroying but rather fulfilling the old law.

From other parts of the New Testament may be gathered a *Domestic Decalogue* for the regulation of family and church life—such as the following:

"Let every man abide in his calling with God" (1 Cor. 7:20–24).

"Fathers, provoke not your children to anger" (Eph. 6:3).

"Children obey your parents in the Lord" (Eph. 6:1).

"Speaking the truth in love"—truthing in love (Eph. 4:15).

"Be clothed with humility" (1 Pet. 4:5).

"Study to be quiet" (1 Thess. 4:11).

"Consider one another" (Heb. 10:24).

"Let your speech be always with grace" (Col. 4:6).

"Support the weak" (1 Thess. 5:14).

"Mind your own business" (1 Thess. 4:11, etc.).

"Deny Thyself" (Matt. 16).

In other words—make God your partner, exercise godly self-control, mix truth with love, cultivate humility, keep the peace, be considerate of others, hold your tongue, mind your own business, help the needy, be self-forgetful.

What a new Eden would come to the race were such a new Decalogue in force!

As the Holy Scriptures draw to a completion and a close, it is noticeable how all law is simplified and narrowed down to a few precepts and finally to one. Comparison of the following passages will be found to unfold a profound philosophy of all legal enactments, to show the uses of legislation and the conditions which make all law needless.

First Timothy 1:9. "The law was not made for a righteous man, but for the lawless and disobedient."

Romans 10:4. "Christ is the end of the law for righteousness to every one that believeth."

Romans 13:8–10. "He that loveth another hath fulfilled the law," etc.

Galatians 3:24. "The law is our schoolmaster to bring us to Christ."

Galatians 5:14. "All the law is fulfilled in one word—thou shalt love," etc. Compare Matthew 22:36–38.

James 2:8. "If ye fulfill the Royal law—ye do well."

These and similar teachings show that no *outward* code is needed when two great *inner* laws control: loving obedience God-ward, and loving unselfishness, man-ward; and thus all law is at last resolved into one: LOVE.

Law is not made for the law abiding, but for the lawless. Its restraints are never felt till they are disregarded; then they become a yoke and a fetter. The holy angels know no law; being in entire sympathy with God, they move in the same direction as He does, without any constraint. We may all do as we please when we please to do as we ought; and the highest end and result of law is to train us to obedience, to show us the blessedness of the "undefiled in the way who walk in the law of the Lord," to reveal to us how they "walk at liberty who seek His precepts," and how, when the law of God is "in the heart," not an external, compulsory code, but an internal, impulsory principle, perfect freedom is attained.

Someone has sought to illustrate this by a fable of the birds, that at their creation they were wingless; that subsequently the wings were created and attached to them as burdens; but when cheerfully and patiently borne on their shoulders, the wings grew fast; the burdens changed to pinions, and what the birds first bore, bore them.

35

Miracles and Discourses

A MONG THESE SCRIPTURE PROMINENCES THREE, not already considered, deserve special mention. Biblical *Miracles, Parables*, and *Discourses*. The first are special exhibitions of supernatural power; the second, of divine illustration of truth; and the third of continuous development of doctrine.

As to *miracles*, there are reckoned about sixty-two in the Old Testament, which someone has carefully compiled and arranged as follows:

Lot's Wife becoming a Pillar of Salt (Gen. 19:26).

The Burning Bush (Ex. 3:2).

The Changing of the Rod of Aaron into a Serpent (Ex. 7:8–12).
    The Plagues of Egypt:

The Turning of the Waters into Blood (Ex. 7:19–25).

The Frogs (Ex. 8:5–15).

The Lice (or Mosquitoes) (Ex. 8:16–19).

The Flies (or Bloodsuckers) (Ex. 8:21–32).

The Murrain upon the Cattle (Ex. 9:1–7).

Boils upon Man and Beast (Ex. 9:8–12).

The Hail Storm (Ex. 9:13–26).

The Locusts (Ex. 10:12–15).

The Darkness (Ex. 10:21–23).

The Death of the Firstborn (Ex. 12:29).

The Pillar of Cloud (Ex. 13:21).

The Dividing of the Red Sea (Ex. 14:21, 22).

The Healing of the Waters of Marah (Ex. 15:23–25).

The Giving of the Manna (Ex. 16:15).

Water from the Rock in Horeb (Ex. 17:6).

The Giving of the Quails (Num. 11:31).

Miriam Smitten with Leprosy (Num. 12:10).

The Judgment of Korah (Num. 16:31–33).

The Budding of Aaron's Rod (Num. 17:8).

The Brazen Serpent (Num. 21:9).

Balaam's Ass Speaking (Num. 22:28–30).

The Dividing of the Jordan (Josh. 3:15–17).

The Overthrow of Jericho (Josh. 6:20).

The Sun and Moon Stand Still (Josh. 10:12–14).

Gideon's Sacrifice Consumed by Fire (Judg. 6:21).

Gideon's Fleece (Judg. 6:36–40).

Samson's Victory with the Jawbone, etc. (Judg. 15:15–19).

The Fall of Dagon (1 Sam. 5:3–5).

Thunder and Rain at the Prayer of Samuel (1 Sam. 12:16–19).

Three Days' Pestilence (2 Sam. 24:15).

The Prophecy against Jeroboam and its Attendant Circumstances (1 Kgs. 13:1–5).

The Slaying of the Disobedient Prophet (1 Kgs. 13:24).

Elijah Fed by Ravens (1 Kgs. 17:6).

The Increase in the Widow's Barrel and Cruse of Oil (1 Kgs. 17:16).

The Raising of the Widow's Son (1 Kgs. 17:17–23).

The Descent of Fire upon the Altar on Mount Carmel (1 Kgs. 18:38).

Elijah Fed by an Angel (1 Kgs. 19:5–8).

God's Manifestation to Elijah at Horeb (1 Kgs. 19:11–13).

The Destruction of the Two Captains with their Companies (2 Kgs. 1:9–16).

The Translation of Elijah (2 Kgs. 2:11).

Elisha Dividing the Jordan (2 Kgs. 2:14).

The Healing of the Waters of Jericho (2 Kgs. 2:21, 22).

The Scoffers Torn by Bears (2 Kgs. 4:38–41).

Defeat of the Moabites (2 Kgs. 3:20).

The Increase of the Oil (2 Kgs. 4:3–6).

The Raising of the Shunammite's Son (2 Kgs. 4:31–37).

The Poisonous Pottage Healed (2 Kgs. 4:38–41).

The Feeding of a Hundred with Twenty Loaves (2 Kgs. 4:42–44).

The Cure of Naaman's Leprosy (2 Kgs. 5:27).

Gehazi Smitten with Leprosy (2 Kgs. 5:27).

The Restoration of the Axe (2 Kgs. 6:6).

The Miracles Wrought by Elisha on Human Vision (2 Kgs. 6:17, 18).

The Raising of the Siege of Samaria (2 Kgs. 7:1–6).

The Resurrection at the Tomb of Elisha (2 Kgs. 13:21).

The Destruction of Sennacherib's Army (2 Kgs. 19:35).

The Going Back of the Shadow upon the Dial of Ahaz (2 Kgs. 20:8–11).

Shadrach, Meshach and Abednego in the Fiery Furnace (Dan. 3:23–27).

Daniel's Deliverance from the Lions (Dan. 6:22).

Jonah's Preservation (Jonah 1:17).

Of these Old Testament miracles there is a basis for at least a *threefold* classification; they serve to exhibit:

I. The powers of *nature*.

    (1) *Inanimate*, water, blood, oil, light, fire, etc.

        (a) Several have to do with water; the Nile plague, the Red Sea, Jordan, Marah, Meribah and Rephidim, waters of Jericho, water to allies in Moab, the iron made to swim, sacrifice at Carmel, etc.

        (b) Two, with *oil*—widow's cruse and oil in the vessels.

        (c) Two, with the *Sun*, Joshua's long day, and Dial of Ahaz.

        (d) Five, with *fire*—Pillar of fire, Shekinah fire, fire from heaven at Carmel, companies consumed, fiery furnace.

        (e) Three, with *food*—Manna, cruse of oil, meal and barrel, and feeding of the hundred men with twenty loaves.

        (f) *Miscellaneous*—Aaron's rod, darkness, thunder and hail, earthquake, Jericho's walls, etc.

    (2) *Animate:*

    Aaron's rod turned to serpent, frogs, lice, flies, murrain, boils and blains, locusts, firstborn, lion's den, Jonah and great fish, etc.

II. The power of *Disease:*
Leprosy of Miriam, Naaman, Uzziah; fiery serpents and brazen serpent; Jeroboam's hand withered, the deadly pottage, etc.

III. Power of *Death:*
Nadab and Abihu, Burning at Taberah, Kibroth Hataavah, Korah and company, Uzzah, Widow's Son at Zarephath and Shunammite's Son, Syrian Army, Sennacherib's Army, Smiting Philistines, Mockers at Bethel, Enoch's and Elijah's translation, and Elisha's bones.

This analysis, however incomplete, may hint the vast scope even of Old Testament wonder working.

The recorded miracles *of our Lord* number thirty-eight, as follows:

1. Water Made Wine (John 2:1–11).
2. First Draught of Fishes (Luke 5:1–10).
3. Demoniac in the Synagogue (Mark 1:23, 24; Luke 4:33–36).
4. Leper cleansed (Matt. 8:2–4; Mark 1:40–56; Luke 5:12–14).
5. Centurion's Servant (Matt. 8:5–13; Luke 7:1–10).
6. Peter's Wife's Mother (Matt. 8:14, 15; Mark 1:30, 31; Luke 4:38, 39).
7. Paralytic, Borne of Four (Matt. 9:2–7; Mark 2:3–12; Luke 5:18–25).
8. Nobleman's Son (John 4:46–54).
9. Tempest Calmed (Matt. 8:24–27; Mark 4:37–41).
10. Jairus' Daughter (Matt. 9:18, 19; Mark 5:22–24; Luke 8:41, 42).
11. Bloody Issue (Matt. 9:20–22; Mark 5:25–34; Luke 8:43–48).
12. Dumb Spirit (Matt. 9:32, 33).
13. Legion of Demons (Matt. 8:28–33; Mark 5:2–20; Luke 8:27–39).
14. Blind and Dumb Spirit (Matt. 12:22; Luke 11:14).
15. Withered Hand (Matt. 12:10–13; Mark 3:1–5; Luke 6:6–10).
16. Widow's Son (Luke 7:11–15).
17. Invalid Man (John 5:2–15).
18. Man Born Blind (John 9:1–39).
19. Blind Man (Mark 8:22–26).

20. Two Blind Men (Matt. 9:27–31).
21. Walking on the Sea (Matt. 14:24–33; Mark 6:47–52; John 6:16–21).
22. Daughter of Woman of Canaan (Matt. 15:22–28; Mark 7:25–30).
23. Deaf and Dumb Man (Matt. 15:30, 31; Mark 7:32–37).
24. Feeding Four Thousand (Matt. 15:32–38; Mark 8:1–9).
25. Exorcism of Mary Magdalene (Luke 8:2).
26. Feeding Five Thousand (Matt. 14:15–21; Mark 6:35–44; Luke 9:12–17; John 6:5–13).
27. Dumb Spirit (Matt. 17:14–21; Mark 9:17–25; Luke 9:38–42).
28. Fish and Tribute Money (Matt. 17:24–27).
29. Woman With Infirmity (Luke 13:11–17).
30. Dropsy (Luke 14:2–6).
31. Ten Lepers (Luke 17:12–19).
32. Bartimeus and Another Blind Man (Matt. 20:30–34; Mark 10:46–52; Luke 18:35–43).
33. Fig Tree Withered (Matt. 21:19, 20; Mark 11:13–21).
34. Lazarus Raised (John 11:1–44).
35. Healing Malchus' Ear (John 22:51).
36. Our Lord's Own Resurrection (Matt. 28:1–10; Mark 16; Luke 24; John 20; 1 Cor. 15:4–8).
37. Second Draught of Fishes (John 21:6).
38. Our Lord's Ascension (Mark 16:19; Luke 24:50, 51).

To these may be added a secondary list for reasons which are apparent:

1. His Escape from Violence at Nazareth (Luke 4:28–31).
2. Many Unrecorded Healings (Matt. 12:15, 16; Mark 3:10–12; Galilee).
3. Great Multitudes Healed (Matt. 15:30, 31; Mark 7:32–27; Galilee).
4. Many Demoniacs (Matt. 8:16, 17; Mark 1:32–34; Luke 4:40, 41; Galilee).
5. Miracles at Jerusalem, Compelling Belief (John 2:23).
6. Healings in Judea Beyond Jordan (Matt. 19:2).
7. Healing of Sick at Bethsaida (Matt. 14:16; Luke 9:11; John 6:2).

8. All Manner of Sickness in Galilee (Matt. 4:23, 24; Mark 1:34).
9. Great Multitude Healed out of Judea, etc. (Luke 6:17–20).
10. Healing Every Sickness (Matt. 9:35).
11. As Many as Touched Made Whole (Matt. 14:35, 36; Mark 6:55, 56; Galilee).
12. A Few Sick Folk at Nazareth (Mark 6:5).
13. Certain Women With Evil Spirits (Luke 8:2, 3).

The Discourses of our Lord, like His parables and miracles, are susceptible of a two-fold classification into major and minor utterances.

Of the former we may reckon:
1. The so-called Sermon on the Mount (Matt. 5, 6, 7).
2. His Instructions to the Twelve Apostles (Matt. 10).
3. John the Baptist and His Mission (Matt. 11).
4. Satan Casting out Satan, Holy Spirit, etc. (Matt. 12:22–50).
5. Parables of the Kingdom of Heaven (Matt. 13).
6. The Externals and Internals of Godliness (Matt. 15:1–20).
7. The Confession and Knowledge of Christ (Matt. 16:13–28).
8. The Magnitude of Small Numbers (Matt. 18:1–20).
9. The True Nature and Patience of Forgiveness (Matt. 18:21–35).
10. The Danger and Destructiveness of Avarice (Matt. 19:16; 20:16).
11. The Peril and Meanness of Ambition (Matt. 20:20–38).
12. Obedience and Disobedience to Divine Authority (Matt. 21:23–44).
13. The Called and the Chosen of God (Matt. 22:1–14).
14. The Guilt and Condemnation of Hypocrisy (Matt. 23).
15. The Signs of Christ's Coming and the End (Matt. 24, 25).
16. The Vineyard and Unfaithful Husbandmen (Mark 12:1–12).
17. The Sermon in the Synagogue at Nazareth (Luke 4:16–30).
18. The Love that is Born of Forgiveness (Luke 7:37–50).
19. Six Wrong Tempers: Intolerance, Ambition, Revenge, etc. (Luke 9:43–62).
20. The Commission of the Seventy (Luke 10:1–24).
21. The Good Samaritan and Love to Neighbor (Luke 10:25–42).
22. The Lesson of Importunity in Prayer (Luke 11:1–13).

23. The Sin and Folly of Covetousness (Luke 12:13–59).
24. The Strait Gate and the Shut Door (Luke 13:23–35).
25. The Feast and the Guests (Luke 14:7–35).
26. The Love of God for the Lost (Luke 15).
27. The Responsibility of Stewardship (Luke 16:1–31).
28. Conditions of Prevailing Prayer (Luke 18:1–14).
29. The Nobleman and His Servants (Luke 19:1–27).
30. The Rebuke of the Sadducees (Luke 20:27–47).
31. The Post-Resurrection Exposition (Luke 24:13–34).
32. The New Birth and Eternal Life (John 3).
33. The Water that Quenches Thirst (John 4:1–42).
34. The Divine Equality and Authority of the Son (John 5:17–47).
35. The Bread Which is from Heaven (John 6:26–71).
36. The Two Fatherhoods, God and Devil (John 8:21–59).
37. The Good Shepherd and the Sheep (John 10:1–38).
38. The Humility of True Service (John 13:1–20).
39. The Great Preparatory Discourse (John 14—16).
40. The Intercessory Prayer (John 17).
Of Minor Discourses we suggest:
1. The True Law of the Sabbath Rest (Matt. 12:1–13).
2. The Leaven of the Pharisees (Matt. 16:1–12).
3. Divorce and Marital Relations (Matt. 19:3–12).
4. The Moral Meaning of His Miracles (Mark 2:3–17).
5. The Vice of Intolerance and Bigotry (Mark 9:38–50).
6. The Resurrection Life and Its Conditions (Mark 12:18–27).
7. The First and Greatest Commandment (Mark 12:28–34).
8. God's Estimate of Human Gifts (Mark 12:41–44).
9. The Last Great Command and Commission (Mark 16:14–20).
10. The Barren Fig Tree and Its Lesson (Luke 13:1–9).
11. Offenses and the Forgiving Spirit (Luke 17:1–10).
12. The Address on the Last Day of Feast (John 7:37–39).
13. The Light of the World (John 8:12–20).
14. The Resurrection, Spiritual and Physical (John 11:25, 26).
15. The Corn of Wheat and the Crop (John 12:21–36).
16. Believing and Rejecting (John 12:42–50).

Among the discourses of our Lord should be ranked those "Seven Epistles" to the churches of Asia Minor which form the unique sevenfold post-resurrection address of the Risen One. Space forbids their adequate treatment here; but they are divisible, each, into the following heads:

1. Our Lord appears in each in a certain character, or with certain characteristic description of Himself adapted to the particular message.

2. There is a word of commendation for what is praiseworthy.

3. A word of condemnation for such things as are undesirable, inconsistent or blameworthy.

4. A word of counsel or exhortation.

5. A promise of reward, with its conditions.

Especially notable is the evident progress of thought in the rewards promised, which are all couched in figures and imagery, drawn from the Old Testament, and following a progressive historic order. There can be no accident in this striking fact. They are all "*to him that overcometh*," the symbolism evidently being drawn from the consecutive history of mankind and of Israel from the creation of Adam to the consummation of the Kingdom under Solomon. To exhibit this correspondence and development we resort again to parallel columns.

1. "Will I give to eat of the Tree of Life which is in the midst of the Paradise of God."	Gen. 2:8, 9.	John 1:12, 13; 3:16–38.
2. "Shall not be hurt of the Second Death."	Gen. 2:17; 3:3.	5:24.
3. "Will I give of the Hidden Manna, A white stone, And in the stone a new name written."	Ex. 16:4–33; 28:9–12; 28:21.	6:26–58.
4. "Power over the nations, and he shall rule them with a rod of iron."	Ex. 17:8–16.	7:37–39; 9:39
5. "Shall be clothed in white raiment; and I will not blot out his name out of the Book of Life."	Ex. 32:26, 33.	10:27–29.
6. "Will I make a pillar in the Temple of My God; and he shall go no more out . . . and I will write on him My new name."	1 Kgs. 7:21, 22.	14:16–23.
7. "To sit with me on My throne, even as I also overcame," etc.	1 Kgs. 10:18, 20.	17:22.

36

The Place and Province of Parables

I T IS DIFFICULT TO EXPRESS the exact idea, that there is in the word of God, a mystical element, a peculiar quality of suggesting a far deeper meaning than at first suspected. This finds illustration in the *prophetic* Scriptures, especially the indirect forecasts of the future; and particularly in the *Messianic* element, pervading the entire Word of God, cropping out where at first thought it would be least expected. It also appears in the *scientific* department, where an elastic poetic phraseology, obscure and enigmatic, provides for an after accommodation to newly discovered facts.

The same mystical element is susceptible of far wider illustration and is continually attracting new attention. As in the works of God, every enlargement of our powers of vision and observation through the lenses of telescope, microscope and spectroscope, brings to light new wonders of the creative hand, so every increase of real insight into the Word of God overwhelms us with evidence that the same Divine Hand has been at work; and, as the "Heavens declare the glory of God and the firmament showeth His handiwork," so the Law of the Lord is seen to be perfect, in its adaptation to its purpose, converting the soul, making wise the simple, etc. (Ps. 19).

This mystical element conspicuously appears in *parabolic form*. Three prominent sorts of Parable are found in Scripture:

(a) Parabolic *utterance*, as in Luke 15 and John 15.

(b) Parabolic *action*, as in the miracles, all of which have a moral meaning.

(c) Parabolic *picture* or *object*, as in the Tabernacle and its furniture.

Our Lord's *spoken* parables are generally reckoned, as, in number, about thirty-three; or counting some doubtful cases, may reach forty. To these, His parables in *action*, or miracles, singularly correspond in number and nature, and might almost be set side by side for comparison. His parables of speech were meant to set forth great leading truths, such as the Love of God, the nature of sin, the law of reward and retribution, the vital union of the believer with Himself, etc. His parables of action were on the other hand, designed, as He declares, to show His power on earth to forgive sins and to remedy their consequences. So the Parabolic pictures or objects or the Word of God set forth in a remarkable way the leading facts and truths about Redemption, the Person of the Redeemer and the blessings of the Redeemed. These parables are found in *two* conspicuous forms, namely: The whole system of sacrifices, offerings and feasts; and the construction and furniture of the Tabernacle of Witness, so closely associated with that system.

The whole New Testament, especially Hebrews 9, is the exposition of the Tabernacle, whose volume of suggestiveness grows more and more upon us. From one point of view it presents a grand picture of the whole work of Christ for the believer; from another, an unusually complete view of the whole life of the believer in Christ.

The Tabernacle was in three courts—the outer, with the Brazen Altar of sacrifice and the Laver; the inner, with the Table of Shew Bread, the Golden Candlestick, and the Altar of Incense; and the inmost, the Holiest of All, with the Ark of the Covenant surmounted by the Mercy Seat. It requires little imagination to see here the work of Christ set forth in order, from His vicarious sacrifice of Himself on the Cross, and the Sending of the Regeneration and Sanctifying Spirit, throughout His whole career, as the Light of the World, the Bread of Life, the Intercessor, including His final entrance within the veil and in the presence of God for us. Or, regarded as teaching the believer how to draw near unto God for us. Or, regarded as teaching the believer how to draw near unto God in Christ, the outer court suggests two conditions: remission of sins through atoning blood and re-

generation of spirit through the Word of God and the Holy Ghost—
the *terms* of communion. Then the inner court suggests the three *forms*
of communion; a living light of testimony, the systematic consecration of substance, and a habitual life of prayer. Then the inmost
shrine may represent the final *goal* and *ideal* of communion, when perpetual obedience is like an unbroken tablet of law, the beauty of the
Lord our God is upon us, and all His attributes and our affections and
activities are in perfect harmony. No one can claim infallibility in interpreting these parabolic pictures and objects, the very beauty of
this form of teaching being in part that it admits of ever increasing
clearness of vision and accuracy of insight, as our life and character
approach nearer to final perfection. But we are sure that there is
here a wealth of meaning, yet unexplored and unsuspected by even
the children of God, and which only the ages to come will fully unveil and reveal.

A parable proper is, in Scripture usage, a similitude usually put in
narrative form, or used in connection with some incident. Parables
are not altogether lacking in the Old Testament, and sometimes appear in the form of short proverbs, dark prophetic utterances, and enigmatic maxims, or metaphors expanded into a narrative form (cf.
1 Sam. 10:12; 24:13; 2 Chr. 7:20; Num. 23:7, 18; 24:3; Ps. 78:2;
Prov. 1:6; Ezek. 12:22; 20:49). The word may be applied to a short
proverb, like "Physician, heal thyself!" or to a mere comparison (Matt.
24:32) to the typical character of Levitical rites (Heb. 9:9) or to single facts in patriarchal history (Heb. 11:19).

For our present purpose it is best to limit the use of the word to
its common application, excluding the fable, the myth and the allegory, which demand separate treatment.

Our *Lord's* parables claim principal attention, as constituting a class
by themselves and possibly meant as a complete system and series of
parabolic teachings. They are generally introduced formally by the
words, or their like: "He spake a parable," etc. In a few cases, the imagery of a parable is implied in a parabolic saying, not so called.

Several features are noticeable:

1. The recorded miracles and parables of our Lord closely correspond
in number; we can trace from forty to fifty of each, and the miracles

all have a hidden parabolic meaning, as the parables have all a deeper than their literal significance.

2. The miracles teach us the significance of the *forces* of creation; the Parables, of the *forms* of Creation (Rev. Dr. Hugh McMillan).

3. When a parable is predictive and prophetic, it is always in allegorical dress; when preceptive and didactic, actual and historical (Rev. Dr. W. G. Morehead).

The Parables may be thus cataloged:

1. The Contrasted Foundations: Rock and Sand (Matt. 7:24, 27).
2. The Sheep in the Pit (12:11, 12).
3. The Creditor and Two Debtors (Luke 7:41, 43).
4. The Sower, Seed and Soil (Matt. 13:3–23; Mark 4:3–20; Luke 8:5–15).
5. The Tares and Wheat (Matt. 13:24–30).
6. The Blade, Ear and Full Corn (Mark 4:26, 29).
7. The Mustard Seed (Matt. 13:31, 32; Mark 4:30, 32; Luke 13:19).
8. The Leaven and Meal (Matt. 13:33).
9. The Treasure hid in the field (Matt. 13:44; Luke 13:21).
10. The Pearl of Great Price (Matt. 13:45, 46).
11. The Dragnet (Matt. 13:47, 48).
12. The Unmerciful Servant (Matt. 18:23–35).
13. The Good Samaritan (Luke 10:25, 27).
14. The Good Shepherd (John 10:1–18).
15. The Friend and Loaves (Luke 11:5–8).
16. The Rich Fool (Luke 12:16–21).
17. Stewards, faithful and faithless (Luke 12:35–48).
18. The Barren Fig Tree (Luke 13:6, 7).
19. The Chief Seats at Wedding Feast (Luke 14:7–11).
20. The Excuses for Non-attendance (Luke 14:12–24).
21. The Lost Sheep (Matt. 18:12-14; Luke 15:37).
22. The Lost Silver (Luke 15:8–10).
23. The Lost Son (Luke 15:11–32).
24. The Unjust Steward (Luke 16:1–8).
25. The Rich Man and Lazarus (Luke 16:19–31).
26. The Unjust Judge (Luke 18:1–8).

27. The Pharisee and Publican (Luke 18:9–14).
28. The Laborers in the Vineyard (Matt. 20:1–16).
29. The Servants and Pounds (Luke 19:11–27).
30. The Two Sons and the Call to Vineyard (Matt. 21:28–31).
31. The Wicked Husbandmen (Matt. 21:33–43).
32. The Marriage Feast and Garment (Matt. 22:1–14).
33. The Vine and Branches (John 15:1–10).
34. The Servant Who Beat His Fellow Servants (Matt. 24:45–51).
35. The Wise and Foolish Virgins (Matt. 25:1–13).
36. The Talents (Matt. 25:14–30).
37. The Sheep and Goats (Matt. 25:31–46).

Beside these are minor Parables, of a second rank, not so prominent as such:

1. New cloth on old garment (Matt. 9:16; Mark 2:21; Luke 5:36).
2. New Wine and Old Bottles (Matt. 9:17; Mark 2:22; Luke 5:37, 38).
3. Old and New Wine (Luke 5:39).
4. Blind Leaders of Blind (Matt. 15:14; Luke 6:36).
5. Strong Man Keeping His Palace (Matt. 12:29; Mark 3:27; Luke 11:21, 22).
6. The Empty House and Seven Demons (Matt. 12:43, 45; Luke 11:24–26).
7. The Householder and Treasure (Matt. 13:52).
8. Things That Defile (Matt. 15:11–20).
9. Leaven of Pharisees (Matt. 16:6–12; Mark 8:15–21; Luke 12:1).
10. Servant and Master and Service at Feast (Luke 17:7–9).
11. Fig Tree and Summer (Matt. 24:32; Mark 13:38; Luke 21:30).
12. Commanding Porter to Watch (Mark 13:34–36).

As to *classification* of the more important:

1. There are certain *"Parables of the Kingdom"* which are the most conspicuous, which we indicate by numbers in the first preceding list: 4, 5, 6, 7, 8, 9, 10, 11, 12, 17, 19, 20, 24, 28, 29, 31, 32, 34, 35, 36—about twenty.

2. A second group, illustrating duties to God and man: Nos. 1, 2, 3, 13, 15, 16, 18, 25, 30—about nine.

3. A third group, illustrating God's attitude to men: Nos. 14, 21, 22, 23, 26, 27, 33—about seven.

In the secondary series we discover various lessons:

1. Consistency of teaching and practice: Nos. 1, 2, 3, 4, 5.

2. The need of purity of heart: Nos. 6, 8, 9.

3. The blessedness of service: Nos. 7, 10.

4. The duty of vigilance: Nos. 11, 12.

Or classifying according to *moral lessons enforced*, out the whole number.

Five specially set forth the Divine character and attributes:

Eight, the history of the Kingdom in this present age;

Nine, the responsibility of stewardship;

Nine more, the importance of obedience as a habit of heart;

Six, the beauty of forgiveness and unselfish love;

Four, the need of perpetual watchfulness;

Three, the importance of consistency in teaching and conduct;

Three others, of humility and importunity in prayer;

And one, of humility in all relations to God.

If it be proper to select twelve that may be ranked as perhaps most important, we should unhesitatingly choose:

1. The Good Shepherd	Christ as Vicarious Savior
2. The Vine and Branches	Christ as Source of life and Fruit
3. The Sower	The Reception of Gospel
4. The Tares	The Danger of Counterfeits
5. The Dragnet	The Duty of Evangelization
6. The Unjust Judge	Importunity in Prayer
7. The Pharisee and Publican	Pride and Humility
8. The Prodigal Son	The Love of God
9. The Two Foundations	The Building of Character
10. The Ten Virgins	The Need of Watchfulness
11. The Talents and Pounds	The Duty of Stewardship
12. Good Samaritan	Love to Man as Man

Three parables are connected with *money* or intrusted goods or property—the parable of the *Talents*, the *Pounds*, and the *Pence* (Matt. 25:14; Luke 19:12–27; Matt. 20:1–16). Together they present God's method in distributing responsibility, and reward for service; but, in each case the teaching is somewhat different, all together giving the complete truth.

The Parable of Talents shows that, so far as the distributions are unequal, if the improvement be equal, the reward will be equal.

The parable of the Pounds, that, where or so far as the distribution is equal, if the improvement is unequal, the measure of reward accords therewith.

The parable of the Pence, that, where the opportunity has been lacking, but, when offered, improved, the reward will be according to the fidelity in the use of such opportunity as was given. The willing mind is here recognized in those who would have worked longer, if any call to labor had come to them, and who therefore received the same penny as the others.

Trench and Arnot reckon some thirty parables of our Lord, as follows:

The Sower, the Tares, the Mustard Seed, the Leaven, the Hid Treasure, the Pearl, the Dragnet, the Unmerciful Servant, the Vineyard Laborers, the Two Sons, the Wicked Husbandmen, the Royal Marriage Feast, the ten Virgins, the Talents, the Seed, Blade and Ear; the Two Debtors, the Good Samaritan, the Importunate Friend, the Importunate Widow, the Rich Fool, the Barren Fig Tree, the Excuses, the Lost Sheep, the Lost Coin, the Lost Son, the Prudent Steward, the Rich Man and Lazarus, the Unprofitable Servants, the Pharisee and Publican, the Pounds.

Carefully examined, several striking particulars appear in this catalog:

Just *half* of the whole number refer *to the Judgment*, and present various phases of that final assize.

Some of them regard and treat that Judgment as the time of the great ingathering of the final harvest, like the parables of the Sower, the Tares, and the Dragnet, with the separation of good and bad.

Others exhibit the judicial penalties and gracious rewards connected with the Judgment, like the parables of the unmerciful servant, wicked husbandmen, vineyard laborers, excuses; others magnify the duty of vigilance and diligence, as the parables of the Ten Virgins, Talents and Pounds.

Others show the penalty of wastefulness and fruitlessness, or the reward of unselfish service, like the parables of the Rich Fool, the Barren Fig Tree, Dives and Lazarus; or the Prudent Steward.

Two are meant to encourage perseverance in prayer, those of the Friend at Midnight and the Widow at Court.

If half of the whole number have to do with some aspect of judgment, the other half exhibit some aspect of *Love* and *Grace*.

Other facts will be seen as the classification is carried further into subordinate groupings; but this suffices to show that such arrangement compensates for much discriminating study.

37

Biblical Figures of Speech

RHETORICAL FIGURES may be classed somewhat as follows:*
1. Those depending on the *kind of words* employed—*tropes;*
and on the *number of words* employed—*repetition* and *ellipsis.*
2. Those depending on the *representative imagery* employed: A change in the presentation of the represented object—in Nature—personification; in relations, vision; in degree, hyperbole. Also these making use of comparison and contrast. Some figures are forms of personation—as apostrophe—and irony, sarcasm, doubt and interrogation are forms of figure.

Biblical figures most common are the following *ten:*

1. *Comparison,* where one thing is compared to another.

2. *Contrast,* where two things are designedly set in opposition.

3. *Simile,* likening one thing to another in express terms.

4. *Metaphor,* when one thing is used for another without expressing the likeness formally.

5. *Parable,* a narrative in which such likeness is drawn out.

6. *Allegory,* similar to a parable, only not, perhaps, capable of literal interpretation.

7. *Type,* where one thing supplies a suggestion or forecast of another.

8. *Apostrophe,* where an individual or an attribute is addressed.

9. *Hyperbole,* overstatement—use of exaggerated terms.

---

* Compare *Standard Dictionary.*

10. *Metonymy*, representing a thing by one of its attributes or accompaniments—a crown for a King, etc.

A few examples from Scripture may serve to make the definitions above more clear.

1. Comparison (Ps. 84:10). Here a day in God's Courts is compared with a thousand elsewhere; and the position of a doorkeeper in the House of God with an abode, even as owner, in the tents of the wicked.

2. Contrast (Prov. 11:1). False balances, contrasted with just weights, and what is an abomination to the Lord with what is His delight.

3. Simile (Ps. 103:11, 16). The greatness of His mercy and grace are likened to the heights of Heaven above earth, and the distance between East and West; and His fatherly pity to that of an earthly parent.

4. Metaphor (Eph. 2:19–22; 6:10–20; 1 Pet. 2:6, 7; Eph. 1:13, 14; Ps. 84:11). The Temple of Believers, The Panoply of God, Christ, the cornerstone, etc.

5. Parable (Matt. 13; Eccl. 9:14, 15; Is. 5). The Parables of the Kingdom; The Little City and the Poor Wise Man; The Vine and Wild Grapes.

6. Allegory (Judg. 9:7–15); Ps. 80:8–16). Jotham's allegory of the Trees that sought a King—the first allegory in Scripture. The Vine—the boar and the wild beast personating destructive forces.

7. Type (Rom. 5:14). Adam, here first declared to be the type of the Coming "Second Man" and "Last Adam," as the Head of the Race.

8. Apostrophe (Is. 51:9; 54:1–5; 1 Cor. 15:55). The arm of the Lord is here addressed as a person; Israel, as a wife; Death and the grave, as individual foes, having power to inflict sting and achieve victory.

9. Hyperbole (Matt. 16:26; Eph. 3:20). "Gaining the whole world" is an exaggerated phrase for the largest worldly success. "Exceeding abundantly above all we ask or think" piles words on words and heaps superlatives together in a vain attempt to express what is inexpressible.

10. Metonymy (Gal. 6:17; Is. 59:1). The marks of the Lord Jesus stand for identity with Him in suffering; the Lord's arm and ear, for His power to save and answer prayer.

11. Impersonation (Prov. 7:12–36; 23:31, 32). Wisdom personified as a wise woman, and hostess, etc. Wine, as a serpent, with insinuating motion, fascinating eye and venomous sting.

12. Riddle (Judg. 14:12–14): Samson's riddle of the Lion and bees. The Books of proverbs and Ecclesiastes suggest many such riddles (30:18, 19). The four "things too wonderful" for Agur, are riddles to be solved. Often prediction takes the form of a riddle, as when Elisha foretold that the Samaritan Lord should "see but not eat of" the supply that relived famine (2 Kgs. 7:19, 20); or it was prophesied that Zedekiah should be carried captive to Babylon, but not see it (cf. Ezek. 12:13; 2 Kgs. 25:7).

The oldest allegory in Scripture is that of Jotham in Judges 9:7–15. There the trees are represented as seeking a King, and successively applying to the Olive, the Fig tree and the Vine, and, at last, to the Bramble. This which is one of the oldest is also one of the most beautiful of all the fables or apologues in the whole range of literature. It teaches incidentally contentment with one's appointed sphere, and the privilege of being of service to God and man in the place where God has put us; and the vanity of the lust of mere promotion. Finally, the Bramble—or rather the Buckthorn or Ramnus, is appealed to—and the answer is very significant: "Come, and put your trust under *my shadow!*" as if it could afford shelter! And, the "fire coming out of the bramble" refers to its inflammable character being easily set in a blaze and rapidly burning. The application is only too obvious. The nobler Gideon and his worthy sons had declined the proffered Kingdom, but this base born and vile Abimelech had accepted it and would prove like an irritating thornbush to his subjects and a fiery destroyer, his course ending like the burning thornbush in the mutual ruin of himself and them (vv. 16–20 interpret the allegory).

Metaphor is often used in a very striking way, but must not be construed literally.

"This is My Body" (Matt. 26:26). Here "*is*" is the equivalent of "represents," as in the parallel passage in Exodus 12:11, "*It is* the

Lord's Passover," where plainly the slain Lamb could not *be*, but only *represent* the Passover.

Perhaps the most majestic metaphor in any language is that of Revelation 20:11–15—The "Great White Throne." Nothing more awfully sublime was ever written, even by inspired pens.

One example of Divine metaphor we expand upon to show its beauty and manifold pertinency. It is found in Ephesians 1:22–24; 4:15, 16; etc. Christ, the *Head of the Body*—the Church.

This will bear indefinite amplification and application. In the human body all five senses are located in the head, and within a few inches of each other—sight, hearing, smell, taste and touch—the last nowhere else so keen as in the lips. Through the nostrils, breath finds its way to the lungs, and through the mouth food and drink to the stomach. From the head, as the great nerve center, the two systems, cerebrospinal and sympathetic, proceed; here is the throne whence are issued all commands to the entire system. So, in the Headship of Christ over the body of believers: all spiritual sensation, supplies for spiritual sustentation, and direction to spiritual activities emanate from Him. "In all things He must have preeminence." On Him is the whole dependence of the Body for reconciliation, union of the members with God and each other; vitality and energy; power to do or bear; sensibility to, or activity in, divine things.

This Headship *implies:*

1. Preeminence (Eph. 1:22). Lordship, Sovereignty.
2. Identity with the Body (4:4–6; 5:30).
3. Dependence and interdependence (4:12–16).
4. Unity of life and work (2:14–16; 4:4–7).
5. Sanctity (4:17–24; 5:25, 26).
6. Present Purpose—Creation unto Good Works (2:10).
7. Future Glory (v. 27).

"How often would I have gathered thy children together *as a hen gathereth her brood under her wings.*" Bunyan counts this a singularly happy simile. The hen has four calls to her brood: A *warning* call, as when the hawk hovers near, a *warning* call, when the night comes with its chill; a *feeding* call, when she has a morsel for hunger; and a *fostering* call, when she would invite them to her cherishing care.

Of comparison and similes none surpass the following:

"They shall mount up with wings *as Eagles*" (Is. 40:31).

"They that wait on the Lord shall renew"—literally *exchange*—"strength"—exchanging exhaustion for replenishment.

Two contrary qualities are noticeable in this king of birds: great capacity for action, sustained effort; and equally remarkable capacity for repose.

It is obviously built for *flight*; its form, the most perfect known for sweeping rapidly through the air with maximum of speed and minimum of resistance; its bones, light, hollow, cylindrical, the peculiar structure that most combines lightness and strength; its feathers, made to move, each as a little wing to propel with the least effort.

The Eagle is built for high altitudes, capable of respiration in the most elevated, attenuated atmosphere; and with an eye that can bear a cloudless sky and look the sun in the face. Thus built to live in the firmament, it belongs rather to heaven than earth.

It is also adapted to meet and master tempestuous winds, fly before them and outstrip them in speed; or, when needful, turn, confront, and fly against them. Not afraid of the storm, the Eagle can grapple with fierce tempests.

On the other hand, it is as capable of long sustained repose. No other bird can stand so still, hold so fast, and rest so perfectly. Grasping the rough crag with its talons, it settles down, bending the legs; and by a curious arrangement of muscles and tendons, as the weight of the body rests on them, the talons fasten only the more securely upon the rock. The great bird sleeps with absolute confidence, for it cannot fall, as its hold cannot relax unless the body, rising, lifts its weight; perched on an inaccessible crag, it can remain motionless for an entire day, renewing strength, recuperating exhausted energy, resting to prepare for a new wrestle with the elements. No bird lives so *alone*. Eagles are solitary, do not move in flocks like inferior fowls, but live in separation, at most accompanied only by a mate; again reminding us of the solitary saint, seeking habitual aloneness with God.

Hence the Eagle's flight is Jehovah's illustration of the tireless and triumphant activity of those whose strength He renews, and suggests:

1. Length of pinions, the wings often, when outspread, measuring from seven to nine feet from tip to tip.

2. Strength of pinions; from the oldest times, the eagle being regarded as the emblem of strength and courage, like the lion among beasts.

3. Loftiness of flight, no bird soaring higher or more delighting in the uppermost realms, far above clouds.

4. Powerfulness of flight, facing violent winds and flying in the face of them, antagonism stimulating energy.

5. Tirelessness of exertion, maintaining continuous flight for many hours and actually resting on the wing.

6. Renewal of vitality. This last emphatic reference is to the reinvigoration following the moulting of the plumes, suggesting the future upspringing of resurrection saints after the exchange of the body of humiliation for the new plumage of glory. This imagery of the mounting up of eagles is continued throughout Scripture from the time of the Exodus, to the ascension of our Lord, the "Great Eagle" of Revelation 12:14.

If doctrine supplies structure for discourse and pillars to uphold the temple of truth, illustrations are as windows to flood it with light, and none are so perfect for their purpose as those God uses. We need to study Biblical similes and comparisons, illustrative narratives and figures of speech. So forcible are God's illustrations that they often convince as arguments, and, like analogies, fit the truth at every point. Note Hebrews 9:15–17. In the Matter of a Last Will and Testament, there are eight necessary conditions:

1. A Legator, or Testator.
2. A Legacy, bequeathed by Testament.
3. A Legatee or body of heirs.
4. A Death of the Testator.
5. A Probate Court, acting on the Will.
6. An Executor or body of Executors.
7. An Execution or carrying out of the Will.
8. An Election on the part of the heirs.

This last condition may not be universal, but prevails in Localities, the heirs appearing at court and electing to "take under the Will"—

as it stands; or to "take under the Law," that is to dispute the Will, and try to break it so as to get a larger share of the estate.

The illustration is as perfect as it could well be.

God the Father wills an estate to heirs, the Lord Jesus Christ being the Mediator of the New Testament. There is an inheritance to be divided; and a body of qualified heirs. There is a judgment-death of the mediator necessary to make the estate available to the heirs. Heaven is the probate court approving the will and declaring its terms fulfilled; Christ, risen and ascended, is His Own Executor and Administrator and the Advocate of His people. There is also an actual division of the inheritance, now, in foretaste, while heirs are in minority; and hereafter in full possession when majority is reached.

The only condition to be fulfilled is that the heirs shall elect to "*take under the will*," and not dispute the provisions of Grace. This is the acceptance by faith of the offer of Salvation. Dr. H. C. Mabie tells of an actual occurrence in his congregation, where a lawyer arose, after a sermon on the subject, and expressed his desire then and there to "take under the will."*

As an example of figurative language, we cite "*Bearing the Mark*" (Gal. 6:17) or more literally: "the brand—*stigmata*—of my Master, Jesus Christ." The word "Lord" means, in this connection, legal owner or possessor, "Stigmata" is the common word for the brand with which masters marked slaves, especially those who had run away or showed signs of so doing. Professor Mahaffy says:

> In the numerous records of manumissions found at Delphi and at other shrines in Greece, we have learned the legal process by which a slave gained his own liberty. He did not bring his master his earnings, and obtain his freedom with his receipt for the money; but went to the temple of the god, and there paid in his money to the priests; who then with this money bought the slave from his master on the part of the god, and he became for the rest of his life a slave of the god, which meant practically freedom, subject to certain periodical religious duties. If at any future time his master or his master's heirs reclaimed him, he had the record of the transaction in the temple. But on one point these documents are silent. If he traveled, if he were far from home, and were seized as a runaway slave, what secu-

---

* *Methods in Soul Winning.*

rity could he have? I believe St. Paul gives us the solution. When liberated at the temple the priest, if he desired it, branded him with the "stigmata" of his new master, Apollo. Now St. Paul's words acquired a new and striking application. He had been the slave of sin; but he had been purchased by Christ, and his new liberty consisted in his being the slave of Christ. Henceforth, he says, let no man attempt to reclaim me; I have been marked on my body with the brand of my new master, Jesus Christ. Probably he referred to the many scars he bore of his persecutions.

38

Typology and Symbolism

THE STUDY OF TYPES has unhappily fallen into disrepute in some quarters, by the fact that some have carried to excess an allegorical and mythical method of interpretation, tracing in every detail of Scripture, some fanciful notion or forecast; as when one writer seeks to prove the doctrine of the Trinity from the first word of Genesis, *bara*—because the three initial letters—beth, resh and aleph—are respectively the initial letters of the words which stand for "Son," "Spirit," and "Father," which may be only a coincidence and without designed significance.

Biblical *types* require a volume of themselves.

There are several distinct sorts:

1. Typical Persons, like Adam, Cain and Abel, Melchizedek, Abram and Isaac, Moses and Aaron, Joshua, Samuel, Saul and David, Ruth, Rahab, Jonah.

2. Typical Events, like Babel's confusion of tongues, the crossing of the Red Sea, lifting up the brazen serpent, smiting the rock, siege of Jericho, Pentecost, etc.

3. Typical Actions, like Zedekiah's making horns of iron, to represent the repulse of the Syrians (2 Chr. 18:10).

4. Typical Structures, like Noah's Ark, Tabernacle, Temple, Solomon's House of Cedar, etc.

5. Typical Furniture, like altar, laver, ark and Mercy Seat.

6. Typical Ritual, like offerings, five great festivals, Passover, etc., day of atonement, year of Jubilee, etc.

7. Typical Robes, like high priest's breastplate and Holy Crown.

8. Typical Rules and Regulations, like laws about unclean contact with the dead, etc.

9. Typical Forms, like cube, pyramid, sphere, or square, circle and triangle.

10. Typical Colors, like blue, red, white, purple, green, etc.

11. Typical Numbers, like four, seven, twelve, forty, seventy, one hundred, etc.

12. Typical Instruments, like trumpets, harps, rod, spear, hammer, etc.

We mention a few prominent types of Scripture which richly compensate study, and about which there is a consensus of opinion.

Babel and Babylon—type of a godless, man-glorifying civilization.

The Beast—of a tyrannical, oppressive heathen monarchy.

Blindness—of ignorance, willful misapprehension and judicial veiling.

Bride—of redeemed church of Christ.

Bridegroom—of Christ in covenant with His people.

Bulls—of violent foes, destroying God's heritage.

Candlesticks—of churches.

Chariots—of hosts of God, or obedient angelic servants.

Crown—of victory and reward.

Cup—of divine blessing in fullness.

Darkness—of gloom, wretchedness, despair.

Dogs—of the impure and vile and persecuting.

Door—of entrance, opening to salvation or opportunity.

Dragon—of Satan in violent assault.

Fire—of Power of God—generally in judgment.

Furnace—deep affliction.

Garments—of righteousness, or sin.

Gates—of power and security especially connected with sessions of judges and armed forces.

Girdle—of strength, particularly in race.

Hail—of sudden divine judgment in retribution.

Harvest—of good or evil brought to ripeness.

Hunger, etc.—of strong yearning, unsatisfied desire.

Incense—of prayer, praise and intercession.

Keys—of authority and control.
Night—of adversity, superstition, affliction.
Oil—of fertility, joy, anointing.
Palms—of victory.
Rock—of fixed truths and refuge.
Rod—of government and correction.
Salt—of influence, saving and savoring society.
Sea—of human society, especially in revolt.
Serpent—of subtlety and treachery—the devil.
Sheep—of disciples.
Star—of a prince or prominent ruler.
Sword—of slaughter or division.
Wilderness—of time or place of tribulation and exile.
Yoke—of toil and restraint.

Blue is for some reason, very conspicuous, as in the Tabernacle. The Robe of the Ephod was "all of blue," and this is the predominating color, appearing in the "gate of the court," the "door of the Tabernacle," the veil and innermost curtains, the ephod, lower fastenings of the breastplate, ribbon which encircled the miter and held fast the holy crown; in the miter itself and the covering for the sacred vessels. We find it again conspicuous in the paved work below, and the firmament above, when the God of Israel was seen by the Elders (Ex. 24:10) and in the wall of the City of God (Rev. 21:19). What the blue *means*, we can only infer from the fact that it is preeminently the *heavenly hue*, as green is the earthly. Blue overarches the whole world, above; we cannot look up without seeing it everywhere and always, and, however clouded, still eternally there. Thus it may well represent the *Divine faithfulness*—God's perpetual love and grace—His unfailing promise and covenant; and, so interpreted, every reference to blue, in the inspired Word, gets a new beauty and meaning. Man may vary, as the earth presents a thousand aspects and colors, from the bright green of grass and foliage to the dull gray of desert sands, or the brown of decay and the black of blight; but over all alike and always is God's heavenly dome of blue.

Such uniform usage of the Scriptures naturally suggests a probability of typical intent and meaning, which sometimes approaches certainty. Here it is well again to note the first mention.

For example, the reference to trees of a certain species is very consistent throughout, each having its own fixed associations and natural suggestions.

The Juniper tree—despondency (1 Kgs. 19:4, 5).

The Mulberry tree—God's signal and man's opportunity (2 Sam. 5:23, 24).

The Olive tree—God's promise—especially as to *Israel*. This is especially interesting (Gen. 8:11; Ps. 128:3; Rom. 11:7–24).

The Palm—Victory and uprightness (Judg. 4:5; Ps. 92:12; Jer. 10:5; John 12:13; Rev: 7:9).

The Cedar—Permanence, Richness and Fragrance (2 Sam. 7:2; Ps. 92:12).

The Fig Tree—Fruitfulness or disappointed promise of fruit (Num. 13:23; Matt. 21:19; Luke 13:6, 7).

The Sycamine or Sycamore Tree—That is deep-rooted and ineradicable (Luke 17:6). Fruit, wild and abundant (1 Kgs. 10:27; Is. 9:10; Luke 19:4).

The Apple Tree—Satisfaction, sustenance, consolation (Song 2:3–5). A very remarkable typical metaphor is the *Olive Tree* (Rom. 11:16–24). Again, the figure is almost an analogy.

1. The Root—Patriarchal ancestry.
2. The Soil—The territory of Canaan.
3. The Branches—The stock ramifying into tribes and families.
4. The Fatness—The rich privileges of the Elect Nation.
5. The Flower—Messiah; the consummate bloom and fruit.
6. The Excision—Cutting off the original branches on account of unbelief.
7. The Grafting—Gentile Scions, incorporated through faith.
8. The Re-ingrafting—Restoration of Israel.
9. The Husbandman—Jehovah; planting, pruning, grafting.
10. The Ultimate Result—Fruitfulness; Glory to God.

There are some three instances when the *Fig Tree* appears very prominent; they appear to have a link of connection. Our Lord's own application of the "Barren Fig Tree" to the Jewish Nation, suggests a possible key to the references to this tree in Scripture, and it seems to unlock many passages in both Testaments. Of the score of references, we select three as most conspicuous:

Luke 13:6–9. The Barren Fig tree spared for another year of culture and opportunity.

Mark 11:12–14, 20, 21. The fruitless Fig tree, cursed and withered away—dried up from the roots.

Matthew 24:32–24. The blossoming of the Fig tree—a sign of the speedy consummation of the age.

Taking these in this their apparent chronological order, the Jewish Nation, even after three dispensational "years" of barrenness, have a fourth period of probation, as from the Crucifixion of Christ to the Destruction of Jerusalem.

Then, the Nation, having failed to fulfill the promise of its history and opportunity, fell under the curse.

Finally, the restoration of the Jew to national unity and covenant relation is to usher in the Millennium.

Still more careful analysis will suggest minuter points of analogy, for example:

The "three years" of Luke 13:7 may represent the three years of our Lord's personal ministry, He being at the time near the end of the third. During the first there had been the preaching of John the Baptist, as well as His own; in the second, conspicuous miracles and appeals to the Jewish people; in the last, His great passion and atoning death. And yet the Jews were spared for the Pentecostal witness to His Deity.

The "fig tree in the way" may suggest the Jew as in the very path of our Lord's career, with ostentatious display of pharisaic zeal and formal obedience, but, while saying, "Lord," "Lord," doing not what He says, but rather making God's Word of none effect, etc.

Compare other recurrences of the reference to the fig tree.

The types and symbols of the Holy Spirit are most instructive:

Air, as breath, atmosphere, wind.

Light, burning in fire or flame, shining in radiance, illumining darkness, beautifying and glorifying that on which it falls.

Water, diffused in atmospheric moisture, condensed in rain, distilled in dew, poured in floods and streams.

One remarkable feature here is that all these are *elemental*, and a peculiarity of all elements is that they are universally pervasive and comprehensive, necessary to life, immeasurable and inexhaustible, independent; and that, while they are in us, we are also in them.

The types used to represent *Service* are very significant.

The first prominent typical lesson of this sort is connected with the *Rod* of Moses, which was probably nothing more or less than a shepherd's crook, which may have been the rudest sort of a staff. But Jehovah said to him: "What is that in thine hand?" And he answered: "A rod." And, He Said: "Take this rod in thine hand, wherewith thou shalt do signs" (Ex. 4:1–5, 17). Here the obvious lesson is that the simplest tool or weapon God can use for a sign or instrument of His power.

With Joshua, the *Spear* was conspicuous.

In the Book of Judges we have a series of such lessons. All the deliverers of Israel by their own weakness or obscurity or the inadequacy of the means they used, glorified the power of God. Ehud was left-handed; Shamgar slew 600 with an ox-goad; Deborah was a woman; Jael took a tent pin and hammer to slay Sisera; Gideon used lamps and pitchers and trumpets to create a panic among the Midianites; Samson slew a thousand men with the jawbone of an ass; etc.

Subsequently, the "Axe" and "Saw," "Hammer" and "Rod" are referred to as passive instruments, wholly ineffective apart from the hand that wields them (Is. 10:15; Jer. 1:23). In both Testaments, a "vessel"—especially an earthen vessel—is used as a symbol of service (Jer. 18:4; 2 Tim. 2:21).

There can be no accident in all this—a rod, a spear, an oxgoad, a tent pin, a hammer, a trumpet, lamp, pitcher, a jawbone, an axe, a saw, a vessel. Here are twelve symbols of human service—all of them powerless in themselves, useful only because passive in the hand of him that uses them. None of them can even lift themselves up or lay themselves down, or move themselves; a trumpet cannot sound of itself, an axe cleave of itself, a vessel fill, carry or empty itself. The join lesson of all this obviously is that we are only powerful as we are passive—surrendered to the Hand and Will of the Great Workman.

In Exodus 21:5, 6, provision is made for a servant who in the Year of Release refuses to leave his master, that his ear shall be bored through with an awl, in token of perpetual and willing servitude. In

Psalm 40:6, 7, "Mine ears hast Thou bored" refers to this custom, and is a typical expression of the reference of the Messianic Servant for His Father's will.

In Hebrews 10:5, "But a body has Thou fitted Me," etc., the quotation from the Old Testament serves a double purpose: first, it explains the reference in the Psalm as Messianic, and again it reconciles an apparent inaccuracy in the quotation. The language in the Epistle to the Hebrews becomes the Spirit's commentary on the sentence in the Psalm, and although the words vary the sense is equivalent. Junius says, "The ear is a member of the body; by the piercing of the ear hearing becomes possible; and only by the hearing does the body become the instrument of obedience." As the slave's body became a declared instrument of obedience when his ear was bored, so by the conception of the Holy Spirit was Christ's body fitted to be the instrument of service to the Father. When the Israelite servant protested his unwillingness to leave his master, his bored ear expressed a body newly surrendered to service, and even the change of words here interprets the Psalm's meaning.

The *indirect* prophetic element has ampler consideration in connection with the study of types, but a singular forecast of coming events sometimes may be detected in a simple historic occurrence.

In Judges 6:37–40, Gideon's two signs of the wet and the dry fleece primarily were meant to assure him that in his difficult task, Jehovah was with him. But compared with Hosea 14:5, Romans 11:30–32, etc., it is easy to see how the two great periods of Hebrew history are forecast: First, the 2000 years during which God was "as the dew unto Israel"; they were made the handful of fleece on the floor, saturated with moisture, while dryness was on all nations round about. Then, for another period, already nearly 2000 years, there have been on Israel, dryness and spiritual death, and the Spirit poured out on the Gentiles round about.

Thus, the close student finds constant surprises in the Word of God, correspondences that are both too frequent and too exact to be accidental. He finds a *pervasive, prophetic elements*, in the bird it is not only the wings that fit for flight, but the hollow, cylindric and air–filled bones and whole shape and structure of the body.

In Solomon's Temple, the wings of the cherubim touched one another in the midst of the Holiest of All, and being stretched forth reached with their tips the side walls, thus spanning the entire breadth of the Sanctuary. Who can think of them without at least being reminded of the two great dispensations, which, touching each other in the midst of history at the Cross of Calvary, where God was manifested in the flesh, reach backward to the limits of past history in Creation and forward to the limits of future history in the new Creation, at the end of the ages!

39

Value of Historic Sidelights

GREAT ORATION IS THE PRODUCT of a threefold sympathy on the part of the orator; sympathy with his *theme*, sympathy with his *audience*, sympathy with the *occasion*. If he be not in sympathy with his theme or subject, he cannot enter deeply into it and unfold it. If he be not sympathetic with his audience, he cannot reach and touch their convictions and emotions and resolves. If he be not in sympathy with the occasion, he will not feel the inspiration of the practical issues, needs and duties which lend to oratory its main value. The first sort of sympathy is rhetorical, the second personal, and the third, actual and practical.

A reader and student of Scripture needs a similar threefold sympathy: First, with the subject of which it treats; then with the divine Author and hymnal writer; and finally with the object for which it is written, and the circumstances that determined both subject and object. Therefore, beside the incidental references in other sections to the historic sidelights thrown upon the narratives and discourses of Scripture, it seems important to give this department further illustration.

In 1 Corinthians 10:1–14 is a brief outline of the history of the children of Israel from Egypt to Canaan, with the distinct statement that "all these things happened unto them for examples, and are written for our learning and admonition"; and we are here taught to find, beneath Old Testament historical narratives, a deeper spiritual meaning. The passage through the Red Sea, the manna, the Rock, are treated, respectively, as types of Baptism, and of Christ as our spiritual food and drink. In 2 Corinthians 3:1—4:6, the glory on Moses' face and the veil which he put on, are used as types of the glory of the divine Word and the veiling of the mind of the Jews to its real teaching.

In Galatians 4:24–31, the story of Sarah and Hagar, Isaac and Ishmael, is treated as "an allegory," illustrative of the fact that the liberty, born of grace, and the bondage, born of legalism, cannot dwell together in harmony in the same believing heart; and that the legal spirit must be cast out to make room for the gracious growth of the spirit of faith.

A key to the Epistle to the Ephesians may be found in Acts 19, Paul's experience at Ephesus, with four incidents of major importance:

1. Twelve disciples, receiving the Holy Spirit, are at once raised to the heavenlies, in a higher knowledge and experience of both truth and life.

2. Seven sons of Sceva, a Jew, undertaking to exorcise evil spirits, are by them overcome, and signally worsted and wounded.

3. Many Ephesian magi, masters of deceitful arts, who have practiced on the credulity of the people, are converted, confess their deeds and publicly burn their costly books.

4. There is a terrible tumult in the Ephesian theater and an appeal to Diana worshipers by the town clerk.

How naturally, in writing to Ephesian disciples, Paul would emphasize the new and heavenly knowledge of the power and love of God into which it was their privilege to enter by the Spirit; the awful power and malignity of demoniac agencies, and the need of the panoply of God if we are to overcome and stand in the evil day; the grand transformations both of character and conduct wrought by the power of God (Eph. 2:1–13; 4:14–29; 5:6–13); and the Spiritual Temple of God, in contrast with the Fane and Shrine of Diana—one of the seven wonders of the world (2:20–22). Also the glorious beauty and symmetry of the divine Temple and the invisible Dweller therein; as also the slight and cunning craftiness of moral impostors, who play on popular credulity by tricks of sophistry and cunning (4:15; 5:11);

and the profane revelry, connected with heathen fanes in contrast with the filling of the Spirit (5:18; 6:19).

Thus the whole contents of this Epistle are illustrated, interpreted and illuminated by placing, side by side, with this letter the brief record of a visit and sojourn at the capital of pagan worship.

In Hebrews 3—12, ten entire chapters, constituting the bulk of the whole Epistle, are occupied with the typical treatment of Old Testament history and prophecy; and with such fullness of detail as to suggest that here we have the essence and substance of that discourse of our Lord on the way to Emmaus which is referred to in Luke 24, but nowhere else outlined.

The two Epistles of Peter are based on the suggestive analogy between the desert wandering and the pilgrimage of God's believing people from earth to heaven.

James constantly refers to the same old-time events, particularly naming Abraham's offering of Isaac, the giving of the Law at Sinai, Rahab's reception of the spies, the trials of Job, the schools of wisdom in Solomon's days, the triumphant prayers of Elijah.

Jude makes at least ten references in his brief letter, to the events of Old Testament history from Adam to Balaam; and as for the Apocalypse, it would be a temple without windows—one dark mystery—but for the constant references to the same Old Testament records which flood it with light. For examples, as we have already seen, the successive rewards promised to the overcomers, in the Epistles to the seven churches, must be interpreted by the history from Eden to Solomon—the "tree of life," the "death" of the fall, the "manna" of the desert, the war with Amalek, the "white raiment" of the priesthood, the building of the temple, and the "throne" of Solomon.

How obvious it is that here, in at least seven or eight conspicuous books of the later Scriptures the illustrations and imagery are so drawn from the earlier, that the two are inseparably interwoven; in many cases the very pattern of the fabric is in Old Testament design and coloring; or, to adopt Paul's own figures in Ephesians 2:21; 4:16, it resembles a temple in which all the parts are fitly framed or joined together, or a body in which they are not only so framed and joined, but compacted into living unity by that which every joint supplieth according to the effectual workings in the measure of every part.

Peter's Epistles, so obviously framed with reference to the desert journey from Rameses to the Jordan, show at least fifty points of illumining correspondence if compared with the narrative from Exodus to Joshua. Every great stage and experience of that forty years may be found hinted more or less obscurely:

In the very names and words used, "pilgrims," "strangers," "sojourning," etc. (2:11; 1:17).

In the reference to pilgrim attire and habits (1:13).

The Paschal Lamb and Bloody Sacrifices (1:18, 19; 2:5).

The Consecration of the Priesthood (2:5, 9).

The Divine choice of the People as an elect nation (2:9, 10).

The need of harmony among pilgrims.

The awful judgments upon the disobedient (4:17).

The appointment of the Seventy (5:1–3).

The Tabernacle and Tents (2 Pet. 1:13).

The Entrance into Canaan (2 Pet. 1:11).

There are many more possible and probable references:

The promises Inheritance (1 Pet. 1:4, 5).

The Trials of Faith (1:7).

The Revelations of Jehovah's Holiness (1:15, 16).

The scorched pastures of the Desert (1:24).

The Exodus from Egypt (2:9, 10).

The flocks and herds of the pilgrims (2:25; 5:2, 4).

The spoils of Egypt, their jewels (3:3, 4).

The Temptations to Lust, Moab, etc. (4:1–4).

The wild beasts encountered (5:8, 9).

The forty-two stations on the route (2 Pet. 1:5–11).

What a flood of Light the Transfiguration throws on the words of Peter (2 Pet. 1:16–21). The four words applied to our Lord, "power," "majesty," "honor," "glory," are nowhere else found in such conjunction. This was the one occasion in His earthly life when His divine characteristics, omnipotence, supreme majesty, essential glory, and exalted dignity were disclosed to moral eyes—when His disguise was swept aside to reveal the star of universal empire, glittering beneath, and the crown of imperial dominion on His brow. In fact, no other commentary is needed, when Matthew 17:1–8, Mark 9:1–9, and Luke 9:26–36, are used as sidelights to illumine the words in Peter's Epistle. Even the reference to the "tabernacle"—a word very rarely used in the New Testament—is explained by his impulsive exclamation on the mount—"let us make here three tabernacles"; the word he uses of his own "decease" is the same which our Lord used on that occasion—"*exodus*"—of His approaching death; and then, when "the Kingdom of God came with power," in that vision of glory, were made known unto Peter the "*power* and *coming*" of the Lord Jesus. That Transfiguration was a revelation of the "excellent glory"—eyes and ears being overwhelmed by what they saw and heard. it was the day dawn of glory, making even the light of prophecy only, in comparison, as a glimmer of a torch in the darkness of night. There is perhaps no one instance in which one paragraph in an Epistle is so lit up with illuminative clearness and transparency of meaning by a narrative in the gospel history, as in this case.

The number so mysteriously found in Revelation 13:18, as the number of the Beast, 666, is found but twice, elsewhere (1 Kgs. 10:14; Ezra 2:13).

Its first occurrence seems to be significant. There is something at least startling in finding, in this simple historical statement, explicitly repeated in 2 Chronicles 9:13, the same number which is thus afterward invested with a significance, so terrible and mysterious—a coincidence which Professor Plumptre says can hardly be looked on as casual. Inasmuch as the "Seer of the apocalypse lives entirely in Holy Scripture," on this territory alone is the solution of the sacred riddle to be sought (Hengstenberg). Is there here, then, any hint supplied of the possible significance of this repeating decimal .666+?

Notice at least three points: 1. The wealth of Solomon represented worldly accumulations largely contrary to the express prohibition of God (Deut. 17:16, 17). In fact, his whole course in this respect was in disobedience to the explicit will of God. This estimate of his annual revenue of gold, exclusive of all payments in kind, represents *mammon*, worldly riches, carnally accumulated.

2. The Apocalyptic Seer writes expressly to set in contrast the earthly Babylon and the Heavenly Jerusalem, the Man of Sin and the

Son of God—the counterfeit apostate woman and the genuine Bride of Christ—the false riches and the true—and it is not unnatural that this number should reappear stamped on the image of the Beast.

3. The Worship of the Beast and the homage paid to Mammon are identical. It reproduces in the latter days the illusive glamour and glory of the former days when Solomon's disregard of the law of God led to these vast multiplications of gold in his coffers. That annual revenue then marked the glory of his riches as not of God but of the Devil—more becoming to Babel than to the city of God.

Revelation 15:3. And they sing the song of Moses, the servant of God, and the son of the Lamb.

This unique phrase is found nowhere else, and must have some marked significance. As to the "Song of Moses," at the shores of the Red Sea, that is the first song sung in the Bible narrative; it is the first great psalm of victory, and is especially ascribed to Moses in Exodus 15:1, As to the "Song of the Lamb," it seems to be referred to in Revelation 14:1–3. There is a curious correspondence between the two: these are respectively the *first* and *last* instances when the word "song" occurs. They celebrate the Deliverance from Egypt and the pursuing foes, on the one hand, and the final Deliverance from Satan and all foes of spiritual life, on the other; they mark the two bounds of Redemption history, and between them lies the whole history of God's ransomed people. The reference to the song of Moses carries us back to the Red Sea, rather than to that dying song of Deuteronomy 32, and hence the title "Servant of God" (Ex. 14:31). The mission of the angels was to renew the plagues of Egypt (Rev. 15). The song of Moses was sung *after* the Hebrews escaped those plagues; the song of the Lamb *anticipates* the final triumph of the redeemed over the enemies of Christ and His church. Thus the song of Moses is renewed and invested with a higher meaning in this new connection.

Moreover, as Israel had stood on the *shore* of the Red Sea, whose waves had stood upright as a wall for their protection, having victoriously passed over and seen the destruction of their foes; so now the victorious saints stand *on the sea itself*, now no longer as treacherous waters wherein the feet sink, but as solid glass under the feet, having a firm footing like their Master on the Galilean Lake; and the sea is no more tumultuous as well as treacherous, but smooth as glass, and reflecting their glory as they stand upon it.

As to reference to the "White Stone" in Revelation 2:17, Professor Ramsay in a learned but lucid article finds the interpretation in the fact that superstitious people would sleep in a temple in the hope that some vision for their guidance would be vouchsafed to them by the god of the shrine. If during such *incubatio* they deemed such a vision was granted them, they henceforth *wore around their necks a white stone, upon which was written a new name, which they took*. In support of this interpretation the learned Professor instances Aelius Aristides, the great rhetorician of Asia Minor in the second century, who always carried within such a "synthema," as a pledge of divine aid in the pursuit of the course marked out for him by his god. Upon this memento was his newly adopted name of Theodorus, "the gift of God."

This is a case in which secular history becomes a sidelight on the sacred narrative.

Of the value of common historic facts to interpret biblical references, perhaps the best illustration is found in the Olympic and Isthmian games, from which Paul especially draws no small proportion of his figurative and metaphorical language, as in 1 Corinthians 9:24–27; Philippians 3:12–14; Hebrews 12:1, etc.

In the first of these three passages a knowledge of the laws of the racecourse and arena of competitive athletics is quite essential to avoid misinterpretation. Before the games began a herald entered the stadium and proclaimed aloud the condition of entrance into the lists, such as these: Competitors must be of pure Hellenic blood; freemen, not slaves; untainted by crime or treason; and must have gone through the prescribed course of training, etc. And this explains Paul's words about possibly being a "castaway"—the word *adokimos* means a "rejected candidate"—one who could not stand the test. It refers not to his *salvation*, which he never questioned, but to his *reward as a racer*. He kept himself in training, lest after entering the racecourse as a herald proclaiming the conditions of acceptable service, he himself should be set aside as unworthy of the race and the prize.

40

Representative Historical Scenes

CERTAIN MEMORABLE EVENTS are bold historic landmarks that both define and divide the territory of the ages; and it is well to make our own maps of Time with those events in their proper location, as converging and radiating centers. In the following list, capitals are used at the beginning of each paragraph, to indicate those of *primary* importance, and those that immediately succeed in the paragraph represent the secondary under the same class.

CREATION—Six successive days of creative energy: last of all, man, woman; Eden and Tree of Life, etc.

THE FALL—Expulsion from Eden. First recorded sacrifice—first murder. Epoch's Translation.

THE DELUGE—Ark building—first world-judgment. New beginning of the human race under Noah, and new occupation.

BABEL—First idol center. Second great act of divine judgment. Confusion of tongues and dispersion of mankind.

CALL OF ABRAM—First formal separation unto God. First recorded covenant of God with man, on basis of *Faith*.

BURNING OF SODOM, etc.—Third great judgment. Sins of carnality and sensuality carried to climax, and compelling doom.

EXODUS FROM EGYPT—Fourth representative judgment. Beginning of an elect nation. Passover, crossing Red Sea, Pillar of Cloud, etc.

LAWGIVING AT SINAI—Beginning of legal code. Tabernacle, priesthood, sacrifice. Revolt at Kadesh Barnea, etc.

ENTRANCE INTO CANAAN—Crossing Jordan. Fall of Jericho. Occupation of land. Moral decline. Civil anarchy—period of Judges.

KINGDOM ESTABLISHED—Samuel's Judgeship. Three reigns. Temple building. Visit of Queen of Sheba. Solomon's idolatry and apostasy.

KINGDOM DIVIDED—Revolt of ten tribes. Jeroboam and calf worship. Baal worship. Ahab and Jezebel. Elijah's translation. Elisha. Sennacherib's defeat. Revival under Josiah, etc.

CAPTIVITY—Israel in Assyria. Judah in Babylon. Jerusalem destroyed and temple.

DECREE OF CYRUS—Daniel in Babylon. Ezekiel, Jeremiah, etc.

RETURN FROM EXILE—Second temple dedicated. City rebuilt. Deliverance of Jews under Esther. Fall of Babylon. Jonah's mission to Nineveh, etc. Synagogue worship, etc.

OLD TESTAMENT CANON—Ezra the Scribe. Septuagint translation. Pharisees, etc. Sanhedrin.

The following belong to the *New Testament* Period:

JOHN [THE] BAPTIST—Last of Old Testament succession of seers. Forerunner of Christ. Baptism of repentance. Reformer.

BIRTH OF CHRIST—Virgin mother. First appearance at temple as "Son of Commandment." Early years at Nazareth. Carpenter.

BAPTISM AND TEMPTATION—Anointing of Spirit. Fasting. Threefold testing. Victory as second man and recovery of Adam's lost scepter.

BEGINNING OF MINISTRY—First gospel message. Initial miracle. Calling of disciples. Sermon on Mount, etc.

TRANSFIGURATION—First full disclosure of deity. Moses and Elijah. Discourse on coming "Exodus."

PASSION WEEK—Triumphal entry as king and rejection by the Jewish rulers. Passover. Last discourse and supper. Gethsemane. Arrest and mock trial.

CRUCIFIXION—Two thieves. Seven sentences on cross. Death, burial, etc. Sealing of sepulcher.

RESURRECTION—Sloughing off grave clothes. Successive appearance to chosen witnesses. Walk to Emmaus. Forty days. Teaching about kingdom.

ASCENSION—Final interviews. Galilee and "Five Hundred." Last commission. Session at God's right hand. Priestly intercession, etc.

PENTECOST—Ten days' waiting. Outpouring at Jerusalem, in Samaria, at Caesarea, at Ephesus. Church established. Judgment of Ananias and Sapphira.

PERSECUTION—Action of Jewish rulers. Dispersion of disciples. Martyrdom of Stephen. Conversion of Saul.

FOREIGN MISSIONS—Church at Antioch. Call of Barnabas and Saul. Three successive mission tours. Europe entered at Philippi. Paul at Rome.

ERA OF DECLINE—Beginning of heresy and apostasy. Twenty-five years of comparative silence. Suspended inspiration, etc.

NEW TESTAMENT CANON—Three synoptic gospels. Epistles of Paul, etc., Jude, etc., John's special ministry to church in decline. Apocalypse.

DESTRUCTION OF JERUSALEM—Final dispersion of Jews and end of Jewish dispensation.

The great *Day of Atonement* was one of the central historic scenes of the Old Testament (Lev. 16) The two goats—one slain for expiation of guilt, the other, "Azazel"—goat of "removal," led away from before the presence of Jehovah and out of sight of the people, beautifully represent, together, sin as both atoned for and borne away to be no more remembered or brought to mind.

Isaiah 1:18:

> Though your sins be as scarlet
>   They shall be as white a snow;
> Though they be red like crimson,
>   They shall be as wool.

The Rabbis explain this by the miracle which tradition affirms to be connected with the Day of Atonement: that when the lot used to be taken of the Lord's goat and Azazel, a scarlet fillet was bound on the head of the latter, which, after Aaron's confession of his sins and those of the people, became white as snow; and it is added that for years before the destruction of Jerusalem by Titus this miracle had ceased. This latter is a remarkable admission of the parties that clamored for our Lord's crucifixion, inasmuch as, if true, it would make the time of the cessation of the miracle coincide with their rejection of the Messiah.

It is a curious fact that, if the most conspicuous events of both dispensations are carefully cataloged and arranged, they number in all about thirty, and that the central one that is a sort of golden milestone to which all roads run and from whence all radiate is the *Cross of Christ*.

Calvary thus becomes, in a double sense, the central historic scene of Scripture and of the world's history. Its significance therefore must be inexhaustible. About those three crosses on Golgotha endless mediation lingers and hovers, with ever new revelations of truth and grace. In the center we see the suffering "Son of Man," the vicarious, atoning Savior. On His right hand a penitent and believing malefactor, who that day is promised to be with Him in Paradise; on the left, as impenitent rejector and blasphemer, who, from the side of that same Savior, goes down to the second death. How sublimely simple the lesson, and how comprehensive. Here every great truth about sin and salvation, mercy and judgment is representatively hinted. Look at the truth taught about SIN:

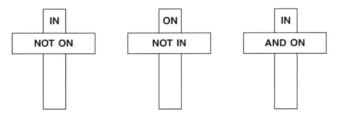

Mr. B. W. Newton well says that in these three crosses we have a whole system of practical theology. Our Lord Jesus Christ is in the midst—the Mediator in whom and through whom we have eternal life. On one side the unbelieving thief, who abides in death; on the other the believing thief, who enters into life: so that, as we look from one to the other, it is though we "passed from death to life, through Jesus Christ our Lord."

The *Transfiguration* should rank in our thought, as, in one aspect, the supreme event of our Lord's human life, being the *only occasion when His Godhead was fully revealed*, the glory and majesty of that disclosure being more than human eyes could bear. Up to that point, His humanity was rather a cloak obscuring than a robe revealing His Deity; and, from that point, until His resurrection and ascension, the obscuration was even more complete. But, to prepare disciples for the awful tragedy before them, He permitted them for once to get a glimpse of the Son of Man coming in His glory and the kingdom of God, not in mystery, but in power.

The Resurrection of our Lord is without parallel as the one greatest event that has ever taken place. Only His Incarnation and Transfiguration deserve to be classed with it; and His final advent will complete the fourfold series with a full, final manifestation of His essential majesty, sovereignty and glory.

The Resurrection must not be regarded as an isolated fact or event, but as incorporated with the rest, and with the whole consistent body of supernatural working inseparable from the whole Christian system and constituting it. A bird is fitted for flight not by its wings alone, but by its whole structure—its shape, and the hollow, cylindrical bones, filled with air, make it buoyant. A pyramid's apex is but the crown of a pyramidal structure, itself a little pyramid, and all the lines and angles of the larger conform to the pattern of the smaller. So our Lord's Resurrection was but one feature and phase of a life that is throughout supernatural and superhuman. He was miraculously conceived, miraculously taught and wrought, miraculously rose and ascended, and His final reappearance will be throughout a miraculous manifestation. The Resurrection has two great aspects which need to be looked at side by side, as they have a close mutual bearing:

1. As related to our Lord Himself.

1. Historic. An unprecedented event. Firstborn from the dead to die no more.

2. Prophetic—crown of all prophecy (Acts 2:24–31).

3. Messianic—Demonstration of His Deity (Rom. 1:4).

2. As related to the disciple.

1. Type and pledge of believer's Resurrection (Phil. 3).

2. Establishing Faith in the Scriptures and in Him.

3. His Resurrection the model and measure of the believer's life (Rom. 6).

4. Miracle—greatest miracle—all miracles in one.	4. The pledge and supernatural life and power in Him.
5. Beginning of Exaltation coupled with ascension (Eph. 1).	5. Making possible and real a life in the Heavenlies even now (Eph. 1).
6. Lordship of universe (Eph. 4). "That He might fill the universe."	6. Secret of the pleroma—fullness of God in believer (Col. 2).
7. Secret of Pentecost (Acts 2).	7. The Indwelling of God by the Holy Spirit.
8. Victory over Satan (Heb. 2).	8. Guaranty of power over all foes, world, flesh, devil, death.
9. Complete Atonement.	9. Justification assured (Rom. 4:25).
10. Precursor of Final Advent.	10. Basis of Missions—gospel to a dying world.

Our Lord's Resurrection is given such prominence in the New Testament that it is more referred to than even His death, and for a sufficient reason, for without resurrection even His death would have had no saving power (1 Cor. 15).

The words of Romans 1:4 are of vast importance: "Declared to be the Son of God with power, according to the Spirit of Holiness, by the resurrection from the dead."

Here is an explicit statement that in this event is to be found the one all sufficient, convincing, irresistible *demonstration of the Deity of Christ*. The whole sentence is emphatic—"declared"—characterized by precision, definitely, distinctively set forth; "with power," "according to the Spirit of Holiness"—a phrase nowhere else found.

The importance of the Resurrection of our Lord is set forth in Scripture from many points of view, and the following should never be lost from view:

1. The fulfillment of a great Prophecy, in fact a center and keystone of all Messianic prediction (Acts 2:24–31).

2. The prefect demonstration of our Lord's Deity, including His ascension, which is connected with it as another stage in His upward progress from the lowest Hades to the highest Heavens. Compare Ephesians 1:19; 4:8–10.

3. The consummation of all miracle, itself not only the chief miracle, but all wonders in one, the deaf hearing, the blind seeing, the dumb speaking, the palsied limbs moving, when His dead body again heard and saw and spoke, and moved and walked.

4. The beginning of all Resurrection, a wholly unprecedented event. There had been reanimation, resuscitation of dead bodies before, but He was the first to rise to *die no more*. It was the inauguration of a new order and era.

5. The basis of all justification to the believer (Rom. 4:25; John 16:8–11). Had He Himself remained under the power of death, how could He deliver others who were under its penalty?

6. The type, pledge and pattern of the believer's resurrection (1 Cor. 15; Phil. 3:10, 11). Hence "the first fruits," a sample as well as a forecast of the coming harvest from the grave of buried saints.

7. The model and measure of the believer's spiritual life (Rom. 6:4; Eph. 1:19; John 11:25, 26). "Like as" He was raised, to die no more, "even so we also," identified with Him in death should be also in resurrection and henceforth walk in newness of life.

8. The basis of the Gospel message to a dying world. In the Acts of the Apostles and all the Epistles, Christ's Resurrection is the engrossing theme of pen and tongue, the central fact to be witnessed, and used to justify faith and hope.

9. The signal judgment upon Satan as having "the power of death" (Heb. 2:14, 15). In the so-called "Golden Legend" there is a singular passage representing all Hades as declaring that if the dying crucified One of Calvary comes hither, He who called Lazarus back from the dead, will break the dominion of the Devil in the realm of death.*

10. The condition of the Pentecostal Gift of the Spirit (Acts 2:32, 33; John 16:7). In both these passages the descension of the Spirit is made dependent on the ascension of our Lord.

From all points it was an event *without parallel*, nothing before or after it, comparable to it. In its manifold relation to our Lord Himself, the vindication of His claims and the consummation of His work; to the believer in his justification, sanctification and glorifica-

---

* *The Psalms in Human Life*, pp. 110–112.

tion; and to the proclamation of the Gospel, it is absolutely unri-valed in importance. Hence, Satan will never cease his efforts to make Christ's resurrection a myth, a tradition, an uncertainty, or even a fabrication, or to rob it of all its essential reality by spiritualizing it as an expression for the survival of the influence of a good life.

41

Links Between the Historical and Ethical

THERE are *parables in action* as well as in diction—lessons taught in acts as well as words. The eye is quicker to see than the ear to hear; and the imagination is more easily impressed and the memory stored with truth which takes visible form. Parables in action like those in discourse are often left unexplained or partially unveiled, to stimulate curiosity and docility, the deeper meaning half hidden behind the veil of a miraculous work, a strange occurrence, to be fully disclosed when prayerful search draws the veil aside.

Scenic representation appeals to the histrionic sense. History is God's age-long drama with its grand acts, its many scenes, its count-less actors, and the whole world and universe the stage and theater; only these are not fictions, but real august transactions. Details may be comparatively unimportant, because they are, like drapery and scenery, mere accessories to the main end—the great lesson God would teach, upon which attention should principally be fixed.

It is a singular fact that every great representative scene in Bible history seems meant to teach some marked lesson, and that such lessons are seldom, if ever *repeated.*

Take for example, the following scenes in Old Testament history, and observe how they stand alone in the peculiar example which each furnishes of some particular grace or virtue:

279

Scene or persons:	*Exemplifying:*
Noah building the Ark.	The Principles of Service
Abram leaving Haran,	The Obedience of Faith.
Jacob at Peniel,	Self-surrender.
Joseph and his Brethren,	Forgiving Love.
Moses interceding for Israel,	Self-oblivion.
Joshua and the Angel of the Lord,	Submission to Leadership.
Gideon and the Three Hundred,	Victory through Weakness.
Samuel brought to the Temple,	Maternal Consecration.
David's encounter with Goliath,	Courage of Faith.
Solomon and his Prayer,	A Wise Choice.
Balaam and the Princes of Moab,	The Evil of Compromise.
Elijah on Mount Carmel,	Power in Prayer.
Daniel in the Lion's den,	Safety in the Will of God.
Nehemiah at the Court,	Zeal for God's House.

Noah was a typical witness and workman. He conformed to a divine message; he preached a hundred years without a convert; and he proved that he believed his own message by building the ark. He thus represents threefold fidelity: to his mission in his long and patient preaching; to his master, in indifference to outward success and a world's verdict; and to himself in consistency with his own doctrine.

Reference has already been made to Abraham as the typical believer, father of the faithful, and example of the obedience of faith. He was a threefold exhibit of how believing in the Lord is the basis of a righteous character, leading him implicitly to trust His word, follow His lead and accept His will, though such trust seemed at times credulous, such obedience blind, and such surrender almost servile. He also shows how trust was vindicated by fulfillment, obedience rewarded by blessing, and surrender compensated by marvelous interposition.

Jacob, at Peniel, teaches us how the highest success is linked to apparent failure, and victory to defeat. It was not while he wrestled that he got the blessing, but when by the shrinking and dislocation of his thigh he could no longer wrestle but only hold on and supplicate, that he got the blessing there and then and the new name of "wrestler of El" as his memorial—a singular illustration of the sanctification that comes not by our works, but by abandoning self-effort and letting God have His own way.

Joseph's treatment of his brethren is perhaps in all the Word of God, the finest example of love, unselfish, sympathetic, forgiving and magnanimous. That forty-sixth chapter of Genesis is the counterpart of the thirteenth of First Corinthians—the latter a description in words unrivaled in literature; the former a delineation in acts unsurpassed in narrative. Hear him, as he bids the guilty brothers "draw near," apologizes for their crime, quiets their accusing conscience, points to the providence behind their treachery and assures them with the kiss of affection.

Moses was a typical *Legislator;* he received his instructions from the universal Lawgiver; he exercised all authority as a mere vicegerent; and he mediated between God and men, transmitting God's Word to them and pleading their cause before Him.

Moses before Jehovah (Ex. 32:30–35), is the noblest example of *Old Testament Intercession*, to the point of complete self-sacrifice. The people had committed a sin so flagrant, blasphemous, presumptuous, that it came near to being unpardonable. With Sinai in sight, and the canopy of God spread upon its summit, with the echo of God's voice of command yet in their ears, they actually made a calf of gold, and set it up as a god, dancing nude heathen dances about their idol! God was very wroth. His holy anger burned like a consuming fire, and there was danger that the whole of the sinning people would be swept away before His indignation; Moses ventures to intercede, and offer himself as a sacrifice, if by such self-offering the sin of the people may be atoned for. He was willing himself to perish, if by such vicarious suffering Israel may have a further probation! It is a case of man's perfect self-oblivion for others sakes. Compare Paul, Romans 9:1–3, in his anxiety for Israel.

Such a spirit, is perhaps, the nearest reflection of Christ's own infinite Love, and is very rare. If we seek modern examples, we may do well to study the life of Francis Xavier, who, misguided as he was, spared not himself any privation or suffering, shrinking not from death itself, to save the heathen. Ignatius, in the arena facing the lion, and saying, "I am grain of God; I must be ground between the teeth of lions to make bread for God's people!" and Captain Allen Gardiner, dying of starvation for the sake of the Tierra del Fuegians, are likewise examples.

Joshua's laying down his authority at the feet of the "Captain of the Lord's Host," is the typical example of the general in chief becoming only a common soldier, when the true Commander appears on the scene. It is the recognition of "Higher Law" and Supreme Authority, man yielding his scepter into a divine hand, and gladly following instead of leading, like Constantine, when laying out his imperial capital at the Golden Horn, saying, "I am following One who is leading me."

Gideon and his 300 are the great example of the fact that God puts no stress on numbers. Sometimes "the people are too many," and will take all the glory of their success, and so He must reduce their strength to weakness, and displace their sharp weapons by broken pitchers and lamps, if they are to see that it is not with the Lord a matter of saving by many or by few—that His is the battle, and His the victory.

Samuel brought to the Temple, as a weaned child, there to minister in his linen ephod, and to become recipient of divine visions, and as a lad be established as Jehovah's prophet in the eyes of all Israel, is the unique example of a mother's consecrating piety and of the potentiality of childhood. As John Tebonius, Luther's teacher, lifted his scholar's cap before his pupils because he saw in them already the future burgomasters, chancellors, doctors and magistrates, we are to recognize the possibilities latent in a pious childhood, and the sacredness of begetting, bearing and rearing offspring for God.

David's encounter with Goliath teaches, as no other example does, how we can do great battle for God if two conditions are met: if we are fighting with trust in Jehovah's name and strength, and if we are using the weapons with which we are experimentally familiar. It is not the learning of the schoolmen or the armor of the controversialist, but the simple methods of the witness that God uses to smite boastful arrogance in the forehead.

To Solomon's wise choice (1 Kgs. 3:5–15), we have adverted. This is made emphatic, that, when the Lord said, "ask what I shall give thee," his "speech pleased the Lord," for he chose what would best fit him to rule—"an understanding heart to judge the people." In the East, absolute despots made even life and death hang on their whim. Hence the supreme need of a clear insight and impartial equity, in administration. Solomon asked both and because he chose unselfishly, not what would please himself but profit his people, not what would gratify self, but glorify God, He gave him what he had not sought, riches and honor and long life—a grand illustration of Matthew 6:33—that when the first things are put first, the secondary are given unsought.

Balaam was the typical *compromiser;* he sought to serve Jehovah and yet a heathen ruler; he had prophetic gifts, but perverted them to divination; he worshiped the true God and yet was a slave to greed. He constantly vacillated and oscillated between two motives—the desire of selfish promotion and the fear of offending Jehovah—and, to an almost incredible degree, ventured in a path of disobedience after direct warning and restraint.

Elijah on Carmel, 1 Kings 18:

The apostasy of Israel was at its height, God's altar broken down, and the sacred fire quenched (16:30–33). Baal being the Sun-god, a test by fire was natural, and Elijah proposed that the true God should be known by His answering by fire. The appeal of Baal's worshipers was all day long, but in vain; the Sun-god sent down no burning ray. Then Elijah drenched his offering and altar, until it became sure that the fire that consumed them could be no *natural* flame, and, after a moment's appeal to Jehovah with no repetition, the descending Fire of God did its work, and the people shouted, "Jehovah is the God!" Then the flood followed the fire, after three and a half years of drought. This great intercessor kept on praying until the "man's hand" raised in prayer was seen reflected on the cloud! Compare James 5:17, 18.

Daniel in the Den (6):

This was the last of the conflicts recorded in the first half of this book. This Hebrew captive was both beyond reproach in his outward life and an excellent spirit was found in him; so that his foes could ensnare him only by his obedience to his God. So they conspired to make his *praying unlawful.* But he not only persisted in prayer, but took no means to hide it, and dared the lions for the sake of duty; and not only was he kept from all harm, but saw that those that plotted against his life lose their own in that very den!

Daniel was a typical *exile:* he maintained separation even in a heathen environment; he educated and elevated the very people that carried him captive; and he compelled his persecutors to acknowledge his faultlessness.

Nehemiah at Court (1:2):

So zealous was this King's cupbearer for God and His ruined city and temple that he could not rest even in a place. Every step was taken in *prayer*, at every new stage lifting his heart for divine guidance, and trusting in His Providence. He was independent and intrepid; making up his mind what God would have him do, he went on whether others helped or hindered, disregarding precedents, refusing to abuse his rulership by self-seeking, and swerving instead of being served. He set about rebuilding walls and reforming abuses, using his authority to stop Sabbath breaking and temple profanation, mixed marriages and all covenant violates. Nehemiah is one of a very few of whom no fault or folly is recorded.

Saul, the king, is evidently a type of *man who begins well and ends ill.*

The one impressive thought in connection with him, is the *disastrous end to which a man may come at last, notwithstanding a promising beginning.* He and his three sons all die in one day. Pursued by the archers and charioteers of the enemy (v. 3; 2 Sam. 1:6) and wounded in the stomach, his shield cast away, Saul fell on his own sword and died. The Amalekite's story (2 Sam. 1) was probably an invention to curry favor with David, by claiming to be the slayer of his enemy. The body, found by the Philistines, was ignominiously stripped and decapitated; the armor deposited as a trophy in the temple of Astarte, and the naked, headless trunk affixed to the wall, the head being placed in the temple of Dagon (1 Chr. 10:10). Perhaps these humiliating details are recorded to show how emphatically this first king of the Jews was forsaken of the Lord. What a forty years' reign!

Note the *steady downward progress of sin*—the final result of yielding to temptation. Every man is sure to be tempted, and there is no escape from one of two courses: he will go down or up, but cannot stand still. We read in James 1:15: "When lust hath conceived, it bringeth forth sin: and sin, when it is finished, bringeth forth death." And again in 3:15: "This wisdom descendeth not from above, but is earthly, sensual, devilish." Sin begins by a wrong desire, which ripens into a wrong act, and finally brings spiritual death—first the *earthly* level; then the *sensual* depths, and at last the *devilish*.

We may represent this by the *steps of a staircase*. Here is a middle landing—

EXPOSURE TO TEMPTATION—

where every man stands.

What are the steps *downward?*

1.—Trifling with temptation.

2.—Yielding to it, with misgivings and reproaches of conscience.

3.—Habitual yielding, so as to be often overcome, and feel less compunction.

4.—Utter slavery to the sin, bound in the cords of habit.

5.—Abandonment by one's self and by God to the power of evil.

6.—Utter enslavement by the devil, as not only his victim, but his agent in tempting others.

7.—Hell.

What, now, are the *upward* steps traced *from the bottom up?*

7.—Heaven.

6.—Becoming a succorer of other tempted people.

5.—Beloved of God, taken up into the sphere of His own love.

4.—Acquiring a gracious self-control.

3.—Overcoming habitually.

2.—Overcoming for the time.

1.—Taking the attitude of resistance to temptation.

The question is:

"WHICH WAY?"

We may trace Saul's downward steps:

1.—Parleying with sin (1 Sam. 13:8).

2.—Yielding and disobeying (13:9–14).

3.—Habitually yielding (15:9–23).

4.—Rejected of God (15:23–35; 16:14).
5.—Self-abandoned (28:6–20).
6.—Aiming to destroy others (18—24).
7.—Destroying himself (31:4–6).

There are two representative cases of our Lords' dealing with the highest human types of *moral excellence* apart from regenerating and sanctifying grace; and they are very significant.

The first is to Nicodemus (John 3) and the other, the nameless young ruler (Matt. 19:16–26) whom Prebendary Webb-Peploe thinks to be identical with Saul of Tarsus.

These two men both appear to be the supreme product of a legal obedience, upright and externally blameless, courteous, sincere, lovable and attractive. The rich young ruler may stand as the last hope of his race, and Jesus, beholding him, loved him. Both Nicodemus and he accepted our Lord as a divinely sent teacher, and both were in their moral characters and conduct above reproach. Yet to Nicodemus, our Lord suddenly revealed the fact that, without a new birth from above he could neither "enter" nor even "see" the Kingdom of god.

To the righteous young ruler He as suddenly revealed the fact that beneath all his faultless external righteousness lay a heart essentially enslaved to greed and worldliness, that he was practically an idolater and needed a supreme master. Both lessons are essentially and ultimately the same though taught in different terms and seen from different points of view. Neither were *hypocrites* but both were *formalists*; ensnared, one by rabbinical learning and self-righteousness; the other by a refined form of selfishness; both needing as much as anyone else the inward change.

42

The Illustrative Typical Element

WHEN OUR BRITISH FOREFATHERS of the Elizabethan age were about to act upon the stage a historic age or epoch they used first to represent in dumb show a scenic representation of the chief personage of the period in a pageant. We may image our great Divine Teacher as affording us such a spectacle, and the various personages of the Sacred narrative, defiling before us in a figurative procession, each meant to convey some wholesome encouragement or warning by showing us how good and evil respectively appear when seen in a true light with their sure, ultimate results. All history thus becomes to us a succession and procession, not of events merely, but of divine lessons in truth and duty, not one needless or useless or out of place.

In Numbers 19:1–10, we have an ordinance concerning the *Red Heifer*. In Hebrews 9—13 is the solitary reference to it in the New Testament, and it is noticeable how, not the *blood* but the "*ashes* of the heifer, sprinkling the unclean sanctifieth to the purifying of the flesh." We are therefore to look in the use made of the *ashes*, for the special typical lesson intended.

The color of the heifer—red—hints the red earth which gave to Adam his name, and the scarlet hue of guilt and of the blood that atones for sin. Every rite connected with the heifer—slain without the camp, and defiling all who had contact with it, etc., all point to a peculiar identification with the corruption of sin. But the main point

287

is the fact that the entire ashes were used to make a lye, five times called a "water of separation" kept especially for sprinkling those who by contact with death and decay had been defiled.

We pass by many interesting points to notice the *them* when this ordinance was instituted—not at Sinai, but as though an afterthought, first coming before us after the sentence of exclusion from Canaan—with the long sojourn before the people. In a desert the system of Levitical sacrifices would demand more victims than could be found. But one heifer's ashes would suffice for a lye for a long period, and it is said that only six were burnt up to the destruction of the second Temple.

The most illumining view is that this Red Heifer typified the permanent effects of our Lord's sacrifice; the "water of separation" hinting how the ordinance of the Lord's Supper, for example, perpetually commemorates and applies the one finished work of Atonement, "cleansing the conscience from dead works to serve the living and true God." Whereas in every other sacrifice there must be each time the blood was sprinkled, a new victim, in this case the ashes of the one victim might be used for thousands of those who required cleansing.

We are more than safe when the Word itself authorizes a typical interpretation of an event.

Take as an example the narrative of the Lifting up of the Brazen Serpent, in Numbers 21:6–9, as interpreted by John 3:14–16; 12:32.

Looking at this event in its declared symbolic import, we find many most suggestive correspondences and contrasts. It is a pictorial exhibition of *Salvation from Sin, by Faith in God's Approved Sacrifice and Substitute.* There is, therefore, a threefold symbolism: of Sin, Sacrifice, Sanctification.

1. Of Sin, as venomous, permeative, destructive—a moral virus introduced into man's very constitution by that old serpent, the Devil—spreading from part to part, burning in the very blood, growing worse and worse and ending in death both physical and spiritual. The sting of a serpent has an immediate effect on the blood, the fountain of life—then the nerves, both sensor and motor, rapidly reaching the brain, the great nucleus of nerve force.

2. Of Sacrifice. The brazen serpent reminds of Him who was made sin for us, though He knew no sin, as the brazen image was like the serpent but without its sting or venom. The fact that the serpent was coiled about the cross piece of a banner staff, is also remarkable, for if so, a cross was before the eyes that looked and lived. And again let us observe that in both cases the efficacy of the means used depended upon the divine will and plan. It was Infinite Love and Grace that sent the Son to be the Savior of the world and connected salvation with the look of Faith.

3. Of Salvation. The Power of God was immediate and complete in its work. Whosoever looked, lived, without regard to the stage of the disease or any other state of the bitten one. The invitation was universal, the condition single and simple, the deliverance instantaneous.

Faith is beautifully hinted in the look which brought healing—something too simple for definition and needing none—faith that led to explicit obedience, submission without reasoning as to the mode of cure or waiting to understand its philosophy—faith that abandoned all self-help, and took a proffered gift of life.

In the Bodleian Library, Oxford, is a picture illustrating a valuable manuscript. A cross occupies the center, dividing two groups. On the left are serpents, on the right, none. Moses is seen, and back of him, one who with arms crossed is looking at the serpent on the cross—healed. On the other side are four representative figures: One, kneeling before the cross, but looking not at the brazen serpent, but at Moses, as though depending on his priestly intervention; another, lying on his back, a serpent at his ear, even in extremity still hearkening to evil suggestion; a third, binding up another's wounds as if expecting some immunity through good works; a fourth fighting off the serpents as if depending on fleshly energy. The picture is too true to life; for alas, how many, instead of simply trusting in God's dear Son, are looking to man's help, resorting to self-help, or still surrendering to the Devil.

Inferior scenes often supply singularly beautiful illustrations of spiritual truth, for example, the narrative in 2 Kings 8:4, 5, of providence and prayer. The woman whose son Elisha had restored to life, after she had been absent in the land of the Philistines seven years because of famine, appeals to the King for her house and land. Just at that very hour the King, talking with Gehazi, had asked him to tell him of this greatest miracle of Elisha; and, while he was reciting this story, in came the woman herself, and Gehazi had the confirmation on the spot of the strange and incredible story he had told the King. What an illustration of the manner in which the Hearer of Prayer can make use of exact coincidences to demonstrate the efficiency of prayer.

An instructive illustration of the *Energy of the flesh* as opposed to the *Power of the Spirit* is found in 2 Kings 2:15–18.

Some who had seen the miraculous crossing of the Jordan by Elijah, but not the rapture into Heaven, urged Elisha to authorize a thorough search for Elijah's body, as though the Spirit of the Lord would lift him up from earth only to cast him down, wounded and helpless, upon some height or into some ravine! With the physical strength of fifty men they propose to supplement the work of the Almighty. Of course, the prophet refuses to sanction a procedure so vain and irreverent. They urge him, until as from sheer wearisomeness with their carnal importunity he withdraws opposition, leaving them to search for ten days in vain; and then he reminds them that from the first he had foretold the futility of their effort.

In 2 Kings 5, the narrative of Naaman's healing from leprosy in an unparalleled illustration of salvation, especially in the following points:

1. The universality of sin and need. Naaman, despite his rank and deeds was a leper, needing cleansing.

2. The insignificance of God's instruments—a little nameless maid who waited on Namaan's wife.

3. The unpurchaseable character of Grace. Cure not to be bought nor rewarded with even princely gifts.

4. The impartiality of a true messenger. No homage paid to the artificial distinctions of human caste.

5. The efficacy of divine ordinances. The waters having no inherent healing power but being God's appointed means.

6. The simplicity of Salvation. No great thing demanded but only an act of simple obedience.

7. The completeness of conditions. No cure until the sevenfold dipping in the Jordan was accomplished.

8. The certainty and immediateness of blessing. The cure instantly followed the absolute compliance.

The visit of the Queen of Sheba to Solomon (1 Kgs. 5) seems to be a forecast of the believer's experimental knowledge of Christ as Savior and Lord; and there are so many suggestions of resemblance that some have construed it as another biblical "allegory." Note some of these very instructive hints:

1. She was drawn to Solomon by *hearing* of him, especially "concerning the name of Jehovah."

2. She came herself to *prove* him with hard questions which nine others could answer.

3. She brought with her a tribute of homage and of worship.

4. She saw for herself and found all reports but confirmed and surpassed.

5. She pronounced those especially happy who were honored with his presence.

6. She found all her secrets unveiled and the questions of her heart revealed.

7. He gave her all her desire and "royal bounty" beside.

John 13:10–14. He that is washed needeth not save to wash his feet, but is clean every whit. Ye also ought to wash one another's feet.

Here beside the primary lessons of humility and service is taught a more hidden or less obvious lesson that, when once regenerated, there is no need of repeating that experience; and henceforth we need only to regulate our daily *walk*. One who comes from a bath is clean, save as by the way, his feet have taken the dust of the road, a simple laving of the feet restores the cleanness of the whole person. So, after cleansing from guilt in the blood, and reception of the new nature by the Spirit, our only further need is that from day to day the washing of water by the word shall keep our walk scriptural and spiritual. We are to watch our daily life as disciples, and apply the teachings of the Word and the example of Christ to the correction of errors of thought, word and deed. And by the same Scripture teaching are we to wash one another's feet, rebuking error and evil, and helping to make the walk of fellow disciples faithful and obedient.

In Galatians 4:21–31, the historical narrative of Hagar and Ishmael is presented as having a deeper allegorical meaning than the mere surface reveals. This Hagar is Mount Sinai, which gendereth to bondage. Sarah represents grace, and Isaac, her son, the liberty of faith. Hagar represents law, and Ishmael, her son, represents the bondage which unbelief engenders. The territory in which both for a time sought to live together is the believer's own experience. But the two are incompatible and irreconcilable. Faith and unbelief, liberty and slavery, love and fear, hope and despair, cannot abide together. And God says to every child of His, "Cast out the bondwoman and her son, for there can be no common inheritance for the son of the bondwoman and the son of the free woman. Give your heart wholly to the dominion of grace and faith."

The same lesson is taught in Hebrews, in that other parable of Sinai and Zion. Leave the mount that quakes and burns, with its blackness and darkness and tempest and trumpet and awful voice of law; and live on Mt. Sion, the place of the King's palace, with its holy memories, experiences and prospects. There you look back to Calvary's cross, up to heaven's daily blessing, and forward to the far but near horizon of the blessed Hope. Faith reconciles, faith saves not only from Hell but from the inward Slough of Despond and the torments of fear. Faith makes real the encampment of God's holy angels about the believer and the fellowship of all redeemed souls in heaven and earth. Faith makes you conscious and confident of your heavenly citizenship, and your interest in atoning blood, which calls not for vengeance but for mercy.

43

Misunderstandings and Perversions

W HEN IT IS SAID THAT DAVID put the Ammonites "under saws, harrows and axes, and made them pass through the brick kiln" (2 Sam. 12:31), it does not mean that he cut them up or burned them up, but put them to certain forms of labor. When Jehovah is said to be a *"jealous God,"* no mean, malicious feeling is ascribed to Him, but only His desire and determination not to allow His worship to be corrupted by idolatry or His people's devotion to Him to be shared with rival deities (Ex. 20). When our Lord declares that He "came not to send peace but a sword," and to set even parents of children at variance (Matt. 10:34–36), we are not to understand this as the motive and design, but as the consequence and result of His mission.

It is a mistake to infer from the use of past and present tenses in Isaiah 53, "He *is* despised and rejected of men"; "He *was* cut off out of the land of the living," etc., that this refers to some servant of God, then living, or who had already died. This is to overlook the fact that there are *prophetic tenses;* and that one way that prediction shows its divine character is that it speaks of future events with the same air of certainty as if already accomplished. It is the assurance of omniscience that foretells and omnipotence that will surely accomplish.

Italicized words, which indicate what it supplied by translators, to make the sense clear, sometimes not only obscure it, but introduce foreign conceptions. Some scholars boldly take the position that all such supplied words are a needless and unwarranted addition; that where the original plainly implies them they need not be italicized; and, where it does not, they should be omitted. Where God's Spirit leaves a blank, we may only at risk, attempt to fill it.

In Acts 2:41, 47, we are told how converts were *added*—translators have supplied *"unto them,"* and *"to the church,"* which latter is not authorized by the best manuscripts. The inspired phrase found later on, "added to the Lord" (v. 14), suggests that the meaning may be in all cases—added to Himself as disciples—a possible hint of the vast difference between divine converts and human proselytes (Matt. 23:15). When man adds converts they are often his own followers or adherents of his sect; they imitate their teacher and leader, reflecting even his vices, and are like Corinthian schismatics who boasted, "I am of Paul," "I of Apollos," "I of Cephas." But when God adds to Himself the bond cannot be too close and involves no risk.

Much misunderstanding invests that whole teaching of John in his first epistle from 2:29 to 3:10. This is often taken to mean that the *commission of any sin invalidates all claim to sonship!* To this we have referred, but it needs more emphasis. This is obviously a *total* misconception, as appears from three points of view.

1. The affirmation of incapacity to sin is made of *"whatsoever is born of God"*—that is so much of the disciple as *constitutes the divine nature in him*—whatever in us does sin it cannot be what is born of God and is His seed.

2. The sinning referred to is a continuous and habitual sinning, not an occasional lapse into sin. He that is born of God does not *go on* sinning—the tense is a continuous present—he cannot go on in sin, because he is born of God; if he does he is a child of the devil, who goes on sinning from the beginning.

3. The inspired writer himself acknowledges that a regenerate disciple may sin and points to the provision for such lapses into sin, in the atonement of the heavenly Propitiation and the advocacy of the heavenly Paraclete. While he writes to disciples so that they *may not go on* sinning, if any *do* sin, he reminds them of the perfect provision made for such failures (1 John 2:1, 2).

How shocking the perversion of Predestination and Election to blank *Fatalism!* God would encourage man in coming to Him by first coming to man; in choosing Him by first Himself choosing man; in depending upon Him by assuring him that He will keep him in such dependence. The practical truth of Election is that, in very step and stage of Salvation it is God who leads the way and makes all the advances. He sought the lost sheep till He found him and then laid him on His shoulders and bore him to the fold. Instead of making us feel helpless and hopeless, Predestination should stimulate us to action and advance by the assurance of His omnipotence beneath and behind our impotence. We should learn to spell "persevere" out of "preserve"—where the same letters are found, and to "keep ourselves in the love of God," by the confidence that He is "able to keep us even from stumbling." To lie back supinely in unbelief and apathy, saying, "If I am to be saved I will be," or, because "God must do all," is not only a shameful perversion of Scripture doctrine, but it is worthy only of an idiot or an incurable fool, and is often a mark either of voluntary rebellion or hopeless folly.

The statement in James 2:17–26, that Faith cannot justify, without works—is grossly misunderstood to mean that works are necessary to justification *in God's sight*—a doctrine so diametrically opposed to the Spirit's teaching in Romans 3, 4, 5, as to seem to some irreconcilable. But we have seen elsewhere how this conflict is avoided.

The *sinner* is justified before God upon the sole ground of faith. Works do not help, but hinder, for they become a basis of supposed merit or desert. The believer should however be, as such, justified *before the world*, and it is by works of love that the life of faith is indicated and vindicated in the sight of men, the fruit showing the tree to be alive and growing. In one case the question is, how is a sinner saved? By believing. In the other, the question is, how is a believer to prove his faith? By bringing forth its proper fruits. The word *justify* here is used, not of making righteous, but of defending oneself against accusation by proving it groundless; after I am justified by faith godward, I am to *justify my faith*, manward.

Few perversions are more serious than that of the so-called *Kenosis* (Phil. 2:7). "He made Himself of no reputation"—literally, "He emptied Himself"—is taken by some to mean that in some strange way our Lord laid aside not the externals of His glory and rank only, but so divested Himself of omnipotence, omniscience, as to become liable to infirmities of weakness and errors of ignorance, like other men. This is resorted to as an apology for His supposed mistakes in His teaching. If a rationalistic criticism seeks to invalidate His endorsement of Old Testament history and prophecy, or get rid of any obnoxious utterance, it is easy to say that He reflected the current errors, traditions, and superstitions of His day!

Such concessions involve us in perplexities far greater than any they solve. *They leave us without any infallible Teacher.* Here a solitary sentence and a single word is assumed as a sufficient basis for impugning the whole and final and decisive authority of the Son of God, and the more positive His teaching the easier to evade its emphasis by making it one of the examples of the Kenosis! Without attempting to enter into a discussion of this mischievous and dangerous theory, its importance demands a few words of caution:

1. No sound exposition ever bases an important doctrine on a solitary text, especially when confessedly obscure, and unsupported by other testimony.

2. No being like the Son of God could divest Himself of the very essentials of His personality. He might sacrifice externals, and consent to a humiliation of outward form and condition, but how could He the all-wise become ignorant, and the Infallible, imbibe and teach error?

3. He constantly averred that, how ever He may have held in suspense His divine nature and attributes for a time, He as a servant, received from the Father both His authority and His message—that what He did He wrought by His power, and that what He spoke, He spoke under His guidance, even to the very words (John 17:8; 8:26; 14:10, etc.).

4. If the Epistle to the Philippians teaches the Kenosis or self-emptying, the companion Epistles to the Colossians and Ephesians even more emphatically teach the *Pleroma* or divine filling. If he emptied Himself therefore it was but the signal for such infinite fullness as defies description. One Epistle must supply a commentary on the other (Eph. 1:22; 4:10; Col. 2:3, 9).

No perversion can well be more ingenious or complete than the wide spread misinterpretation of 1 Corinthians 11:27, 29. To this day, among the highlanders of Scotland, many believers dare not come to the Lord's table from fear of eating and drinking "unworthily," of being "guilty of the body and blood of the Lord, and so eating and drinking damnation to themselves."

No interpretation has ever more overturned both the obvious meaning of the Scripture in this passage or its general teaching throughout. The unworthiness, referred to here, is not the unworthiness of the *participant*, as a person, but of the *participation*, as an act—that is, it concerns the *intelligent way* of commemorating our Lord's death. The Corinthian church had perverted the Lord's Supper to a semi-pagan feast, and sometimes a drunken revel, in which its real significance was of course entirely lost sight of, the rich and poor separated instead of being united in fellowship, and instead of profit, damage rather insulting to spiritual life. The table of the Lord became a banquet board and the significance of the bread and cup was lost; there could be no discerning of the Lord's body and blood in such a Bacchanalian revel, and the whole celebration, instead of being a tribute to His atoning work, became rather a travesty of the solemn tragedy of His death.

The word "damnation" is absurdly out of place; the meaning is that there could be no divine approval of such conduct, but rather disapproval, no blessing but rather correction and chastisement. Hence, the further admonition in verses 30–33, where the Corinthians are warned that such a course only brings spiritual sickness and feebleness and torpor instead of health, growth and service.

How subtle Satan is! If the Lord's Supper means anything, it is a confession and constant reminder of our absolute dependence upon Another's death and life, His merit and desert; and the devil uses this very memorial of such dependence on Him to turn the eye inward in morbid self-examination, to find if possible some ground of self-complacency, to justify our approach. The very rite that was meant to rebuke legalism is made to foster it! The very caution meant to help us to come rightly, hindering us from coming at all!

44

Dispensations, Ages and Covenants

THE CONCEPTION OF *Covenant* seems inseparable from that of dispensations, and fundamental to it. God, from time to time, has chosen to enter into a covenant or compact with man, a mutual agreement, binding upon each party, implying, therefore, mutual obligations, and conditions. By the terms of a covenant, unfaithfulness, on the part of either party, or failure to fulfill the conditions, or terms of the compact, forfeits the compact.

These covenants with man implied more or less intimate fellowship with God, and promise of blessing; and the condition on man's part was *always obedience*, But the compacts differed in minor respects, both as to promises and conditions, and as to the seal or sign connected with them, as also in the human parties contracting. To understand these features is essential to the perception both of God's faithfulness and of man's faithlessness and failure; likewise to appreciate the nature, necessity and perpetuity of that "new covenant" which ultimately displaced all the rest.

Each of the first five books of the Bible has a distinctive character. Genesis is the book of beginnings: this idea of beginnings is its dominant, ruling conception. The Divine purpose is manifest and apparent in its structure, for there is a *threefold* beginning: first, with *Adam;* second, with *Noah;* third, with *Abram;* with each of these three history makes, in a sense, a new start.

Each of these beginnings is marked by a *covenant:* with Adam, a covenant of life, of continuance in the favor of God, of preservation in a state of innocence, happiness and exemption from that death which was the penalty of transgression. With *Noah*, it was a covenant of possession; the earth purged by a flood, was given to him as a dwelling place, with promise of continuance, and preservation from another flood—in a word, a pledge of continuance of the existing natural order. With *Abram*, it was a covenant of blessing, for himself and his seed, and, through them, for all other families of the earth, in the Messiah. Here, for the first time, grace, instead of law, appears in the covenant and marks a stage of revelation.

Each of these covenants had a condition: with Adam, obedience to one restrictive command; with Noah, occupation of the desolated earth by multiplication and diffusion of the human race; with Abram, faith, as manifested in renunciation of home and kindred, and separation unto God.

And to each covenant there was a seal of confirmation: with Adam, the tree of life; with Noah, the bow in the cloud; and with Abram, the rite of circumcision; each seal being singularly fitting: the tree in Eden, the sacramental sign of continued life; the bow in the cloud connecting heaven and earth, God and man, in harmonious relations; circumcision in the flesh, an expression of separation and consecration in the spirit, a type of the subjection of the carnal to the spiritual.

Each covenant had its method of violation and forfeiture: in Adam's case, by eating of the forbidden fruit; in Noah's by concentration and centralization, instead of diffusion, as shown at Babel; and in case of Abraham's descendants, by compromise with idolatry.

Two other covenants are referred to in the Pentateuch—one at Horeb (Ex. 34:27), and one in the land of Moab, which is expressly declared to be "beside that which Jehovah made with them in Horeb" (Deut. 29:1).

The covenant at *Horeb* was one of *Theocracy*, Israel accepting their great Deliverer and Emancipator as King; hence, it was signalized by the promulgation of law—a new code; and its condition was loyalty to a Divine Ruler, its sign and seal *two tables of stone*, inscribed by the finger of God.

The covenant at Moab was one of special promise of *national prosperity*, prominence and permanence. Its condition, separation from idolaters and submission to the only true God; and its singular *seal* was the *two peaks of Ebal and Gerezim* at the gateway of the land, a constant reminder of their solemn Amen to all its provisions. It also hinted for the first time a larger promise and more glorious destiny—a circumcision of heart which forecast the Pentecostal outpouring and the Messianic Era.

The new covenant differs from all the rest. It is one of *spiritual,* not *temporal* blessing, and made with our Lord Jesus Christ in behalf of man, and hence forever irreversible and unchangeable. Its *sign* is the *blood of the cross* and it is *without conditions*, since our Lord is the contracting party in man's stead and cannot fail or be faithless.

There is a beautiful hint of the ultimate recovery through the "New Covenant" of all blessing, lost and forfeited through the old, as represented in all three primitive covenants, which may be traced in the Apocalypse, where each forfeiture, under the penalties of law, seems offset by a new favor, under the final triumph of grace. The death, temporal and spiritual, which followed the first sin, is at last remitted and banished: "there is no more death"; and hence, again appears the tree of life in the midst of the Paradise of God. The confusion of tongues and forcible dispersion that followed God's visitation on the sins of Noah's posterity at Babel give way to one tongue among the celestials and a new community in the City of God; and hence, the rainbow appears round about the throne, the new pledge of continuance to the new order. The degeneracy and destruction that followed Israel's idolatries and apostasies give way to regeneration and restitution; hence, the twelve tribes appear permanently incorporated in the very foundations of the new Jerusalem.

This contrast between the beginning and the ending of the race's history can be seen only as the first chapters of the first book of the Bible are compared with the last chapters of the closing book. Such comparison will make all biblical history seem like the perimeter of a golden ring, where, after a vast sweep of thousands of years, we reach the point of starting in the point of finishing. What was first found in Genesis, is last found in Revelation: Eden, in Paradise regained;

the tree of life; the rivers of Eden in the river of the water of life; the companionship and converse of God in the cool of the day restored in the tabernacle of God with men, where there is no decline of day; and, whereas the curse came on the original Eden, in the new Paradise "there shall be no more curse." What appeared as finally forfeited in the fall, is thus seen to have been only suspended privilege, to be recovered and restored when God makes "all things new." It is a wonderful vision of the consummation of grace. All that lies intermediate, between Eden and Paradise, is the working out of this amazing scheme of redemption; and the shadows of the midnight, with its darkness that might be felt, can only be understood in the glories of the eternal noon, with the light and luster unspeakable of the final inheritance of the saints.

In addition to this covenantal conception is that of successive *periods* in which all time, and in fact all duration, is divided.

History, in God's plan, is constituted of AGES, each having its own specific character and purpose; and these distinctive features need to be examined with discrimination; the promises, prophecies, ordinances and utterances of the Word, appropriate to one period, may and often do so pertain, principally, if not exclusively thereto, as to be misapplied if referred to any other. "Distinguish the times," said Augustine, "and the Scripture will be consistent with itself."

Five great ages, at least, clearly appear in Scripture, all referred to as distinct, in the one Epistle to the Ephesians:
1. "Before time began"—"before the foundation of the world."
2. "Before Christ came."
3. "The present evil age."
4. "The coming age" (Millennial).
5. "The age of ages"—when time shall be no longer.

Of these we should get clear conceptions, and there is a hint of an age, following the millennial, but preceding the Eternal—when the triumphs of our Lord shall most fully be realized.*

The two ages, which are so contrasted in the Epistles to the Hebrews—the outgoing and the incoming order—the former preparing for the latter, and forecasting it—do not lie in the same plane, and the

---

* G. F. Trench, *After the Thousand Years.*

points of difference are more numerous than those of resemblance. The former was the shadow, type, prophecy, of which the latter is the substance, prototype and antitype and fulfillment; the former, ethnic, national, temporal; the latter cosmic, racial, eternal. One had more to do with the earthly; the other with the heavenly. Christ was far greater than Moses, Aaron and Joshua combined; the coming inheritance infinitely superior to the Land of Promise, and the New Jerusalem to the old, and the throne and Kingdom of the Son of Man to that of David and Solomon. To judge the future by the past or the present, is to misunderstand them all and misconceive their relations. As a clear-minded man has his pigeonholes for distributing his papers, a Bible student needs to have clearly defined departments of truth, so that he can pigeonhole a precept or promise or prophecy or observance where it belongs and not refer to one dispensation or age or economy what belongs to another. And connected with these distinctions is that other so plainly referred to by Paul, "the *Jew*, the *Gentile*, and the *Church of God*," which are never confused in the Word of God (1 Cor. 10:32).

There is a distinct line which separates the *writings of John* from other New Testament Scriptures.

Though all parts of the Word of God are equally necessary to its entirety, all are not equally important for the instruction of disciples. Even among New Testament books some have a special *present* application.

Almost the last words of a saintly teacher, now with the Lord, were, "Brethren, do not neglect the *ministry of John*." He referred to a fact, often overlooked, that this New Testament writer wrote his Gospel narrative, Epistles and Revelation last of all of those who contributed to New Testament literature. This gives John a unique place among New Testament writers, and the more so because, before he took up his pen a very conspicuous change had begun in church life. So far as dates are known, there is a very noticeable order in New Testament writings. Up to about the year 65 A.D., the primitive apostolic order survived in its essential features as appears from 1 Timothy, Titus, and 1 Peter. There are only two orders, bishops and deacons, both officially recognized, but no sharp line between "clergy" and "laity," and a distinct line of separation between the church and the world.

That some marked change took place within about one year appears from the altered tone of 2 Timothy, 2 Peter, and Jude, which are supposed to date about 66 A.D. The Church, as a witness for God has already begun to fail. Deceivers and corrupters had crept in; heathen usages, legalism, Judaism, antinomianism and various other forms of leaven already permeated the whole lump. In the church assembly an order so new had begun to prevail that individuals loving to have the preeminence, were fast assuming authority, so that one of them refused to receive even John himself. Whether God, by His servant, approved or disapproved these changes and this new order, which appears to behave become general, we are not left to doubt; for when John wrote, it was of the church as having failed on earth and needing to be judged. This conspicuously appears in his Epistles, and in the seven Epistles to the churches in Revelation 2, 3.

Another remarkable fact must be weighed. For about 25 years inspiration seems to have ceased and no new writings were given to the church from about 66 to 91 A.D., when once more the Spirit spake by John. His writings, therefore, form the *last messages* to the church. It is scarcely an exaggeration to say that the writings of the beloved disciple thus make a dispensation, the last before the Lord's second appearing, the period of church decline, and the partial withdrawal of the Spirit's and presidency in the church, the cessation of miracle and largely of supernatural intervention.

Many, even among believers, strenuously oppose all such views, denouncing them as pessimistic. But there is a deeper question once asked by the High Priest, *"Are these things so?"* (Acts 7:1). Now what is most agreeable to the natural man and carnal heart, or most flattering to human pride or self-satisfaction; but what is true, and scriptural, is the prime matter of importance and interest. If continuous prayerful study of the New Testament reveals anything with certainty, it is that, about a generation after our Lord's ascension, decline in doctrine and piety manifestly began in the primitive church which has ever since continued; and that decline was marked by the following conspicuous features:

1. Loss of unity and equality among disciples, the multiplication of sectarian jealousies and divisions, the caste spirit, and the erection

of an ecclesiastical hierarchy, with clerical and lay distinctions, originally unknown, and a multitude of ranks and orders wholly foreign
to the apostolic age.

2. Loss of spiritual power and separation—conformity to the world,
worldly maxims, methods and spirit; introduction of salaried offices,
often very lucrative, which appealed to avarice and ambition; gradual
transformation of the original assembly into a religious club with
large pecuniary outlay and barriers to the poor.

3. Loss of common witness to the truth, and the Christ-disciples
as such ceasing to bear testimony and relegating distinctive Christian
service and activity to a clerical class; absorption in temporal interests,
identification with the world in its pursuits and spirit; practical union
of church and state with consequent corruption of church life and com-
plication with political aims and compromises.

4. Loss of Holy Spirit control; human government and influence
rapidly displacing the invisible Sovereignty of the divine Paraclete.
Artistic and aesthetic standards taking the place of the spiritual; simplicity of worship corrupted by formalism and ritualism, robes, rites,
elaborate ceremonies and spectacular effects; costly buildings, choirs,
clergy and church conduct generally.

51. Loss of missionary and especially martyr spirit; the declension and final cessation of evangelistic activity; neglect of souls, and
finally a thousand years of the dark ages, when the church scarcely survived, and there was only a godly remnant; when all signs of supernatural intervention ceased and prevailing power in prayer.

The Reformation, under such men as Wycliffe, Huss, Luther,
Calvin, Knox, Savonarola—revived evangelical doctrine; and the
missionary movements, under Carey and his contemporaries, revived Evangelism. But, despite the multiplication of missionary organization and activity, the church has never recovered the spiritual
separateness and power of apostolic days. The present decay of doctrine under the rapid growth of rationalistic criticism, assailing the
Pentateuch, then the prophetic and even Messianic element in the Old
Testament; then the infallibility of Christ as a teacher, and finally even
His Resurrection and actual historic *existence*, may indicate some of
the signs of the Times.

45

The Mystical Element and the Mysteries

UNDER THE GENERAL HEAD OF "MYSTERY" may be included:
1. The *Mystical*—occult or obscure, demanding special study, and spiritual insight and illumination.

2. The *Paradoxical*, involving seeming contrariety and contradiction, but not inherently inconsistent.

3. The *Mysterious*, in the proper Biblical sense of "mystery," hidden from the natural man, but an open secret to the spiritual.

1. The Mystical.

It is difficult to express this exact idea, that the Word of God has a peculiar quality of suggesting a far deeper meaning than at first suspected. This has already found illustration in the *prophetic* element, especially in indirect forecasts of the future; and particularly in the *Messianic* element, which pervades the entire Scripture, cropping out where at first thought it would be least expected. It also appears in the *scientific* department, an elastic poetic phraseology, obscure and enigmatic, providing for an after accommodation to newly discovered facts.

The same general truth is susceptible of far wider illustration, and is continually attracting, on the part of reverent minds, new attention. As in the works of God, every enlargement of powers of vision and observation through the lenses of telescope, microscope, and spectroscope, brings to light new wonders of His creative hand, so every increase of real insight into His Word overwhelms us with evidence that the same Divine Hand has been at work; and, as the "Heavens declare the glory of God and the firmament sheweth his handiwork," so the Law of the Lord is seen to be perfect, in its adaptation to its purpose, converting the soul, making wise the simple, etc. (Ps. 19).

I. This mystical element as we have seen conspicuously appears in *parabolic form*, of which there are three prominent sorts in Scripture:

(a) Parabolic *utterance*, as in Luke 15 and John 15.

(b) Parabolic *action*, as in miracles which have a moral meaning and bearing.

(c) Parabolic *picture or object*, as in the Tabernacle and its furniture.

To our Lord's spoken parables, generally reckoned as from thirty to forty, His parables in action, or miracles, singularly correspond in number and nature, and might almost be set side by side for comparison. His parables of speech set forth such leading truths, as the Love of God, nature of sin, law of reward and retribution, vital union of the believer with Himself, etc. His parables of action were meant to show His power on earth to forgive sins and to remedy their consequences.

So Parabolic pictures of objects set forth the leading facts and truths about Redemption, the Person of the Redeemer and the blessings of the Redeemed; and in two conspicuous forms, namely: The whole system of sacrifices, offerings and feasts; and the construction and furniture of the Tabernacle of Witness, the sacrifices, offerings and feasts, of which the whole New Testament is the exposition; of the Tabernacle especially in Hebrews 9.

The Tabernacle has a volume of suggestiveness. From one point of view it presents a picture of the whole work of Christ for the believer; from another, an unusually complete view of the whole life of the believer in Christ.

The Tabernacle was in three courts—the outer, with the Brazen Altar of sacrifice and the Laver; the inner, with the Table of Bread, the Golden Candlestick, and the Altar of Incense; and the inmost, the Holiest of All, with the Ark of the Covenant surmounted by the Mercy Seat. Here the work of Christ is set forth in order, from His vicarious sacrifice of Himself on the Cross, and the Sending of the Regeneration and Sanctifying Spirit, throughout His human career, as the Light of the World, the Bread of Life, and the Intercessor, to His final appearance within the veil and in the presence of God for us. Or regarded as teaching the believer how to draw near unto God in Christ, the outer court suggests two terms of communion; remission of sins through atoning blood and regeneration, through the Word of God and the Holy Ghost. Then the inner court suggests the three forms of communion: a living light of testimony, the systematic consecration of substance, and habitual life of prayer. Then the inmost shrine may represent the final goal and ideal of communion, when perpetual obedience is like an unbroken tablet of law, and the beauty of the Lord our God is upon us, and all His attributes and our affections and activities are in perfect harmony. We claim no infallibility in interpreting these parabolic pictures and objects, the very beauty of this form of teaching being in part that it admits of ever increasing clearness of vision and accuracy of insight, as our life and character approach nearer to final perfection. But of this we are sure: that there is here a wealth of meaning yet unexplored and unsuspected by even the children of God, and which only the ages to come will fully unveil and reveal.

II. A paradox is a statement or expression, seemingly though not necessarily, absurd, self-contradictory, or self-inconsistent. It is doubtful whether such apparent contradictions do not necessarily inhere in a divine book, from the lack of capacity in a finite being wholly to grasp divine ideas; and, in some cases, the paradox, like the parable, may be meant to provoke deeper study, awaken curiosity, and stimulate investigation.

In Holy Scripture contradiction and contrariety of teaching and testimony must be of course only apparent. Nevertheless such paradoxes abound, and serve one or all of three ends: First, to present a problem, afterwards to be solved; to arouse attention and challenge discrimination; and to impress the majesty and mystery of the Divine Author, as one whose thoughts are higher than man's and defy perfect comprehension.

The paradoxes, or seeming contradictions, should not be stumbling blocks to faith, but stepping stones to a higher knowledge of God and His truth. If one aspect of which seems to contradict another, as in so many cases, it is because the finite mind is grappling with the infinite. Neander says that God is both self-revealing and self-concealing; He must needs be both. The true rendering of Job 11:6 is: "The secrets of wisdom are double of understanding." Or as Rotherham phrases it, "The secrets of wisdom are double to that which actually is." A rhythmical version is:

> And shew thee wisdom's hidden depths,
> Truth's twofold form.

Lange makes Zophar to say that God's wisdom is "two-fold in knowledge." Perhaps all these are imperfect attempts to convey a great fact, that necessarily, when God speaks to man in human language, truth has more sides and aspects than any one statement will cover.

But the source of contradiction lies deeper than language—in the *thoughts* of God themselves. Rays of light, emanating from one orb, may at the vast distances suggested by astronomy be so parallel, as that no human instruments can measure their convergence; yet they do meet in their source, they have a common focus, only our measurements are inadequate.

The Paradoxes of the Bible are both inseparable from it as the Word of God and confirmatory of its claims as such. The apparent contradiction has its origins, first in the infinite grandeur of the truth expressed; and, secondly, in the finite limits of the understanding addressed. Many a statement in science and art which, to a beginner in study, is mysterious and unintelligible, perhaps even absurd to that same student, when himself a master in those studies, becomes as simply and obvious as a maxim. How can *God* speak to *Man* about infinite and eternal verities and *not* transcend the limits of a finite and temporal experience! Take, for example, Hebrews 2:14, *"Mors mortis morti mortem nisi morte tulisset aeternae vitae Janua clausa foret."* "Had not death, by death, borne to death, the Death of Death, the gate of Life Eternal would be closed."

A notable *prophetic* paradox is found in Jeremiah's and Ezekiel's predictions that Zedekiah should be carried captive to Babylon but should not see it (Ezek. 12:13). When the Chaldeans at Riblah put out his eyes, the deprivation of sight, before he was carried to the capital of the conqueror, explained the paradox.

Some of the most prophetic paradoxes are associated with the Jews, all, thus far, exactly fulfilled in History:

1. Scattered among all peoples, but mixed with none.
2. A hissing and a by-word, yet a controlling power.
3. Plundered for centuries, yet holding large wealth.
4. Despoiled for long ages, yet not destroyed.
5. Yearning for their own land, yet kept from possessing it.

This last is a historical marvel. Palestine is an insignificant country. It has no geographical, historical, commercial or political importance in itself, and contributes but little to the world's general prosperity. No nation values it but the Jew; and the Jews are rich enough to purchase it at thrice its value, and yet, after all their efforts to possess and colonize it, they cannot yet get control of it.

As to *ethical* paradoxes, the "imprecatory psalms" are needlessly stumbling blocks to many. Those commonly so classed are these four: 7, 35, 69, 109, all characterized by the invocation of a curse on the foes of God and righteousness. No doubt there is something about them out of tune with the mercy and compassion so pervading the New Testament. But there are few relieving considerations:

1. In many cases the imperative may be equally well rendered by the future—instead of "*let it be so*," "it *shall* be so"—turning an imprecation or malediction into a prediction—an apparent prayer into a prophecy.

2. These curses were invoked on *foes of God, as such;* and, in a period, when the mission of believers in the salvation of Gentile sinners was so dimly suggested as to form no distinct part of the faith or duty of the body of believers. Hence, they thought of such wicked men as only so many hopeless hindrances to God's glory and the advance of His cause, and jealousy for Him rather than private animosity prompted these imprecations.

3. The common interpretation now is the *impersonal one*—that the parties so cursed represent not individuals but systems of wrong—principles of evil; these are names, figures, emblems of the wicked or of wickedness as such.

4. But beyond all these, we must recognize a righteous and legit-imate sentiment of retributive justice and judgment. Wrath in God is not a blemish, but a perfection—only another aspect of love and benevolence. Vengeance is not revenge—it is not vindictive but vin-dicative—not a personal retaliation, but a governmental and judicial vindication. There is no perfect love without holy hate—mercy must be balanced by justice and compassion by consideration for right-eousness. Law must be upheld and penalty follow crime. Otherwise, the moral cosmos would fall into chaos.

Many paradoxes, however, are not hopeless of reconciliation; we see their harmony when we get a right point of view.

Law and grace are not a proper paradox, for they do not pertain to the same economy. Law rests on exact individual obedience; grace, on imputed obedience; law pays wages; grace offers a gift.

Neither do faith and works present a proper paradox. The con-tradiction is only apparent; the inspired writers perfectly agree. We need to find and hold the balance of truth.

The unity and Trinity of the Divine Being present another para-dox, but we must remember that the unity is in a common *nature,* shared by all, and the Trinity is of persons, peculiar to each. No bet-ter illustration can perhaps be found than the union of the light, heat and life in the one sunbeam, yet each has its own ray—the light, the yellow; the heat, the red, and the actinic life, the blue; yet all in the white light, and blended in sunshine.

Other seeming contradictions about God vanish when we get a true conception:

For example, His *ability* and *inability.* Omnipotence is all-power, yet He cannot lie (Matt. 19:26; Heb. 6:18). But power is to be mea-sured by the gauge of power and within its proper sphere. Moral im-possibilities come from ethical conditions, physical impossibilities from physical conditions. God's incapacity to sin, lie, or forget is not a sign of imperfection but a part of His infinite perfection.

Again, His *Love* and *Wrath.* If wrath in God is conecived, not as a passion, subject to capricious changes, but as a changeless princi-ple of eternal hatred and antagonism to evil, it is seen as the other pole of Love—a part of infinite benevolence.

Again, His *Immutability* and His *Mutability*. He cannot change, yet He repents and reverses His plans (Mal. 3:6; James 1:17; 1 Sam. 15:10, 11; Jonah 3:10, etc.). He is essentially, but not relatively unchangeable. In His attributes and utterances, always consistent; but His attitude relatively changes towards man when man's attitude absolutely alters toward Himself, somewhat as when we turn about, what was behind is now before, and what we were departing from we are now approaching to. God changes from a retributive Judge to a reconciled Father when we abandon sin and accept salvation.

Other seeming paradoxes equally disappear when we avoid all needless extremes of opinion and prayerfully seek a right point of view.

A notable, proverbial paradox is found in the proverb, five times found in our Lord's sayings:

"For he that hath to him shall be given;

"And he that hath not, from him shall be taken even that which he hath" (Matt. 13:12; 25:29; Mark 4:25; Luke 8:19; 19:26).

Three times it is applied to hearing, what and how we hear. Twice to *receiving* in trust from God for use. There seems to be also a discrimination between hearers—those who hear the Word, without understanding; and those who both hear and understand and therefore are under a higher obligation to obey.

There are thus three concentric circles: the outermost, of the multitude of simple hearers; next, the smaller circle of instructed disciples; and yet within and smaller, of those specially endowed. But with all the law is—USE OR LOSE. To a dull ear, God ceases to speak; to a rebellious will, He ceases to bestow blessing; to an unfaithful steward, He ceases to confer entrustments.

III. As to the mysteries, we have the clear scriptural fact to begin with, that the word "mystery," as Inspiration uses it, has *three* distinct senses: 1. Something not hitherto revealed, but now disclosed; 2. Something not yet revealed, whether it ever can be, and will be, or not; 3. A meaning compounded of these two—something partly revealed and partly not. In either case, it is a mystery.

The word once meant to Greeks, in a form now lightly changed to us, *secret, i.e., explained to the initiated, though still a secret to the uninitiated.* Chiefly, it denoted theatrical or scenic shows on religious occasions, into which there was an initiation by the priests. In process of time men applied it to all kinds of secrets, even to implements, the uses of which had to be explained by instructed persons or experts. Finally, all matters of knowledge that required any teaching, were, in the gross, mysteries. In some quarters, the word even became synonymous with trade, though probably by corruption from mastery or maistry. Phrases, also, of similar importance in Scripture, are used in the three senses now distinguished, the discriminating use of which we now exemplify. Difficulties in understanding the mind of the Spirit often disappear with a little attention to the exceedingly and richly varied scriptural use of words.

The "*mysteries*" proper, need very careful study and there are at least *seven*: namely, the mystery of:

1. Godliness (1 Tim. 3:16; Heb. 1, 2), or the Incarnation.
2. Of Christ (Eph. 3, 4; possibly same as 'of the Gospel' Eph. 6).
3. Of Christ and the church (Eph. 5:32). Bride of Christ.
4. Of Iniquity—the man of sin (2 Thess. 2:7).
5. Of the Kingdom—itself sevenfold (Matt. 13; Mark 4:11).
6. Of Israel's Excision and Ingrafting (Rom. 11:25).
7. Of Resurrection and Translation (1 Cor. 15:51).

Looking at these seven, there is about them a singular symmetry and completeness. God incarnate in the Son of Man, and Satan, incarnate in the man of sin, the union of Jew and Gentile in one body, and of Christ and the church in wedlock; the national restoration of Israel and the actual resurrection of believers; and the sevenfold mystery or history of the Kingdom.

The other mysteries "of His Will," "of the Gospel," "of God," "of faith," "of Babylon the great," "of the woman," etc., are probably either equivalents for the others or involved and included in them. Compare Ephesians 1:19, 6:19; Col. 1:26, 27; 2:2; 1 Tim. 3:9; Rev. 17:5–7).

There are few if any locked chambers, to which the key is not divinely provided, and hung close by the lock itself. He might have put before us an open door. But it pleased Him both to incite and reward patient study, so he confronts us with closed doors so that truth may challenge study; yet He supplies the key, so that he who will search may not do so in vain.

46

Occult References and Intimations

PSALM 23. This psalm is most remarkable as expressing both New Testament and Old Testament conceptions of discipleship. Up to the end of verse 4, the figure is that of a sheep under care of the shepherd; from this point on, that of a son in his father's house, or at least a subject in the palace of a king, or a guest with his host.

The precise difference in the two dispensations is thus here expressed. To the Old Testament saint God was a Shepherd; to the New Testament saint, He is a Father, Sovereign, Host, all in one. And it is not accident, surely, that at the point of transition we find a *table* and an *anointing;* for it is at the table of the Lord that the Old Testament Passover passes into the New Testament Lord's Supper; and at the Pentecost Anointing that the disciple first apprehends fully the Sonship in his Father's House. It is, furthermore, noticeable that the idea of a blissful immortality was reserved for the New Testament to unfold fully. It was but simply hinted in the older times; but after the Lord's Supper and Pentecost came to be clearly revealed and understood. The Death and Resurrection of Christ, His Ascension and the coming of the Holy Spirit, were the necessary preliminaries to its full disclosure. So that this Psalm becomes a sort of enigma of both dispensations.

Occult hints of the Trinity are found in unexpected forms and places, not only in that first consultation in the godhead, "Let *us* make man in *our* image after *our* likeness (Gen. 1:26), and in that

315

strange union of a *plural* noun "Elohim" uniformly with a *singular* verb; but in the so-called "trisagion"—"Holy, Holy, Holy," in Isaiah 6:3, etc.

In Matthew 23:7–10, our Lord forbids His disciples to call others, or themselves be called, "Rabbi"—"teacher"—"Father" or "Master." He uses three separate words, "*pater*," "*didaskalos*," and "*kathēgetos*." It would seem that the first specially refers to the Father, the second to Himself, the Son; and the third to be the Holy Spirit. God alone they are to address and recognize as Father, the Lord Jesus Christ, as "Master," and the Holy Spirit, as Teacher.

Dr. E. W. Bullinger points out that the name Jehovah is found no less than four times in the Book of Esther, in acrostic form, namely, in chapters 1:20; 5:4; 5:13 and 7:7.

Reverend Evert J. Blekkink, of Cobbleskill, New York, while verifying the references in the Hebrew Bible, noticed that in 1 Kings 8:42, there is a similar concealment of the name Jehovah.

"They shall hear of Thy great Name, and of *Thy strong hand and of Thy stretched out arm.*"

The italics indicate that in which the Hebrew acrostic is found; and how it is in close connection with the express mention of the "*Name.*" By way of representing the Hebrew peculiarity to the English eye, he frames a couplet:

> The stranger shall Learn Of Righteous Deeds
> Wrought by Thy hand for Thy people's needs.

Just as here, the initials of the name LORD appear, so, in that unique Book of Esther, the Hebrew reader sees the name JeHoVaH, twice in the natural order of the letters, LORD, and twice also, in reverse order, DROL. In two of these instances, it is the *initials*, and, in the other two, it is the *finals* that spell for us the Name. Owing, however, to the Hebrew lack of *capital* distinctions, the eye does not so readily detect the singularity; though it is said that in three ancient manuscripts, Dr. Ginsburg has discovered the acrostic letters written in larger characters than the others.

The peculiar manner in which the name was *hid*, would indicate the fact that none but the covenant people possessed the oracles of God, while at the same time the peculiar manner in which it was *shown*, would indicate according to the teaching of 1 Kings, that "the stranger" was yet to learn it. Hidden for the very purpose of being revealed, first to the Jew alone, afterward to the Gentile—and by Him who is the Aleph and the Tau, the Alpha and the Omega, the first and the last, the beginning and the end.

The Time Element in Scripture is often very important. Vast interests may lie between two consecutive sentences; two conspicuous instances will recur to every student's mind.

"In the Beginning God created the Heavens and the Earth."

"And the Earth was without form, and void."

No human being can tell how many millions of years may stretch between these two statements. The first tells of a beginning when God created the present visible order, but gives no hint as to when. The second tells of a condition of the earth when He began the present work of its preparation for the abode of man. But, between the original production and the after reconstruction and preparation, all the ages seemingly demanded by geology, may be accommodated without violence to the narrative.

Again, in Isaiah 61:2:

"To proclaim the acceptable year of the Lord"—"And the Day of Vengeance of our God."

No one who heard or read those words, as originally written or spoken, would have supposed that thousands of years would elapse between the two proclamations. But already about nineteen centuries have passed since the first proclamation was made, when significantly our Lord, having read the first part of this double sentence, abruptly closed the Scroll, and sat down saying, "This day is *this* Scripture fulfilled in your ears" (Luke 4:19), but of the Days of Vengeance He made no mention then, nor until the close of His ministry (21:22), when He took up the unfinished strain and foretold of a coming time when this also would be fulfilled.

Such examples should make us cautious how we infer that, because two statements are closely connected in Scripture, they necessarily imply an equally close contiguity of events.

In 1 Corinthians 15:20–25, four great events are singularly gathered into one view: Christ's Resurrection; afterward that of those who are Christ's at His coming; then the End of His Mediatorial

Reign, and the destruction of the last foe. No one who first read this letter of Paul to Corinth could have told of the intervals that might lie between these events. After all these centuries, the Saints' Resurrection has not yet come; and beyond that lies the final conquest of Death as the last Enemy, and the Delivering up of the Kingdom may be the last in the series of events, beyond that age of ages, which seems to stretch even beyond the millennium.

There are occult hints of a peculiar divine *method of reckoning time*, as first found in connection with the institution of the Passover: "This month shall be the *Beginning of Months—the first month of the year* to you"—literally, "the head of months," first in rank as well as first in order. This was a marked change: the *seventh* month of the *civil* year becoming henceforth the *first* of the *sacred* or ecclesiastical. This simple decree affects all the whole after career of Israel, revealing a new philosophy of history, in God's reckoning of time when He "writeth up the people" in His register (Ps. 50:6). This marks, also, for all coming time, the establishment of a *New Calendar*, and includes several particulars:

1. A final break with Egypt. Hitherto the Egyptian mode of reckoning had controlled, the calendar being regulated by the inundations of the Nile. Now this last link was to be severed, and God's emancipated people was to be also a separated people.

2. A new starting point in history. During the Egyptian sojourn the notion was treated as civilly dead, and the Exodus was regarded as a national resurrection, and the beginning of newness of life—the paschal night, "a night to be much observed"—a birthnight with labor pangs (Ex. 12:42).

Thus, the common civil year was, in Jehovah's dealings with Israel, displaced, and a new era began, dependent upon their new relation to Him as His redeemed people. This prepares us to understand that new philosophy of history, already referred to according to which all time in which they practically went back into Egypt, and lived in alienation from God and subjection to His enemies was treated as a blank and not honored with any recorded history. How significant that the Lord should in His reckoning take note only of the times when His people were so far loyal to Him as not to be abandoned to the oppressive rule of their enemies.

The 490 years of Daniel 9:24, it is hard to make out as accurate unless certain years are omitted when the Hebrew people were practically indifferent and disobedient.

However this may be, certain it is that, from the time of the rejection and crucifixion of their Messianic King, Israel disappears from the records of Holy Writ, especially after the judgment which destroyed their city and dispersed their nation.

The deeper significance of all this it is not hard to read. Until we separate ourselves from sin, accepting salvation through the blood of sprinkling, we do not even begin to live and to walk with God, but are dead in trespasses and sins. However, in men's eyes active and successful, in God's eyes we are nothing and have done nothing. Despite all accumulations of wealth and learning, honor and fame, we are as He judges us, poor and destitute and dead, having not even seen life; and any day not spent with God and for God has no entry in His Book of Remembrance. This is God's unique philosophy of history.

Thus God has also His own *calendar*. He reckons times in a way of His own, and in writing up history often leaves great gaps of silence, chasms of oblivion, where there is nothing worthy of a record. Some of the period of years cannot be made out as accurate without some such omissions or additions as may make His chronology correspond with man's. The long centuries of sojourn in Egypt have practically no record, nor have the forty years of desert journeying when His people were under the ban; between the two encampments at Kadesh Barnea, little more than a bare list of stations! The 480 years between the Exodus and the temple building referred to in 1 Kings 6:1 seem to fall short of the actual time computed to be 573 years, by some 93 years. But there were just that number of years during which they were given over to captivity to their foes as recorded in the Book of Judges, as follows: Mesopotamia, 8; Moab, 18; Canaan, 20; Medea, 7; Philistia, 40 = 93. Is this the explanation of an apparent discrepancy? If so, it not only solves an enigma but reveals a principle of God's philosophy of reckoning.

This God of the Bible has His own *mathematics*. "One day is with the Lord as a thousand years, and a thousand years are but as yesterday when it is past, or as a watch in the night" (Ps. 90:4). He is not limited by man's notions of numbers. "One can chase a thousand, and two put"—not *two* thousand, but "*ten* thousand to flight" (Lev. 26:8). In His addition table in this case, one and one make not two but ten.

As we have found in our studies, there are many proofs that the God of the Bible has His own *grammar*. The word "Elohim," translated "God," is plural, but it is always joined to a singular verb, as though to hint that, while there are three *persons* in the Trinity, they are not three Gods, but one God, and so take a singular verb. The gender, number and case of nouns, and the voice, mood and tense of verbs are never found used in the Word of God without a reason which often only close study unveils.

He has also, His own *Lexicon*. He uses language in a way of His own. For example, in Numbers 21, He calls His pilgrim nation, "Israel" up to the point where their rebellious murmurings began; then, seven times, only "the people," until they are penitent, humbled and restored to His favor; and then "Israel" nine times—it is "Israel that" set forward, "sang this song," "sent messengers to Sihon," "smote him," and "possessed his land," "took all these cities," and "dwelt in them." Surely there can be no accident in such reservation of the elect name for the time when they obedient!

The Word of God thus hints that this unique and solitary Being had His own "ways" of thinking and doing everything.

The Bible, without being a scientific treatise, cannot avoid incidental references to scientific subjects, and, whenever it touches the domain of general knowledge and universal fact, reveals the omniscient mind, which is behind it, as the general intelligence of an author shows itself in the treatment of special themes. Knowledge cannot be hid, and He who made the universe never could betray ignorance of His handiwork.*

There are in the universe at least Ten Great Forces, to which the Scriptures more or less clearly refer, which may be studied in a definite order, beginning with the lower and more material, and ascending to the higher and more subtle and spiritual. The study of them

---

* This department finds ample tratment in the author's *Many Infallible Proofs, God's Living Oracles*, etc.

and especially of their correspondences and mutual relations will amply repay any amount of pains and patience.

1. Gravitation, or tendency of bodies to move toward a center.
2. Cohesion and Adhesion, or mutual attraction of particles.
3. Crystallization, the subtle force that determines symmetry.
4. Chemical affinity, the force that promotes new combinations.
5. Vegetation, or the force which develops vegetable life and growth.
6. Animation, the essential life principle in the animal realm.
7. Ratiocination, the force that regulates the reasoning process.
8. Emotion, the affectional force that corresponds to heat.
9. Resolution, or the volitional force residing in the will.
10. Spiritual Affinity, the force that unites holy beings.

Light, Heat, Actinic Life, Electricity, etc., appear to be modes of motion, largely entering into all the operations of the material universe.

47

Pictorial Helps to Impression

VISIBLE FORM or representation addressed to the eye is found greatly helpful both in the impression and retention of ideas. Hence, the value of charts, maps and drawings in connection with Scripture study and exhibition of truth.

A few examples will suffice, as this matter also has ampler illustration in another volume from the same pen.*

An outline of the *Tabernacle and its Courts* is of primary importance not only in the understanding of the structure itself but in the interpretation of numerous Scripture references to it and its various articles of furniture, as in Hebrews 9, etc.

We add a General Summary of Teaching from Romans to Thessalonians.

The drawing that follows is meant to show how the earthly life of a disciple is, at all vital points, represented by and identified with some corresponding experience in the career of the Lord Jesus Christ. The semicircle hints the whole scope of Christ's experience from His incarnation to His final enthronization. The central vertical line indicates the method and principle of the union and identification of the believer with his Lord, namely, His ascent to Heaven and the descent of the Spirit, these two great facts linking Heaven and earth. The base horizontal line stands for the daily earthly walk of the believer as essentially one with the Christ-life, which spans it from beginning to end

---

* *Bible and Spiritual Life,* Gospel Publishing House, N.Y.

323

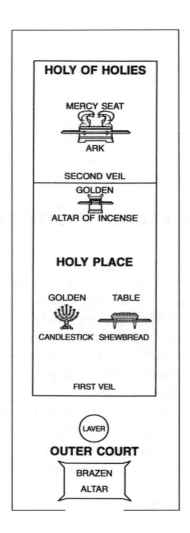

like a rainbow. The various radii are intended to mark the parallel experiences of the believer with those of his Lord, at every point. It is hoped that such diagram, however imperfect, may impress on the mind the truth addressed to the eye.

A chart of *Dispensations* is also very helpful. Dispensational truth is doubly important; it serves both for the interpretation and illumination of Scripture. All history is a plan of God in which two factors are prominent:

God, in judgment and mercy; law and grace;
Man in disobedience and condemnation, faith
    and obedience.

There is no hope save in divine management and mastery; for man has always been a failure. Dispensations express and exhibit God's ways of excessive dealing with man in successive periods and experimental methods.

Certain distinguishing marks characterize every dispensation, and in something like the following order:

A new advance in clearer, fuller revelation of God and truth.

A new decline in man's faith and faithfulness toward Him.

A new assimilation to the world and amalgamation with it.

A new advance in a worldly and godless type of civilization.

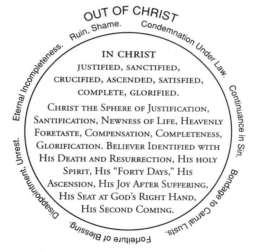

From "In Christ Jesus," published by Funk and Wagnalls.

THE EARTHLY WALK OF THE BELIEVER IDENTIFIED WITH CHRIST

A new parallel development of good and evil—wheat and tares.

A new apostasy or practical denial of God and His truth.

A new crisis of judgment, a catastrophe of destruction.

These particulars may all find illustration in the antediluvian era. It began with a Messianic promise and the institution of worship and sacrifice. There followed rapid declension and departure from God; then the practical wedlock between the sons of God and the daughters of men, with a gigantic race of men renown but godless. Worshippers of God and idolaters grew side by side, until the apostasy was so prevalent that but one righteous family remained, and the flood swept away mankind.

This general historic outline has been strangely repeated in every successive dispensational period. It is still accurate as the type of the present Christian dispensation. This opened with Pentecostal Light; there was even in the apostolic age rapid spiritual declension; the church became worldly and lost separateness; a great imperial civilization developed, but introduced the Dark Ages spiritually; the parallel development of wheat and tares still goes on; the final apostasy from the faith is even now alarmingly progressing; and it only remains for Christ's Coming to bring the catastrophe of judgment.

Many attempts have been made, familiar to most Biblical students, to represent God's dispensational dealings with man under law and under grace, and all follow essentially one scheme. Between the Eternity Past and the Eternity Future, the whole duration or period of time is usually divided into at least five subordinate periods:

1. Creation to Deluge. 2. Deluge to Abram. 3. Abram to Christ. 4. Christ's Advent to Millennium. 5. Second Advent to the End.

This is general accord in the following scheme of dispensations as in harmony with the Word of God:

I.	II.	III.	IV.	V.	VI.	VII.
In Paradise.	Antediluvian.	Postdiluvian.	Abrahamic.	Mosaic.	Church.	Kingdom.
Creation to Fall.	Fall to Deluge.	Deluge to Abram.	Abram to Moses.	Moses to Christ.	Christ to Second Advent.	Second Advent to End.
	About 1650 years.	About 450 years.	About 450 years.	About 1450 years.	2000?	1000?

We add a drawing of the Triclinium, or threefold reclining table, used at meals and probably such as our Lord sat at in the Passover Supper.

TRICLINIUM

If this be correct, it shows by the numbers which were the chief seats and why James and John had asked to sit "at the right hand and left hand"; what is meant by "sitting down in the lowest room" and being bidden higher; and how our Lord could give a sop to Judas at the table, as next to Him on the left. If this chart be accurate, as we believe, it explains many another reference in the Word.

PROPHETS IN ISRAEL AND JUDAH
A TABLE of the Prophets, showing when they prophesied.†

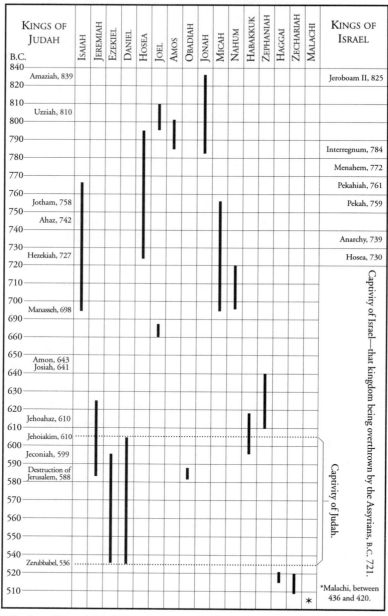

The date after each king's name indicates the commencement of his reign.

Joel is placed twice, as it is doubtful at which period he lived.

† From Angus' Bible Hand-book.

TABLE OF COMPARATIVE CHRONOLOGY

Showing the ascertained or probable time when the various portions of the New Testament were written, and the corresponding events in history. Interrogation points mark the more doubtful times of events.

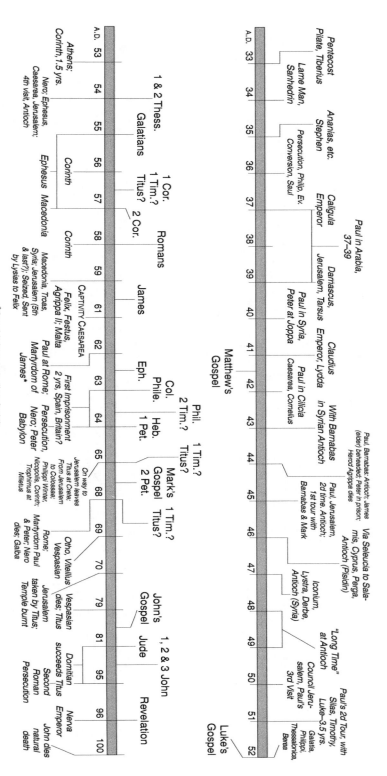

* Son of Alpheus, and author of epistle.

48

The Humorous Element in Scripture

B IBLICAL EXAMPLES MIGHT BE COLLATED of every sort of weapon to be found in the whole armory of humor—wit, satire, irony, retort, ridicule, raillery, drollery, play on words—these and other forms of the ludicrous are employed by prophets, apostles, and some of them even by our Lord Himself, as means to rebuke and expose error and wrong and vindicate truth and right.

One man at least is evidently meant as an example of mischievous *abuse* of the ludicrous—Samson—who is the representative wag of Scripture, in whom humor runs mad, the element of the ridiculous in this case being carried to the extreme, as if for warning. But in general the use of humor is carefully restrained and restricted within its lawful domain and province.

Samson after his slaughter of the Philistines celebrated his victory by a play on words—the original word for "ass" and "heaps" being nearly the same. Wordsworth reproduces the poetic paranomia thus:

"With the jaw bone of an ass, a mass, two masses," etc.

A Jewish student suggests—"*I ass-ass-inated them*" as an approach to the witty original.

What awful sarcasm when Hezekiah, finding the children of Israel still burning incense to the brazen serpent, 750 years after it had served its purpose, broke it in pieces and contemptuously called it "Nehustan"—a mere *piece of brass!* (2 Kgs. 18:4). Ewald paraphrases it "the Brass God."

The Gileadites compelled the Ephraimites at the fords of the Jordan, to pronounce a Hebrew word, "Shibboleth." The Eastern tribe seems to have had a dialectical provincialism in the utterance of this word, and the Ephraimites could not bring their organs to pronounce it, but said "Sibboleth." The former word means a "stream," and the latter a "burden," and the test word was naturally suggested by the locality of the stream. A Frenchman finds similar difficulty in pronouncing the diphthong "th" (Judg. 12:6).

There seems here a designed reference to the paltry differences which often array men against each other and lead even to persecuting hatred. The word "Shibboleth" has passed into our language to indicate the test word, pet phrase, or trifling peculiarity which becomes the watchword of a party or the test of orthodoxy, and may give rise to bitter warfare between sects and persecuting bigotry and intolerance. The difference between the two words was that of a mere aspirate—the sound of "h," and the inability to sound it doomed them to death. How like the controversies of the ages!

What a bitter *irony* is found in that sentence applied to the idolater: "*He feedeth on ashes!*" (Is. 44:9–20; Jer. 10:1–6).

He hews down a tree—cuts up a part of it for fuel for his fire, to warm himself and cook his food; and of the residue he carves a wooden god to worship—he does not see that he is trying to feed his soul on ashes—that the log he burns and turns to ashes is identical with the god he adores. Can a god be burnt upon a fire? Or such a god feed the worshiper with anything better than the ashes which is all that remains of him?

The Bible sometimes makes even *History* humorous—as in poetic retribution in which with all the tragedy there is a hint of comedy. Compare Judge 1:5–7, where Adonibezek who has made seventy captive kings with thumbs and great toes cut off, pick up food under his table like dogs, has his own hands and feet maimed in exactly the same fashion.

Or, far more signally, watch the irony of History, when Haman who built a gallows of great height to hang Mordecai, himself first swings from it with his ten sons! The reader can scarce suppress an outburst of laughter when, before the final catastrophe, this dastardly autocrat asks, "What shall be done to the man whom the King delighteth to honor?" Thinking himself the favorite, Haman lays out a royal program of distinction—not stopping short of the King's own charger, apparel and crown, with a princely herald to go before and publicly proclaim his high estate. And then what a sharp turning point in his scheme when the monarch quickly replies—"Yes! that is the thing to do! carry out that very program—only let it be you that do it to Mordecai!"

The writings of Solomon are full of subtle humor.

Proverbs 6:6. "Go to the ant, thou sluggard, consider her ways and be wise: which having no guide, overseer, or ruler, provideth her meat in the summer and gathereth her food in the harvest."

This is no error in Entomology. The *Atta Providens, Atta Barbara* and *Atta Structor* are not carnivorous but herbivorous. They prepare the soil, plant seed, weed out the soil, reap and store the crop, and when the grain gets wet, bring it to the surface and dry it in the sun.

The emphatic word is "sluggard"—and the ant is put before us as an example of industry and energy. Don't lie abed and dream or fold your hands and mourn that you have not much brains. Neither has the ant, but what brain it has is all gray matter, and not putty. Get up and go to work. Make the most of what you have. What you need is the formic acid of a persistent effort. No matter if you are very small and black and live in an ant hill, if you have only grit. The ant is famous for industry, energy, ingenuity, economy; for division and combination of labor. Whether as masons, agriculturists, carpenters or carvers of wood they furnish examples for admiration and imitation.

"Where no oxen are the crib is clean; but much increase is by the strength of the ox" (Prov. 14:4).

The lesson is simple; if you keep no oxen you will have a clean crib—no fodder to furnish, not litter to clear away; but you cannot avail yourself of the strength of the ox, and the increase it brings.

Occupation is the ox. To do hard work costs something, but it also counts for something; it is easier to be lazy, but it is hard to go hungry. To do nothing gratifies indolence, but indolence has no reward in attainment or accomplishment. Better buy an ox and feed him than to have no ox when you have a field to plough or a load to pull. There is a life of contemplation that is in a sense cleaner than one of action; it keeps us away from the turmoil and dust of the field and street; but it forfeits the increase of work done in the world for the world's good.

"A living dog is better than a dead lion" (Eccl. 9:4).

Founded on popular estimates of the dog and lion in the East, the dog, wild and wolfish, slave of beastly vices, being held very low—the lion, strong and majestic, ranked as king of beasts.

A lower order of man, inspired by a purpose, is better than the highest in rank, unfitted with an aim. When ciphers precede the units they diminish their value; when they follow, they increase it.

Society is an inclined plane—down which the dead lions slide, and by which the living dogs climb, and they pass each other on the way. Down from the highest plane drop those who are inert and purposeless, who have not enough manhood to maintain themselves where God has placed them; up from the lowest level rise those whose innate nobleness and resolution are superior to their natural and social position.

"Wisdom is better than weapons of war" (Eccl. 9:18).

This is the conclusion of a little allegory (vv. 14–18): the allegory of a little city, and a few men within it; and there came a great King against it and besieged it and built great bulwarks against it; and there was found in it a poor wise man and he by his wisdom delivered the city.

The little city is the family, the church, the state, or even the little city of the man's own self. The great King with all his host is the devil; and the poor man is simply a wise heart. The pen is mightier than the sword—brains stronger than brawn. One wise man offsets an army of mere fools—right is stronger than might. As Bacon said, knowledge is power. The man of talent and tact, who has insight to see what is needed, and the foresight to suggest the remedy, is the salvation of society. After nations have wasted millions in war, it is the sagacity and capacity of a few wise men that suggest the basis of a permanent peace, and the same counsels called in earlier might have saved war's awful cost.

"If the iron be blunt and he do not whet the edge then must he put to more strength" (Eccl. 10:10).

"A whet is not let." Sharpness is a form of strength. The purpose of education is to whet the iron—not a dead mass of accumulations, but power to work with the brain. Arnold would have the boy study Latin "not for what he would do with the Latin, but for what the Latin would do with him." Culture is a form of force. A sharp weapon enables us to do as much work with much less muscle.

Education whets and sharpens the dullest tools and helps the workmen to excel and surpass those who have more and better tools, but do not use the grindstone.

The maxim of a heathen moralist is true that "Ridicule sometimes cuts deeper than severity," and is amply illustrated in the books of Proverbs and Ecclesiastes.

"A sluggard who dips his hand into the dish, will not so much as bring it to his mouth"; and "will not turn himself in bed but must be rolled over by others" like a door that cannot turn itself (Prov. 26:14, 15). This is biting sarcasm.

Again, among the four unendurable things, are instanced a servant who becomes a sovereign, and carries the servile spirit into his rule; and an ugly "woman who comes to be married" (30:21–23).

Again, Solomon compares one who meddles with others' strife to a man who grasps a dog by the ears—he can neither safely hold on or let go.

Paul often betrays a keen sense of humor, as for example in some of his paradoxes: "Idle tattlers and busy bodies" (1 Tim. 5:13)—people at the same time idle, as to all that was good, and industrious about all that was evil—hands hanging down for want of work, but tongues always swinging with gossip—active in meddling and mischief making.

He refers to those who, loving fables more than facts, and having itching ears, "heap to themselves teachers," etc.; the metaphor is amusing for it refers to swine that, having the scurvy, seek relief for itching ears by rubbing them against stone heaps.

Listen to an instance of divine sarcasm!

"The Lord shall have them in derision" (Ps. 2:4). His foes conspire to defeat His plans and burst the cords of His restraints and overturn

His throne: but He only derides their impotence as though with a watering pot they would put out the stars, or seek to plant their shoulder against the burning orb of the midday sun and roll it back into night!

Again: "The Lord shall laugh at him: For He seeth that His day is coming" (Ps. 37:13).

He sees the wicked plotting to upset the foundations of justice, but He laughs at his folly and patiently waits the day of retribution when Righteousness shall triumph.

Isaiah 5:7 is a fine example of most exquisite use of play on words. Jehovah "looked for judgment, but behold oppression; for righteousness, but behold a cry." No translation can convey the beauty of the original. He looked for *meshpat* but lo! *mespach*; for *tsedakah* but lo! *tseakah*." Observe the point: He looked for cultivated grapes and found only wild grapes. The difference between the two is one of flavor not of appearance. Externally, a close resemblance, but internally how unlike, and, to express this, in both cases, two words are chosen, so similar in letters and sound as to be almost indistinguishable but meaning opposite things. We might convey some idea of this by a similar use of terms though not an equivalent; He looked for equity and lo, iniquity; for a scepter and lo, a specter.

What withering irony was that of our Lord!

Many good works have I shown you from My Father: *For which of those works do ye stone Me?* (John 10:32).

If the blind lead the blind, both shall fall into the ditch (Matt. 15:14). One has only to see Tissot's picture to realize the awful irony of these words. It portrays a procession of blind men, each with his hands on the shoulders of the man before him, all stumbling forward over unseen obstacles, and the foremost just plunging into a deep ditch.

"He that is without sin among you, let him first cast a stone at her" (John 8:7). What sarcasm that drove those accusers out one by one, self-convicted and condemned!

"Go ye and tell that *fox*"—Herod (Luke 13:32). In one word He described Herod—his cunning, subtlety, cruelty, and dissimulation. No animal is more famous for slyness and ingenuity both in artifices for obtaining prey and averting capture.

49

Finding Hid Treasure in God's Word

THIS CONCEPTION OF THE WORD OF GOD as a treasure house is a ruling thought of Psalm 119, where we constantly meet such expressions as these:

"I have rejoiced in the way of Thy testimonies as much as in all riches" (14).

"Open Thou mine eyes that I may behold wondrous things out of Thy law" (18).

"Make me to understand the way of Thy precepts" (27).

"The law of Thy mouth is better unto me than thousands of gold and silver" (72).

"Thou, through Thy commandments hast made wiser than my enemies." I have more understanding than all my teachers; I understand more than the ancients (98, 99, 100).

"How sweet are Thy words unto my taste" (103).

"The entrance of Thy words giveth light" (130).

"I rejoice in Thy word, as one that findeth great spoil" (162).

These are a few specimens only of what the psalmist found in searching the Word of God. All figures are exhausted to describe it— a flood of light and joy; more understanding than all his enemies, teachers or ancient sages; food both nutritious and delicious; wondrous things, all riches, thousands of gold and silver, great spoil, etc. The whole Psalm contains at least fifty such tributes couched in every form of speech.

Hence the *prayer*, "Open Thou mine eyes"; and the promise so often repeated, that they who search the Scriptures shall find the testimony of Christ, the witness to themselves, and the secrets of holy obedience and experience.

The plan of God is that the reverent study first to know and then to *do* the Will of God as herein set forth shall have a reward so ample as to be inexpressible—"visions and revelations of the Lord."

Compare such Scriptures as the following: Matthew 11:25, 26; John 7:17; Romans 11:25–36; 1 Corinthians 2; 12:1–31; 15:14–21; Ephesians 1:15–23, etc.

He who would find the hid treasure must observe the laws of *uniqueness.*

Whatever stands alone in Scripture may be assumed as having special importance. Not only does its presence in the Word imply a purpose, but its solitariness shows that such purpose is to be discovered within itself, because it has no co-related Scripture. It is meant to be complete, having some function of its own not shared by other parts of the Word, and will reveal some special symmetry and unity. This is another illustration of that universal law that nothing in Scripture is aimless or useless.

That is always unique which stands alone and by itself, either in quantity or quality, in kind or singularity.

For instance, where any person, fact or subject has but one mention in Scripture it is usually designed for emphasis, and the lesson to be conveyed is also unique. Like a single spot of bright color which may give to a dark picture a vernal touch, or a solitary ornament in a building which may complete its whole design, so a solitary mention of a person or an event may contribute a necessary element to the whole body of Scripture teaching.

A *word* which is used but once generally has some unique force. "*Avouch,*" found only in Deuteronomy 26:16, 17 carries remarkable significance. By declaring Jehovah to be their chosen God, the people of Israel evoked His responsive declaration that they were His chosen people. This double avouchment or avowal is a sort of bridal vow, in which each partly plights troth to the other in a marital covenant. This thought, from this point on, pervades Scripture, that such an affirmation on the part of either God or man evokes and elicits a responsive affirmation from the other. Of Jehovah's challenge and man's response, Psalm 27:8 is a good example; also the call to Samuel and his answer. Of man's appeal to God and God's response, Pentecost is the most conspicuous illustration. But all avouchment of Jehovah is sure of a counter avouchment on His part.

The prayer of Jabez stands alone (1 Chr. 4:9, 10).

And Jabez was more honorable than his brethren: and his mother called his name Jabez, saying, Because I bare him with sorrow. And Jabez called on the God of Israel, saying, Oh that Thou wouldest bless me indeed, and enlarge my coast, and that Thine hand might be with me, and that Thou wouldest keep me from evil, that it may not grieve me! And God granted him that which he requested.

This is all we know of Jabez. He was a son of sorrow, like Benjamin. But he was distinguished above his brethren by a high sense of honor.

This prayer bears careful study, and is recorded for a permanent purpose, as a lesson for all time. There are four petitions here and they are very comprehensive:

1. The initial request, which includes all the rest is for a True Divine Blessing.

2. A second request is for enlargement—"that Thou wouldest enlarge my coast," which seems to be equivalent to an increased measure of usefulness.

3. That God's Hand might be with Him—an expression which in the Word of God always carries the idea of Divine strength and co-operation.

4. That he might be kept from evil that it might not grieve or overcome him, which is a petition for a sanctified character and life.

These four requests might be expressed in a way to show more completely their comprehensiveness and symmetry, thus:

Jabez craves and supplicates of God.

1. The Truest, Highest Blessing from God.

2. Increased Sphere; Working for God.

3. Increased Power; Co-working with God.

4. Increased Sanctity; inworking of God.

Notice also *Azariah's Solitary Prophecy:*

And the Spirit of God came upon Azariah the son of Oded: And he went out to meet Asa, and said unto him, Hear ye me, Asa, and all Judah and Benjamin:

The Lord *is* with you,
While ye be with Him;
And if ye seek Him;
He will be found of you;
But if ye forsake Him,
He will forsake you (2 Chr. 15:1, 2).

These thirty words comprise the whole of the recorded utterance of this prophet, who is here mentioned for the only time. There must, therefore, be some peculiar significance in these words, which are the more pregnant with meaning as we are told in the next verse that "for a long season Israel had been without the true God, and without a teaching priest, and without law." It was a prolonged season of spiritual death and darkness, and this prophetic utterance lights up the midnight gloom and interprets the situation, while it affords all needed guidance as to the secret of returning blessing.

There is here a Principle of Divine Dealing, applicable to all ages of history. The expression, "The Lord is with you," is the great assurance which in the Word of God includes all that is most desirable—from Genesis to Revelation it seems to stand for *Fullness of Blessing.* And here we are taught that this comprehensive good is not bestowed by arbitrary caprice, but obeys certain fixed law. There is an attitude of mind, heart and will which commands blessing or forfeits it. James gives us the nearest equivalent of Azariah's prophecy, when he says: "Draw nigh to God and He will draw nigh to you" (James 4:8). And David in 2 Samuel 22:26, 27, when he declares that with the merciful, God will show Himself merciful, with the upright and pure, upright and pure; and with the froward, He will show Himself froward.

We cannot well mistake this plain teaching—the substance of which is that the vacillations in our spiritual experience and history are due not to changes in God, but to changes in ourselves. To the unstable He is unstable, but to the steadfast and faithful, He is found and felt to be the immutable God. The Headlight on the promontory of rock may seem to be moving, but it is the ship that is tossing.

This short prophetic address is recorded for our learning, for it carries a weighty lesson for all coming time, which may be briefly stated, thus:

1. *God is practically, to every man, what his own life makes him.* "Thou thoughtest that I was altogether such an one as thyself" (Ps. 50:21). Our moral and spiritual attitude and aptitude constitute a lens through which God is seen; and if the lens is not clear, true and colorless, it distorts and discolors all conceptions of God.

2. *God is essentially changeless in His relations to man.* To get into right relations with Him, therefore, is to insure on His part right relations to us. And hence, also, rectification of what is wrong or abnormal may immediately restore blessing.

3. *God's Power is always at the command of the penitent and obedient.* There is one great sentence we would write as in letters of flame on every Christians' memory: OBEY THE LAW OF THE FORCE AND THE FORCE OBEYS YOU. The natural world is full of mystic and subtle forces—light and heat, gravitation, magnetism, electricity, etc. They obey fixed laws, and so far and so long as man conforms to those laws, he controls those forces. Light becomes his photographer, heat his refiner, gravitation his engineer, magnetism his pilot, electricity his messenger, motor and illuminator. So in the spiritual realm there is a similar reign of law. Even the Holy Spirit has His chosen methods and channels as even the winds have their currents; and to know and conform to His elect modes of operation and get into the channels of His streams is to find Him filling our weakness with the strength and power of God. Even *prayer* commands blessing only when coupled with *obedience*. As Abraham's servant said: *"I, being in the way, the Lord led me"* (Gen. 24:27).

The lesson of Azariah's prophecy is enforced by Canon Evanson, who well observes, that "There is a mutual interaction between the rain of heaven and the mists of earth. These two kindred moistures produce and reproduce one another. When rich rain falls on soft ground, in due time, a grateful mist rises and makes fresh clouds.

These again break in fresh rain. God, knowing the hearts of all men, gives His grace to all whom He sees to be receptive of it; and to such as use it will He give it in larger measure. The more work done, the more grace given" (1 Cor. 15:10; cf. Heb. 6:7, 8).

Jonah's so-called "prophecy" is unique. He was the *first foreign missionary*, and the lessons of his career are most unique and valuable. They are mainly these:

1. That a missionary may be distinctly called of God and refuse to go—in fact, so turn his back on his call as to go to the farthest *opposite* point, as he started for the West—Tarshish or Tartessus, Spain, instead of Nineveh in the remote East.

2. That when a man, called of God, turns his back on God, there is nothing before him but disappointment, darkness and disaster, until he repents.

3. That when a call is repeated, one may go and practically not go—formally undertaking the sacred duty but heartlessly. A *loveless obedience* is in such case little better than a *lawless disobedience*.

50

Gathering up Fragments

THERE ARE ABOUT TWELVE OR THIRTEEN conspicuous symbols used to express the range and scope of the application of Holy Scripture to daily needs. They abundantly repay study from their great suggestiveness and comprehensiveness. Taken alphabetically, they are the following: Bread, fire, gold, hammer, honey, lamp, laver, light, meat, milk, mirror, seed, sword. Here four symbols refer to food, and food in its nutritious and delicious qualities; four more to the uses of the Word in self-revealing, self-cleansing and self-guiding; four others to its power as a force or weapon, etc.

Througout the Word most valuable hints are scattered on the *philosophy of suffering* which in no one place are gathered up and presented at one view, an exception to an otherwise almost uniform rule. If we search we shall find some six or seven forms or phases of suffering distinguished. We may for want of any better terms call them—

1. The Retributive or Judicial (Romans 2:2–11; 5:23).
2. The Administrative, or organic and hereditary (Ex. 20:5, 6; Rom. 5:12–21).
3. The Punitive or penal (2 Sam. 12:13–19; Heb. 12:15–17).
4. The Corrective or Paternal (Heb. 12:5–12).
5. The Educative or disciplinary (Heb. 2:10; 1 Pet. 1:6, 7).
6. The Vindicative or exemplary (Job 1:2; Dan. 6; Eph. 6:10–20).
7. The Redemptive or voluntary and vicarious (Col. 1:24).

The wealth of suggestion found here only deep study can reveal. Retributive suffering is the final judicial infliction of punishment upon the rebellious, impenitent, unbelieving. It may be wholly escaped by repentance, faith and self-surrender, so that the believer will never come into judgment.

What we have called the administrative pertains to God's method of administering human history. He has established an organic connection between parent and offspring, ancestry and posterity, and a corporate connection between members of the same society, or as we significantly call it "common-wealth," whereby the sins and follies, as also virtues and excellencies of the sire are measurably entailed on the son; and if one member of the body politic suffer, all the members suffer with it; or if one be honored, all rejoice with it. To suspend this organic law would not only arrest the evil consequences of others' wrongdoing, but prevent the blessings which are conveyed in the same channel. Hence our duty is to adjust ourselves to this law by such moderation of our indulgences and virtuousness of habit as both modify the evil consequences of parental sins, and prevent a like inheritance in our children.

By the punitive is meant suffering which even forgiveness does not wholly obviate or prayer remove. "God is not mocked; whatsoever a man soweth that shall he also reap." David's sin was put away, but the child born of it could not be spared. Esau's repentance and remorse could not undo the barter of his birthright, or recall the prophetic blessing that went with it. Nor could even Moses enter the land after his dishonoring of God at Meribah-Kadesh.

Corrective suffering is of the nature of paternal chastisement. It can be got rid of immediately by correcting the fault, for not father continues his chastisement when the child is penitent and obedient. Hence in 1 Corinthians 11:30–32, we are taught that "if we would judge ourselves we should not be judged." It is our lack of self-correction that makes the Father's needful.

Suffering may likewise be educative, preparing us for service and maturing in us virtues only ripened in sorrow, like patience which obviously must be learned when there is something to be patient about, to be borne patiently. Even our Lord had to be perfected through such suffering, for the captain of a company prepares for his captaincy by enduring hardship as a good soldier, sharing the training with the members of his company. Gold can only be rid of alloy by furnace fires. It has three stages of history: in the *mine*, in the *fining pot* or crucible, and in the *vessel*: and it gets to be in the vessel and on the master's table only by passing through the fire.

Vindicative suffering is what we endure in vindication of God, as Job did when the Devil challenged Jehovah to produce a man that served Him without respect to temporal advantage. The Lord needed such a witness in Babylon and Daniel went into the lion's den to vindicate God by proving that a praying saint will not give up even his prayers or conceal them to save his life.

Redemptive suffering is that which is voluntarily endured to save others. In the nature of the case it must be voluntary in order to be truly vicarious. It is never compulsory, God puts no cross on us; if we bear it at all it is because we *take it up* after Christ. Paul could not atone for human guilt, nor redeem men, but he could fill up what was behind in the sufferings of Christ by identifying himself with the Redeemer in voluntarily self-denial for His sake and bringing to the knowledge of the lost the fact of salvation. This suffering, so far from being evaded or avoided, should be regarded as the consummate privilege of the believer.

The wisdom which finds expression in the book of Proverbs and Ecclesiastes is a mine of gems, much neglected. The collection itself challenges the reader to search its contents:

"Have I not written unto thee excellent things in counsels and knowledge, that I might make thee know the certainty of the words of truth that thou mightest answer the words of truth to them that send unto thee?" (Prov. 22:20, 21).

Here is a fine expression of the grand purpose of all Holy Scripture and especially of these words of practical counsel—a gift from God of words of truth, that man might *know* their certainty, and *answer* with them all challengers.

We cite a few conspicuous instances:

"The Fear of the Lord is the Beginning of *Wisdom*," of "*Knowledge*" (Prov. 1:7; 9:10).

This grand saying is repeated at important points. In Job 28:28, it appears as an oracle, at the close of a sublime poem on the mysteries of nature as the key to their solution. In Psalm 111:10, it comes as the choral close of a temple Hymn, as the keynote of all true worship; and here, it is the watchword of all true education, intellectual wisdom.

The word "beginning" means "principle part," head and front. It indicates either a starting point, or a goal, or both; what is first in order, or first in importance. The substance of the lesson is, in all pursuit after wisdom or knowledge *start with God*.

Even in intellectual matters, everything depends on a right *point of view*. "Inspiration Point" in the Yosemite is socalled because it reveals and interprets the whole valley of wonders. Astronomy was misconceived for thousands of years, because the Earth was conceived as the center of the planetary and stellar universe. The moment that the sun was seen to be the center of the solar system and the Earth conceived as a planet moving round it the confusion of the Ptolomaic gave way to the order of the Copernican. So, if in the pursuit of knowledge you take God as the center, the universe becomes a harmonious system. Atheism is folly, intellectually as well as morally. The only rational interpretation of Nature is to put God on its throne as Creator and Ruler.

"Keep thy heart with all diligence, for out of it are the issues of life" (4:23).

Nothing compares in importance with what is *inside:* if taken care of, the *outside*—"mouth," "eyes," "feet"—will take care of themselves. *"Mores"* means both morals and manners. Literally, "above all thy keeping, keep thy heart, for out of it flows Life's great streams." As God is the center of all Truth, the heart is the fountain of all virtue. When we cry "Create in me a clean heart, O God," He replies, *"Keep* thy heart with all diligence." These are the two sides of one great matter. Even our intellectual power and success depend upon diligent keeping of the inner life. From the heart flows the *blood*.

"Watch thy heart above all thy keeping; for from it are the outflowings of Life." Man has under his own charge the making and guarding of his own life fountain, and his first duty is to keep it pure.

"There is that scattereth and yet increaseth and there is that withholdeth more than is meet, but it tendeth to poverty" (11:24).

Increase comes by imparting, and decrease by withholding. If you want to get, give, and if you want to lose, keep. Even mental riches come by constant spending of intellectual capital. A thought or fact is a seed; to be sown if you want a crop. No man learns so fast as he who teaches. Acquisition comes by impartation. There is gain in grain only as it is sown in the soil. "Sowing in the field is better than sewing in a napkin." All gifts are for trading. Coin is for currency.

"He that walketh with wise men shall be wise; but a companion of fools shall be destroyed" (13:20).

Goethe says: "Tell me with whom thou art found and I will tell thee who thou art." Much depends on your companionship. Wisdom and folly are both contagious. Your company suggests your habits and thoughts, directs your aims, refines or degrades your tastes. You will be intellectually and morally assimilated to your chosen companions. Wise men make sages, fools make fools.

"Wherefore is there a price in the hand of a fool to get wisdom, seeing he hath no heart to it."

Money cannot buy learning, nor take the place of brains; there is no "royal road" to wisdom. The rich have no advantage over the poor. He who has a *heart* for his work is bound to succeed; nothing is impossible to the man that wills. What is needed is not preeminently money nor books, but understanding. There is enough latent brain power in any complete man to make him a scholar. In fact, those who have made most of themselves have generally had *least* advantages.

"Train up a child in the way he shall go," etc., literally, *"according to his way"—his bent* (22:6).

The Arabs have a proverb: "You may bathe a dog's tail in oil and bind it with splints and you can never get the crook out of it." Every man has a native *bent* which adapts him to a particular work or sphere. True teaching and training will find out that *bent;* for, even when he is old, he will be likely to pursue it.

"It is the glory of God to conceal a thing, but the honor of kings is to search it out" (25:2).

God has a purpose in concealing truth; to stimulate man to search it out. The effort which leads to discovery is more beneficial than the discovery itself. Secrets are left in nature and Providence, in God's works and Word, to incite study. And it is a royal privilege that a king my covet to explore truth. A great sage said that if he could have his choice to know all that can be known, or forever to seek after more knowledge, he would choose the latter.

This proverb embodies a fundamental law. "God" here is Elohim—god of creation. He is verily a god who concealeth Himself (Is. 45:15). But it is not to evade but to provoke inquiry and investigation. He hides creative mysteries to stimulate the human mind to exploration, and find the reward of search in discovery. It is God's glory to hide: man's glory to seek—even kings, with their high intelligence and large resources, are well employed in searching into what He has concealed.

The glory of Elohim is to conceal; the glory of man is to reveal.

The *Self Life* is another of the subjects which permeate Scripture teaching. Gathering up a few of the fragments we find that the following are the main aspects in which it is presented:

1. *Self-righteousness* or self-trust; as the great hindrance to the acceptance of God's savior and salvation (Rom. 10:1–3).

2. *Self-dependence* or self-help. Even after conversion there is a constant tendency to rely upon our own efforts (Gal. 2:20; Zech. 4:6; John 15:4–6).

3. *Self-seeking* (Jer. 45:5; 1 Cor. 10:33). Constant proneness also to seek self-promotion, advancement, emolument (Matt. 16:24, 25).

4. *Self-pleasing*. To set before ourselves our own gratification and indulgence is perilous to spiritual life (Rom. 15:1–3).

5. *Self-will*. The center of all self life is a carnal, selfish will; and hence the need of its absolute renunciation (James 4:13–15; 1 Pet. 4:2; John 6:38).

6. *Self-defense*. We find it hard to abstain form vindicating and justifying ourselves instead of leaving it to God (1 Pet. 2:12, 15, 19–23; 3:16; 4:19).

7. *Self-glory*. All seeking of human praise detracts from the glory of God and is idolatrous (Dan. 5:23; John 8:50; 1 Cor. 10:31; Gal. 6:14). Though the forms of self life are legion, all may be included under the above seven heads.

On the Times Building in London two books are sculptured in stone. They represent respectively the Past and the Future of human Literature. On one, the Past, ivy is graven to indicate how the writings of past ages are overgrown with antiquity like the ruins of an old cathedral. On the other rests the scythe of Time to indicate how all future writings of men will be severely tested by Time as to whether they can endure, while all that is mortal perishes. On the Bible Society Building in the same street one Book is sculptured—the Book of God, with the sentence: *"The Word of the Lord endureth forever."*